My Name is
LAZARUS

My Name is
LAZARUS

EDITED BY DALE AHLQUIST

34 *Stories of Converts*
Whose Path to Rome was
Paved by G.K. *Chesterton*

ACS BOOKS

ISBN: 978-1-5051-1386-0

ACS Books is an imprint of TAN Books
PO Box 410487
Charlotte, NC 28241
www.TANBooks.com

Printed and bound in the United States of America.

THE CONVERT

By G.K. Chesterton

After one moment when I bowed my head
And the whole world turned over and came upright,
And I came out where the old road shone white,
I walked the ways and heard what all men said,
Forests of tongues, like autumn leaves unshed,
Being not unlovable but strange and light;
Old riddles and new creeds, not in despite
But softly, as men smile about the dead.

The sages have a hundred maps to give
That trace their crawling cosmos like a tree,
They rattle reason out through many a sieve
That stores the dust and lets the gold go free:
And all these things are less than dust to me
Because my name is Lazarus and I live.

Written the day he was received into
the Catholic Church, July 30, 1922

CONTENTS

INTRODUCTION
"Will a Man Take This Road or That?"
By Dale Ahlquist

PEOPLE WHO HAVE NOT READ THE BOOK *The Path to Rome* usually assume it is a book about conversion. But it's not. It's Hilaire Belloc's amusing account of actually walking from France to Rome. The book ends when he gets there.

Belloc was a close friend of G.K. Chesterton's and part of a circle of early 20th century English literary stars, almost all of whom were Catholic converts. The only one in the group who was a cradle Catholic was Belloc. A fearless defender of the Catholic Church and an unabashed critic of Protestants, Muslims, Jews, Atheists, and any other non-Catholics, Belloc was not exactly a maker of converts. As a matter of fact, he never thought Chesterton would become a Catholic. He was stunned, along with much of the rest of the world, when Gilbert

Keith Chesterton took the figurative path that Belloc tread literally.

We will let Chesterton tell the story of his conversion in his own words in the opening chapter of this book, but the point is that when Chesterton reached Rome it was the beginning, not the conclusion, of the story. He arrived bringing others with him. Both inside and outside that literary circle there was a group that was not moved by Belloc but *was* moved by Chesterton, and there was a ripple effect. The ripple continues to be felt over eighty years after Chesterton's death. People who encounter his writings are drawn to his faith. They want what he has.

This is a book that easily could have been two thousand pages long with hundreds of personal testimonies. Consider first this list:

ஃ Oxford chaplain Msgr. Ronald Knox, an Anglican clergyman who became a Catholic priest, translated the entire Bible, was a fellow author of detective fiction with Chesterton, and preached the panegyric at Chesterton's Requiem Mass.

ஃ The social critic H. Marshall McLuhan, who gave the world the term "The medium is the message." He called Chesterton "a practical mystic" with "an unfailing sense of relevance."

ஃ The great Catholic historian Christopher Dawson.

ஃ Evelyn Waugh, the author of *Brideshead Revisited*, who called Chesterton "a lovable and much loved man, abounding in charity and humility."

ஃ The sculptor and print artist, Eric Gill, who called Chesterton "a holy man, beyond all his contemporaries. Thanks be to God he also loved and befriended me." Also, Gill's brother Cecil, who had been an Anglican clergyman.

๛ The poet Alfred Noyes, who wrote "The Highwayman," and was one of the last Englishmen in history who actually made a living from writing poetry.

๛ Novelist Graham Greene, who found in Chesterton his first real hero.

๛ Writer and skier Arnold Lunn, who first wrote a book criticizing Chesterton and other "Roman Converts" before writing a book, *Now I See*, crediting Chesterton for helping show him the way to the Catholic Church.

๛ Iconic actor Alec Guiness, who once played Chesterton's famous priest detective Father Brown, which led to him investigate the Catholic faith.

๛ E.F. Schumacher, of *Small is Beautiful* fame.

๛ Nobel laureate Sigrid Undset.

๛ Author and Jewish convert Gladys Bronwen Stern.

๛ Author and diplomat Sir Shane Leslie, cousin of Winston Churchill.

๛ Two writers with similar names but of no relation to each other: Wyndham Lewis and D.B. Wyndham Lewis.

๛ Two scholars with very different names who were husband and wife: Peter Geach and Elizabeth Anscombe.

๛ American novelist Francis Parkinson Keyes.

๛ John Moody, financial analyst and founder of the *Wall Street Journal*.

๛ Poet and professor Theodore Maynard, who wrote: "The effect of Chesterton's *Orthodoxy* has been enormously powerful upon the young men of this generation. For one of these young men I can speak. I was sliding, at the age of nineteen, from the Calvinist theology in which I had been brought up, into a vague humanitarian scepticism, when I read *Orthodoxy*, and that book began in me a reaction which, by the grace of God, three years later carried me into the Catholic Church."

❧ Aurel Kolnai, a Jewish philosopher from Hungary, who wrote: "Like so many other converts of my time, I was won for Catholicism largely, if not chiefly, by the wisdom and wit of Gilbert Keith Chesterton. One of my prevailing moods in these years could be phrased thus, 'Not to share Chesterton's faith is, after all, a thing of rank absurdity.'"

That is only a sampling of Chesterton's well-known contemporaries, who were drawn by him into the Catholic Church. Some of them (Knox, Dawson, Maynard, et al) even arrived before he did. Chesterton once observed that he was standing at the door of the Church, ushering others in without having entered himself.

For obvious reasons, we have only a few names of lesser known personalities, such as Guy L. Cooper, who first heard Chesterton talking on the radio in 1930 about Prohibition; H.W.J. Edwards, a former Quaker who met GKC in 1930s, got involved in the Distributist League, and attended Chesterton's funeral; Cecil Botting, who taught at St. Paul's School, Chesterton's alma mater; a Franciscan friar named Leo Rowlands; a former Episcopalian priest named Michael Chapman; and Joan Lamplugh of Birmingham, England, who is known only for the fact that she wrote a letter to Chesterton's widow, which is preserved among Chesterton's papers in the British Library. Most of the names and certainly the numbers of Chesterton's other contemporaries who would have credited him with playing a key role in their conversion will never be known, and they are no longer around to testify.

After Chesterton's death in 1936, his star faded and his influence waned for a bit, but with the recent revival of interest in his writings has come a new wave of conversions. Consider now this list:

- The late Stratford Caldecott, editor of *Second Spring*.

- Two former editors of *Touchstone* magazine, Leon Podles and David Mills.

- Former editor of *Chronicles*, Thomas Fleming.

- Former editor of the *Social Justice Review*, Tom Hoover.

- Dawn Eden Goldstein, who went from writing about rock-and-roll to writing about chastity and teaching theology at a Catholic seminary.

- Walter Hooper, who was secretary to C.S. Lewis.

- Mark Shea, author of several books on Catholic apologetics.

- Radio personality Laura Ingraham.

- David Moss, Founder of the Association of Hebrew Catholics.

- Msgr. Stuart Swetland, President of Donnelly College.

- Mark Brumley, President of Ignatius Press.

- Science fiction writer John C. Wright.

- Bestselling novelist Dean Koontz.

- Publisher Conrad Black.

- Marjorie Dannenfelser, President of Susan B. Anthony's List.

- *New York Times* columnist Ross Douthat.

- Pro-life activist Lila Rose.

- The late Regina Derieva, acclaimed dissident Soviet poet who was a Jewish Atheist.

- William Oddie, a former Anglican priest, who is now a columnist for the *Catholic Herald*, and who wrote an article over twenty years ago calling for Chesterton's canonization.

Converts all. And escorted to Rome by G.K. Chesterton.

I have been maintaining a list with hundreds of names of converts on it—former Baptists, Lutherans, Presbyterians, Methodists, Episcopalians, Anglicans, Unitarians, Pentecostals, Eastern Orthodox, Quakers, Mormons, Muslims, Atheists and Agnostics. Jewish converts, too. And one gentlemen approached me after a talk I gave and told me that he was a convert because he'd read Chesterton. I asked him what he was before that. He answered, "A golfer."

For some Protestants, it was Chesterton's classic apologetics—arguments from reason, from history, from lucid analogy—the same kind of arguments with which C.S. Lewis once thrilled them to "mere Christianity," but with which G.K. Chesterton took them to something further: to the historic Church. For some it was social justice, the clear alternative offered by Chesterton's Distributism where other social and political and economic theories were incomplete, incoherent, and unsatisfactory. For some it was a poem. For some it was simply beauty. For all, it was goodness.

LeRoy Smith went to a priest and told him he wanted to become Catholic. The priest asked him if he knew any Catholics who could sponsor him. Mr. Smith replied, with complete sincerity, that he knew only one Catholic: G.K. Chesterton, who was the reason he wanted to join the Church. He now runs a local Chesterton Society in Arizona.

Some were happily cornered by truth. At a certain point they felt an almost whimsical inevitability to their decision. A 22-year-old woman from Texas, closing the book *The Everlasting Man* with a sigh of resignation, used a coarse word, and said: "Now I have to become Catholic." Whereas a 70-year-old woman from New Mexico read just one passage in *Orthodoxy* and knew she had to become Catholic. Sam Guzman, a former

Evangelical from Milwaukee, said to me: "I had been reading Chesterton, I was thinking about becoming Catholic, but I avoided reading *The Catholic Church and Conversion*, because I knew that would be too easy. I didn't want to convert simply because Chesterton did. When I was about 99% sure that I wanted to become Catholic, I read it. It was the final nail in the coffin." And speaking of coffins (and inevitability), add to the list Marcus Daly, who is a coffin-maker on Vashon Island in the Puget Sound.

For some the road was longer and harder and more painful. And costly. If they were Protestant ministers, it meant losing their jobs. In some cases, they lost their spouse. The road to Rome is not easy. And some are still on it. Chesterton is their companion.

And many Catholics have experienced what they call a "deeper conversion" after encountering Chesterton. One life-long Catholic told me: "You know that sword in Mary's heart? I had a sword in my heart, too, but Chesterton pulled it out, and now I am healed."

A woman in Spain came up to me and said, "Chesterton saved my life." Another woman who suffered the pain of being abandoned by her husband told that what saved her sanity and calmed her soul was reading G.K. Chesterton.

And some men, both converts and cradle Catholics, have found that Chesterton played a role in their vocations. Fr. Andrew Luczak, from Illinois, read *Orthodoxy* and *Everlasting Man* in the 1960s, and said the books were instrumental in him making his decision to become a priest. He still reads the author now because, he says, "Chesterton makes me feel young."

I once spoke at a conference and was followed at the podium by Fr. Robert Spitzer, S.J., who began his talk by saying, "Chesterton was the catalyst for my vocation to the Jesuits. I was a child of the culture, and G.K. Chesterton awakened me out of my dogmatic slumber."

So what is it about Chesterton and the Catholic Church? That is what this book proposes to explore through a wide variety of personal stories. Chesterton says that the Church is a house with a hundred gates; and no two men enter at exactly the same angle. Here are over thirty different angles. As I say, the book could have been much bigger.

Not included are the fascinating stories that I know only bits and pieces of. One gentleman told me that Chesterton saved him from Buddhism. Another had been involved in the occult. Another told me that his entire Baptist family converted. And one told me that his entire Episcopalian church converted. There are, of course, many other stories I don't know about.

And then there is the intriguing story of former chess champion Bobby Fischer. Chesterton said that poets don't go mad but chess players do. Bobby Fischer might be a good example of that. The young genius once took the chess world by storm, winning the World Chess Championship in 1972 but eventually relinquishing the crown by refusing to defend it, and then alienating the whole world with eccentric behavior that included bizarre conspiracy theories and anti-Semitic rants that were especially weird considering the fact that Fischer was Jewish. He became a fugitive from the law when he defied a presidential order in 1992 forbidding him travel to Belgrade to play a rematch with his old opponent Boris Spassky in the former republic of Yugoslavia. In 2004, he was arrested in Japan for attempting to travel with an expired passport. An American attorney, Robert Vattuone, acted as Fischer's counsel and helped negotiate an agreement whereby Fischer could live in exile in Iceland, the site of his famous victory over Spassky in 1972. Mr. Vattuone, a Catholic, when he met with Fischer in

Japan, gave him copy of my book *G.K. Chesterton – The Apostle of Common Sense*, and the two of them discussed religion. And Fischer went off to Iceland. After that we don't quite know what happened. Except this: Just before he died in 2008, he arranged for a private Catholic funeral. Vattuone wondered if this was "Bobby's final brilliant move—to the chagrin of his detractors?" His detractors might say it was his final act of madness. Others would say it was a final act of sanity.

Chesterton says:

All Christianity concentrates on the man at the cross-roads. The vast and shallow philosophies, the huge syntheses of humbug, all talk about ages and evolution and ultimate developments. The true philosophy is concerned with the instant. Will a man take this road or that? —that is the only thing to think about, if you enjoy thinking. The aeons are easy enough to think about, any one can think about them. The instant is really awful: and it is because our religion has intensely felt the instant, that it has in literature dealt much with battle and in theology dealt much with hell. It is full of *danger*, like a boy's book: it is at an immortal crisis. There is a great deal of real similarity between popular fiction and the religion of the western people. If you say that popular fiction is vulgar and tawdry, you only say what the dreary and well-informed say also about the images in the Catholic churches. Life (according to the faith) is very like a serial story in a magazine: life ends with the promise (or menace) "to be continued in our next." Also, with a noble vulgarity, life imitates the serial and leaves off at the exciting moment. For death is distinctly an exciting moment.

The Chief Event of My Life

By G.K. Chesterton

THERE WAS SOMETHING ABOUT MY CHILDHOOD, my youngest years, that can only be described as a white light. The very opposite of a dream. The world had a greater reality, a greater solidity, than at anytime in my adult years. It was not merely a material reality, but a spiritual reality as well. A complete reality. And part of this reality, this real world, was the world of imagination. Imagination is the opposite of illusion. Imagination is a thing of images, and we, after all, are made in the image of God. And my childhood was filled with images. One of my most vivid and fondest memories is of a toy theatre which was built for me by my father. I liked the toy theatre even

---

Editor's note: Chesterton refers to his conversion as "the chief event of my life" in the preface to *The Everlasting Man*. The present essay, however, is a composite that I put together drawing from his *Autobiography, Orthodoxy, The Catholic Church and Conversion, The Thing, The Well and the Shallows*, the essay *"Why I am a Catholic,"* and a few other uncollected sources. I used this same text for the basis of an "interview" with Chesterton by Marcus Grodi for a special edition of *The Journey Home* on the Eternal Word Television Network.

when I knew it was a toy theatre. I liked the cardboard figures, even when I found they were made of cardboard. I never felt tricked. The white light of wonder shone on the whole thing. The figures of wood and of cardboard gave me glorious glimpses into the possibilities of existence. Perhaps my appreciation of the toy theatre was in part an appreciation of the carpenter who built it, which ultimately helped me appreciate another Carpenter.

At the same time, you must not imagine that I had a completely comfortable childhood or that I passed it in complete contentment. I was often unhappy in childhood like other children. I was very often naughty in childhood like other children; and I never doubted for a moment the moral of all the moral tales; that, as a general principle, people ought to be unhappy when they have been naughty. But I wanted to mention how terribly important my childhood was to the rest of my life. I have had many experiences. Without giving myself any airs of being a globe-trotter, I may say I have seen something of the world; I have travelled in interesting places and talked to interesting men; I have been in the major political quarrels of my country; I have talked to statesmen in the hour of the destiny of states; I have met most of the great poets and prose writers of my time; I have travelled in the track of some of the earthquakes in the ends of the earth; I have lived in houses burned down in the tragic wars of Ireland; I have walked through the ruins of Polish palaces left behind by the Red Armies; I have heard talk of the secret signals of the Ku Klux Klan upon the borders of Texas; I have seen the fanatical Arabs come up from the desert to attack the Jews in Jerusalem. There are many journalists who have seen more of such things than I; but I have been a journalist and I have seen such things; but none of those things are as real to me as the cardboard figures in that toy theatre of my childhood. Because I was subconsciously certain then, as I am consciously certain now, that there was a white and soli road, a worthy beginning of the life of man; and the man afterwards darkens it. He goes astray from it in self-deception. It is only the grown man who lives a life of make-believe and pretending; and it is he who has his head in a cloud. I knew that morning light. I did not know that it could be lost. I knew even less if it could be recovered. And I did lose it, and I did recover it.

What surprises me in looking back on youth, is how quickly a young man can think his way back to fundamental things; and even to the denial of fundamental things. I had thought my way back to thought itself. It is a very dreadful thing to do; for it may lead to thinking that there is nothing but thought. At this time I did not very clearly distinguish between dreaming and waking; not only as a mood but as a metaphysical doubt, I felt as if everything might be a dream. It was as if I had myself projected the universe from within, with its trees and stars, as if I were their creator. As if I were… God. These, of course, are the thoughts of a madman. Yet I was not mad, in any medical or physical sense; I was simply carrying the scepticism of my time as far as it would go. And I soon found it would go a great deal further than most of the sceptics went. While dull atheists came and explained to me that there was nothing but matter, I listened with a sort of calm horror of detachment, suspecting that there was nothing but mind. I have always felt that there was something third-rate about materialists and materialism ever since. The atheist told me so pompously that he did not believe there was any God; and there were moments when I did not even believe there was any atheist.

I could imagine the maddest crime, when I had never committed even the mildest crime.

I was going through a kind of spiritual suicide. I had never heard of Confession in those days; but that is what is really needed in such cases. And I fancy they are not uncommon cases. I dug quite low, low enough to discover the devil. I knew the reality of evil and the reality of sin.

When I had been for some time in these dark depths, I had a strong inward impulse to revolt; to throw off this nightmare. But as I was still thinking the thing out by myself, with little help from philosophy and no real help from religion, I invented a rudimentary and makeshift mystical theory of my own. It was substantially this: that even mere existence, reduced to its most primary limits, was extraordinary enough to be exciting. Anything was magnificent as compared with nothing.

There were writers who helped me find my way out of this darkness, even though they were not religious writers, per se. Charles Dickens with his endless hope. Robert Louis Stevenson with his "belief in the ultimate decency of things." The poet Robert Browning, who wrote "God must be glad one loves his world so much," The poet Walt Whitman was a hospitable giant who delivered me from the decadent cynicism that swept away so many young men of my time. And there was another poet who attracted me. A poet whose whole life was a poem. St. Francis of Assisi. He was never a stranger to me. I was drawn to St. Francis very early, when I had no more idea of becoming a Catholic than becoming a Cannibal.

When an enthusiast discovers through experience and sympathy that there is another half of the truth that he has not been told, then there is presented to him a perilous alternative. If he goes on to the whole truth, he will become more wise, but he will also become more ordinary, which means the acceptance of an order. The people who do not accept an order are left with chaos. Those are the only two choices, though modern people try to avoid making the choice. In most modern people there is a battle between the new opinions, which they do not follow out to their end, and the old traditions, which they do not trace back to their beginning. If they followed the new notions forward, it would lead them to Bedlam, to Madness. If they followed the better instincts backward it would lead them to Rome, to the Catholic Church. And so what they try to do instead is remain suspended between two logical alternatives, trying to tell themselves that they are merely avoiding two extremes.

I went to art school and failed entirely to learn how to paint or draw, but I met a fellow student named Ernest Hodder-Williams. He and I often talked about literature, and he conceived a fixed notion that I could write; a delusion which he retained to the day of his death. He gave me some books on art to review for a magazine called the *Bookman*, which was published by his family. I tossed off some criticisms of the weaker points and misdirected talents of some great artists, and I found I had discovered the easiest of all professions; which I pursued ever since.

I am a journalist and so am vastly ignorant of many things, but because I am a journalist I write and talk about them all. If you are writing an article you can say anything that comes into your head. I would sooner call myself a journalist than an author; because a journalist is a journeyman.

The ultimate goal of any journey is to get home. But I have had a very jolly time as a journalist, and never asked to be anything better. The definition of journalism, as I have said, and as I have good reason to know, is writing badly. I really am forever conscious of how badly and clumsily I am using the English language in writing and speaking except when I am at the white heat of controversy, and at the hammer and tongs stage I get the illusion that I am doing things rather well. It's the best fun in life, this argument business, and what makes being a journalist really worth while.

I never realized the great common sense of the Christian creed until the anti-Christian writers pointed it out to me. I was not defending any particular theological points, I was merely defending plain old human morals. I was defending Responsibility, which is sometimes called the question of Free Will. It was not that I began by believing in supernormal things. It was that the unbelievers began by disbelieving even in normal things. It was the secularists who drove me to theological ethics, by themselves destroying any sane or rational possibility of secular ethics. It was the Scientific Determinist who told me, at the top of his voice, that I could not be responsible at all. And as I rather like being treated as a responsible being, and not as a lunatic let out for the day, I began to look around for some spiritual asylum that was not merely a lunatic asylum. On that day, in short, I escaped from an error, which still entangles many better men than myself. There is still a notion that the agnostic can be content with knowledge about worldly things and never settle the questions about "other worldly" things. But it is not true. The questions of the sceptic strike direct at the heart of our human life; they disturb this world, quite apart from the other world; and it is exactly common sense that they disturb most. There could not be a better example than this determinist shouting to a mob of millions that no man ought to be blamed for anything he did, because it was all heredity and environment. Logically, that would stop a man in the act of saying "Thank you" to somebody for passing the mustard. For how could he be praised for passing the mustard, if he could not be blamed for not passing the mustard?

I met Fr. John O'Connor when I gave a lecture in Yorkshire. He was a small man with an elfish expression. I was struck by the tact and humour with which he mingled with his very

Protestant company; and I soon found out that they appreciated him, even though I suppose they really thought that he had his house fitted up with all the torture engines of the Spanish Inquisition. I liked him very much; but if you had told me that ten years afterwards I should be a Mormon Missionary in the Cannibal Islands, I should not have been more surprised than at the suggestion that, fully fifteen years afterwards, I should be making to him my General Confession and being received into the Roman Catholic Church.

It has been pointed out that my fictional detective Father Brown was based on Father O'Connor. Well, Father Brown's chief feature was to be featureless. The point of him was to appear pointless; and one might say that his conspicuous quality was not being conspicuous. His commonplace exterior was meant to contrast with his unsuspected vigilance and intelligence; and that being so, of course I made his appearance shabby and shapeless, his face round and expressionless, his manners clumsy, and so on. My friend, Father John O'Connor, as a matter of fact, did not have any of these external qualities. He was not shabby, but rather neat; he was not clumsy, but very delicate and dexterous; he not only was amusing but looked amused. He was a sensitive and quick-witted Irishman. My Father Brown was deliberately described as a Suffolk dumpling from East Anglia.

And yet, there is a very real sense in which Father O'Connor was the intellectual inspiration of these stories; and of much more important things as well. I never knew a man who could turn with more ease than he from one topic to another, or who had more unexpected stores of information, often purely technical information, upon all. But I was also surprised to find out what else he knew. He knew about evil. I had imagined for myself any amount of iniquity; and it was a curious experience to find that this quiet and pleasant celibate had plumbed those abysses far deeper than I. After talking to him, I learned of horrors that I could not have imagined. If he had been a professional novelist broadcasting such filth on all the bookstalls for boys and babies to pick up, of course he would have been a great creative artist of the modern world. But he told me these things reluctantly, in strict privacy, as a practical necessity to prevent me from error.

Afterwards we fell into special conversation with two hearty and healthy young Cambridge undergraduates. They began to discuss music and landscape with my friend Father O'Connor. The talk soon deepened into a discussion on matters more philosophical and moral and, when the priest had left the room, there fell a curious reflective silence, at the end of which one of the undergraduates suddenly burst out, "All the same, I don't believe his sort of life is the right one. It's all very well to like religious music and so on, when you're all shut up in a sort of cloister and don't know anything about the real evil in the world. But I believe in a fellow coming out into the world, and facing the evil that's in it, and knowing something about the dangers and all that. It's a very beautiful thing to be innocent and ignorant, but I think it's a much finer thing not to be afraid of knowledge."

To me, still almost shivering with the appallingly practical facts of which the priest had warned me, this comment came with such a colossal and crushing irony, that I nearly burst into a loud harsh laugh in the drawing-room. For I knew perfectly well that, as regards all the solid Satanism which the priest knew and warred with all his life, these two Cambridge gentlemen (luckily for them) knew about as much of real evil as two babies in the same perambulator.

But the incident of the Cambridge undergraduates, and their

breezy contempt for the cloistered virtue of a parish priest, stood for much more serious things in my life than the heap of corpses that littered my detective stories. It brought me face to face once more with those morbid problems of the soul, the problems I alluded to earlier. It gave me a great and growing sense that I had not found any real spiritual solution to those problems. I had this sudden glimpse of the pit that is at all our feet. I was surprised at my own surprise. It was easy to believe that the Catholic Church knew more about good than I did. But that she knew more about evil than I did seemed incredible.

When people ask me, "Why did you join the Church of Rome?" the first essential answer is, "To get rid of my sins." For there is no other religious system that does *really* profess to get rid of people's sins. It is confirmed by the logic, which to many seems startling, by which the Church deduces that sin confessed and adequately repented is actually abolished; and that the sinner does really begin again as if he had never sinned. And this brings me back to what I said earlier about the innocence of childhood, that strange daylight, which was something more than the light of common day, that still shines in my memory. Well, when a Catholic comes from Confession, he does truly, by definition, step out again into that dawn of his own beginning and look with new eyes across the world. In that brief ritual, God has really remade him in His own image. He is now a new experiment of the Creator. He is as much a new experiment as he was when he was really only five years old. He stands, as I said, in the white light at the worthy beginning of the life of a man. The accumulations of time can no longer terrify. He may be grey and gouty; but he is only five minutes old.

The Sacrament of Penance and the equally staggering doctrine of the Divine love for man, these doctrines seem to link up my whole life from the beginning, as no other doctrines could do; and especially to settle simultaneously the two problems of my childish happiness and my boyish brooding. And they specially affected one idea; which I hope it is not pompous to call the chief idea of my life. I will not say it is the doctrine I have always taught, but it is the doctrine I should always have liked to teach: the idea of taking things with gratitude, and not taking things for granted. Thanks are the highest form of thought. We should be thankful for life, but we should be even more thankful for *new* life. The Sacrament of Penance gives new life. It reconciles a man to God, and to all the living, but it does not do it as the optimists and the hedonists and the heathen preachers of happiness do it. The gift is given at a price, and is conditioned by a confession. In other words, the name of the price is Truth, which may also be called Reality; but it is facing the reality about oneself.

The sins of Christianity is one of the doctrines of Christianity. And the Church is not justified when her children do not sin, but when they do. The world really pays the supreme compliment to the Catholic Church in being intolerant of her tolerating even the appearance of the evils which it tolerates in everything else.

The difficulty of explaining "why I am a Catholic" is that there are ten thousand reasons all amounting to one reason: that Catholicism is true. And the difficulty of treating the matter personally and describing my own conversion is that I have a strong feeling that this makes the business look much smaller than it really is. Numbers of much better men have sincerely converted to much worse religions. But what I can say about the Catholic Church that cannot be said of any of its rivals is that it is catholic, that is, it is universal. It is not only larger than me, but larger than anything in the world; it is indeed larger than the world.

One of the notions that Catholics have to be continually refuting is the accusation that the Catholic Church is always the enemy of new ideas. Indeed, those who complain that Catholicism cannot say anything new, seldom think it necessary to say anything new about Catholicism. As a matter of fact, a real study of history will show it to be curiously contrary to the fact. In so far as ideas really are new ideas, Catholics have continually suffered through supporting them when they were really new; when they were much too new to find any other support. For instance, nearly two hundred years before the Declaration of Independence and the French Revolution, in an age devoted to the pride and praise of princes, Cardinal Robert Bellarmine laid down lucidly the whole theory of real democracy. But in that age of Divine Right he only produced the impression of creeping about with a dagger to murder the king. Again, the Casuists of the Catholic schools said all that can really be said for the problem plays and problem novels of our own time, two hundred years before they were written. They said that there really are problems of moral conduct; but they had the misfortune to say it two hundred years too soon. They merely got themselves called liars and shufflers for being psychologists before psychology was the fashion. It would be easy to give any number of other examples down to the present day, and the case of ideas that are still too new to be understood. There are passages in Pope Leo's Encyclical on Labor, *Rerum Novarum,* which are only now beginning to be used as hints for social movements much newer than socialism. And when Mr. Belloc wrote about the Servile State, he advanced an economic theory so original that hardly anybody has yet realized what it is. A few centuries hence, other people will probably repeat it, and repeat it wrong. And then, if Catholics object, their protest will be easily explained by the well-known fact that Catholics never care for new ideas. Nevertheless, the man who made that remark about Catholics meant something. What he meant was that, in the modern world, the Catholic Church is in fact the enemy of many influential fashions; most of which still claim to be new, though many of them are beginning to be a little stale. A new philosophy in general means the praise of some old vice. In so far as he means that the Church often attacks what the world at any given moment supports, he is perfectly right. The Church does often set herself against the fashion of this world that passes away; and she has experience enough to know how very rapidly it does pass away. The Catholic Church is the only thing that frees a man from the degrading slavery of being a child of his age.

The Catholic Church is more fundamental than Fundamentalism. It knows where the Bible came from. It knows there were many other Gospels besides the Four Gospels, and that the others were only eliminated by the authority of the Catholic Church. It does not, in the conventional phrase, believe what the Bible says, for the simple reason that the Bible does not say anything. You cannot put a book in the witness-box and ask it what it really means. The Fundamentalist controversy itself destroys Fundamentalism. The Bible by itself cannot be a basis of agreement when it is a cause of disagreement; it cannot be the common ground of Christians when some take it allegorically and some literally. Protestants appealed from priests to the Bible, and did not realize that the Bible also could be questioned. There is no end to the dissolution of ideas, the destruction of all tests of truth, that has become possible since men abandoned the attempt to keep a central and civilized Truth, to contain all truths and trace out and refute all errors. Since then, each group has taken one truth at a time and spent the time in turning it into a falsehood. But in all probability, all that is best in Protestantism will survive only in Catholicism.

I grew up in a Protestant world, but I was lucky that among my own family and friends there was none of that strange mania against Mariolatry. There was none of that mad vigilance that watches for the first faint signs of the cult of Mary as for the spots of a plague. No one ever presumed that she was encroaching upon Christ. My family and friends knew nothing about the Catholic Church; but they did know something about this sacred figure, that she represented an idea that was noble and beautiful. In England we called her the Madonna, instead of "Our Lady," an expression which reveals the English instinct for compromise, so as to avoid both reverence and irreverence!

I may still say that my personal case was a little curious. Mary and my conversion are the most personal of topics, because conversion is something personal. But also the cult of Mary is in a rather peculiar sense a personal cult. God is God, Maker of all things visible and invisible; the Mother of God is in a rather special sense connected with things visible; since she is of this earth, and through her bodily being God was revealed to the senses. In the presence of God, we must remember what is invisible, what is intellectual; the abstractions and the absolute laws of thought; the love of truth, reason and logic. But with Our Lady, we are reminded of God Incarnate. She gathers up the elements of the heart and the higher instincts. They do, in a sense, cut through reason. They are the legitimate short cuts to the love of God. And they can only be experienced personally. At least that is how I experienced them. And I hope I am not misunderstood when I describe my personal experience. I don't know if it was a special favour of heaven, but the fact is, I always had a curious longing for this particular tradition, even in a world where it was regarded as a legend. I was always haunted by the idea. In fact, I can scarcely remember a time when the image of Our Lady did not stand up in my mind quite definitely, at the mention or the thought of all the things which are considered Catholic. I was quite distant from these things, and then doubtful about these things; and then disputing with the world for them, and with myself against them; for that is the condition before conversion. But whether the figure was distant, or was dark and mysterious, or was a scandal to my contemporaries, or was a challenge to myself—I never doubted that this figure was the figure of the Faith. She was only human, but she was a complete human being, and she embodied everything that the Catholic faith had to say to the world. The instant I remembered the Catholic Church, I remembered her; when I tried to forget the Catholic Church, I tried to forget her; when I finally faced the freest and the hardest of all my acts of freedom, that final decision that no one else could make for me, it was in front of a gilded and very gaudy little image of her in the port of Brindisi. And it was there that I promised that I would become a Catholic, if I returned to my own land.

Before arriving at Catholicism I passed through different stages and was a long time struggling. The various stages are hard to explain in detail. After much study and reflection, I came to the conclusion that the ills from which England is suffering: Capitalism, crude Imperialism, Industrialism, Wrongful Rich, Wreckage of the Family, are the result of England not being Catholic. The Anglo-Catholic position takes for granted that England remained Catholic in spite of the Reformation or even because of it. After my conclusions, it seemed unreasonable to affirm that England is Catholic. So I had to turn to the sole Catholicism, the Roman. Before my conversion I had a lot of Catholic ideas, and my point of view in fact had but little altered.

Catholicism gives us a doctrine, puts logic into our life. It is not merely a Church Authority, it is a base which steadies the judgment. For instance, here everyone is writing about fashion, discussing short skirts, undressed women, but criticisms from no fixed standpoint. I'll tell you why: they don't know the meaning of chastity, whereas a Catholic does know, and so he knows why he condemns the fashions of to-day. To be a Catholic is to be all at rest! To own an irrefragable metaphysic on which to base all one's judgments, to be the touchstone of our ideas and our life, to which one can bring everything home.

The change I have made is from being an Anglo-Catholic to being a Roman Catholic. I have always believed, at least for twenty years, in the Catholic view of Christianity. Unless the Church of England was a branch of the Catholic Church I had no use for it. If it were a Protestant Church I did not believe in it in any case. The question always was whether the Church of England can claim to be in direct descent from the mediaeval Catholic Church. That is the question with every Anglo-Catholic or Higher Churchman.

It appears to me quite clear that any church claiming to be authoritative, must be able to answer quite definitely when great questions of public morals are put. Can I go in for cannibalism, or murder babies to reduce the population, or any similar scientific and progressive reform? Any Church with authority to teach must be able to say whether it can be done. But Protestant churches are in utter bewilderment on these moral questions—for example on birth control, on divorce, and on Spiritualism.

The point is that the Church of England does not speak strongly. It has no united action. I have no use for a Church which is not a Church militant, which cannot order battle and fall in line and march in the same direction.

I ought to say first that, saving the grace of God, my own

conversion to Catholicism was entirely rational; and certainly not at all ritualistic. I was received in a tin shed at the back of a railway hotel. I accepted it because it *did* afford conviction to my analytical mind. But people can see the ritual and are seldom allowed to hear of the philosophy.

The great temptation of the Catholic in the modern world is the temptation to intellectual pride. It is so obvious that most of his critics are talking without in the least knowing what they are talking about, that he is sometimes a little provoked towards the very unchristian logic of answering a fool according to his folly. But we must never despair of explaining the truth, nor is it so very difficult to explain.

MAGIC

By Brent Forrest

SERENDIPITY IS A LIMP EUPHEMISM for the providence of Almighty God. Our greatest discoveries are those we weren't looking for. The best gifts are those we could not have imagined. So it was when I was received into the Catholic Church. Becoming Catholic was so thoroughly unlikely that I can only account for it as an act of God. I am still surprised.

I was born in Fort Myers, Florida, in 1952 and grew up there working in my family's grocery store. I earned my under-graduate degree in Journalism, traveled several years, then in 1981 moved to San Antonio where I now live and have built a successful investment management firm. In my earlier years I made my living as a magician, performing thousands of times for groups large and small. Once, for publicity, and to prove my great powers, I drove a car on the streets of Fort Myers. I was 19 years old and completely blindfolded. I don't know who had more courage: me, or the car dealer who lent his brand new Lincoln convertible for the stunt.

I was raised in what Flannery O'Connor called the "Christ-haunted South." If you were to ask about my denominational background, I'd probably say "a mix: Methodist, Pentecostal, Baptist, New Age, pragmatist, Platonist, skeptic..." The truth is I'm a religious mongrel. I think that sums up a majority of Americans—at least if they attempt to address religion at all. Many try to escape the confusion by declaring they are "spiritual, not religious." That convenient dodge works, so long as you don't think about it much. I am going to tell you how a kid, who loved magic and tried to discover the secrets behind everything, struggled to unriddle the mystery of his own life. How he came to find himself hopelessly bound and fettered with irreconcilable beliefs. And how that jovial giant of a journalist, G.K. Chesterton, provided the key for this magician to effect an escape.

Most boys and some girls, at one time or another, want to be a magician. It happened to me when I was six. A magician came to school and did amazing things with ropes and boxes and colorful scarves. That evening I told my mother, "I am going to be a magician." The declaration stuck and the art of magic occupied much of my life for the next thirty years.

I never met a practicing magician who believed much in the supernatural. We are skeptics by training and temperament. The wizard told Dorothy, "Pay no attention to that man behind the curtain," but that's all we've ever wanted to do...look behind the curtain to see how it all works. Moreover we've seen how easily even the best and brightest among us can be fooled. Will Rogers said we are all ignorant; but just about different things. Truth is we are all gullible fools; but just about different things. The modern man who is too thoroughly educated to believe in the idea of the Real Presence of Christ in the Blessed Sacrament, is perfectly willing to accept certain incredible and useless implications of quantum theory, such as the idea of infinite parallel universes.

Skepticism can be very useful—but dangerous. It can turn on itself. You can eventually lose confidence in the last instrument you trust: your own mind. My adolescent hero, Emerson, said "Nothing is at last sacred but the integrity of your own mind." I loved that when I was young. Now it doesn't impress me so much. Recently I watched my parents disappear into dementia (which, by the way, is something that also happened to Emerson). No one of us can rely on the integrity of his own mind. It's too easy to lose our way...or our mind for that matter. If you would be safe in this universe you need to rely on something greater than your own mind.

My passion for arcane knowledge extended beyond stage illusions, hypnotism, mind reading, and the like. I wanted to understand the workings of everything, even the grandest things. I spent nearly fifty years in a self-directed quest for the secret of life, the true philosophy. Of course, I was looking for God. Even in the times when I tried to be an atheist. And I tried on about everything my built-in biases could tolerate. My foundational bias was Protestantism. I use that term not in a formal sense, but to describe an unconscious assumption, an attitude of mind. Americans have Protestantism in their DNA... even Catholic Americans. After all, wasn't our nation born from violent protest against those with titular authority? We take pride in our independence and we love to question authority. My unquestioned assumption was the preeminence of my own conscience, my own judgement over any outside authority. I would always go it alone. Being a product of my culture, it never occurred to me that there could be an external authoritative source of truth. Like many, I was the arbiter of what came in. I was, shall we say, my own pope. Worse yet, though I read prolifically, I had no formal training in philosophy, theology, or logic. Take it from me, the truth seeker who directs his own search has a fool for a guide.

Over many years I embraced then discarded a menagerie of "philosophies." My first great love was Emerson, followed by Thoreau. In college I took a turn with Alan Watts, the brilliant East-meets-West charlatan. Then Krishnamurti, the Theosophists, the I Am Movement, (a bizarre cult born in the 1930s). William James and his offspring, the positive thinkers, were next. Napoleon Hill, of "Think and Grow Rich" fame, Dale Carnegie, and those who baptized that movement, Norman Vincent Peale and Robert Schuller. Joel Osteen is, by the way, the present day heir to that movement and Oprah Winfrey is its New Age harlot. Both have a frightfully bewitching charm.

I took a brief run at Carl Jung, Astrology, the I Ching and related things. Then I fell into despair. Nothing. Nothing had been good enough. I began to think: there is death and then nothingness. I fell into a fearful depression. I've heard that if an honest searcher lives long enough, he will go mad, kill himself, or become a Catholic. In low moods I was sympathetic with suicides. I wasn't yet ready to go mad, and there was no way I would consider being a Catholic. Oddly, a brief glimpse into Spinoza's *Ethics* rekindled my craving for God. I prayed, cried out to Him, then leaped tearfully and desperately into the Evangelical movement of the late 70s. This was "born again" Christianity with a Neo-Pentecostal twist: the Charismatic Movement. Those enthusiasms lasted for many years and over time I mellowed into a traditional Southern Baptist. By then, I had memorized much of the New Testament, taught Sunday School and even preached some. Naturally I wrestled with the all the usual distractions: the Rapture, Post-, Pre-, or A-millenialism; can you lose your salvation?; what about predestination?; is there a second Baptism in the Holy Spirit?; and so forth. These are valid questions, but I wasn't equipped to handle them, and the attempt nearly drained what little charity I had. Enrolling in Wake Forest Baptist seminary, I spent a year and a half grinding toward a Master of Divinity degree. Happily I never finished, or I might have hardened into a respectable Baptist minister. Fortunately, a serious taste for beer-drinking and the sweet memories of show business night life derailed things. I dropped out of seminary and went back to show business. I was nearly thirty. God can use anything to redirect us. Even Budweiser.

Having seen professional religion backstage, I was disenchanted again, and soon disgorged Evangelicalism like an emetic. I was done with Christianity—as I understood it. This time I dug deeper and discovered Nietzsche: the greatest Protestant of them all. He was also a great magician. He knew the tricks. He had been backstage, all the way back. He had seen and unriddled it all. And he invited his reader to peek behind the curtain. If ever a man was haunted by God, it was this guy. He was brilliant. His prose could dance like Nureyev, and with a touch of his toe, could knock down whole edifices of religious and philosophic humbug, stuff that had stood for centuries. And for him, it was all humbug. I devoured his work. He would destroy all the trappings, all the props and illusions, revealing at last the spiritual essence with the dross completely burned away. It was exhilarating.

Serendipitously, I discovered an obscure book written by the popular magician, James Randi. It was not a book about conjuring. In the tradition of Houdini, Randi set about exposing frauds. His book *Flimflam* was a blistering exposé of every form of occult or supernatural manifestation that was purported to be the real thing. Randi deliciously unmasked and destroyed a long parade of characters in the witching business: spiritualist mediums, crystal gazers, psychics of every stripe, spoon benders, water witchers, so called ESP researchers, and my favorite, faith healers. That too was exhilarating. I felt safely anchored to the rock of rational materialism. The trouble is, the rational materialist can touch the What and the How, but not the Why of anything. And until he encounters the Who, he will remain forever locked in a prison of his own certainty.

It took about four years to ingest Nietzsche, and a couple more years to reach disillusionment with him. It had all been a boyhood enthusiasm. Not sustainable. I had been fooled again, and again sunk into depression. Reading Spinoza revived me for a time. An Enlightenment Jew in the tradition of Descartes, Spinoza was a sweet soul and a brilliantly disciplined philosopher. An isolated genius suckled on scholarly Judaism and trained in mathematics, he gave us one of the most beautiful philosophies ever crafted. It was a healing place for a recovering Nietzschean. But, like all heresies, even the kindest ones, it was incomplete and could not satisfy.

Entering my fifties, the love of alcohol slowly replaced the love of wisdom. My drinking escalated, I was drinking alcoholically; and the alcohol became the medicine for my soul. That's the great reality for alcoholics. Alcohol is not the problem, it is the solution. And it can be very effective for a very long time. I'm of the type that can never be satisfied with the routine pleasures that seem to satisfy so many in our world. Golf, politics, televised sports, endless small talk, and the drudgery of daily maintenance have always bored me. I sometimes wondered why everyone wasn't depressed. Can't they see how empty it all is...even their religious notions? Those of you who read Walker Percy can understand my type.

Ayn Rand intrigued me for a while. Her *Atlas Shrugged*, written in 1945, is a timeless spot-on dissection of the socialist, progressive, and crony capitalist evils of our day. Rand was an atheist, a fierce anticommunist, and a rigidly logical thinker. Like Schopenhauer, she believed her philosophy explained everything. It was coldly logical, air tight, within itself irrefutable. This bugged me. There was something there. There was truth there. There was truth in everything I had pursued. All of it, everything I had believed, all true in some ways...but none satisfying. I continued to drink. I was at my wit's end and had all but given up. I was trapped in a metaphysical prison and bound with contradictions. Then I read *Orthodoxy* by G.K. Chesterton.

Orthodoxy answered for me, in hours, what I had wrestled with for years. Chesterton has an analogy of the One Key that fits the lock. Well, I heard those tumblers falling perfectly into place. Of course Ayn Rand had irrefutable logic. Her system complete. A bullet, Chesterton says, like the world, is perfectly round, but it is not the world. It's too small. Of course Emerson's or Nietzsche's prose was as beautiful and inspiring as the Northern Lights. Brimming with truth...but not the whole truth. It was not universal. It was not Catholic. Chesterton pegged me as the man who tried to get the cosmos into his head...only to have his head burst. The Christian is invited to get his head into the cosmos where there is unlimited room to move around, and no end of things to discover and enjoy. Simple notions to many readers perhaps, but for me, they were fireworks.

In 2011, God arranged for me to find the newly formed local Chesterton Society in San Antonio. I met kindred souls, most of them Catholic. I nearly shipwrecked the meetings with endless questions about the Church and all the usual

Protestant objections. They were patient with me. Books that helped: Weigel's *Witness to Hope*, the biography of John Paul II, William F. Buckley's spiritual autobiography *Nearer My God*, and a collection of sermons by John Henry Newman. I was struck that such brilliant and learned souls were also devout Catholics. Of course I read lots of Chesterton. His small book *The Catholic Church and Conversion* was especially helpful. In it he describes three stages of adult conversion: First, being fair to the Church, then falling in love with the Church, then running away from it—because you realize that what you have been judging and evaluating is now beginning to evaluate you, and it has put before you an inescapable question that requires more than a theoretical response. Michael Dunnigan, a good friend and canon lawyer who eventually sponsored my confirmation, asked what was holding me back from joining the Church. "Mike", I said, "I just don't want to be fooled again."

One day Mike took me to Mass at the beautiful Saint Joseph's Downtown Church. Following the service he introduced me to the parish priest Fr. Mario Marzocchi. It seemed as though barely ten words were spoken—something about Chesterton sparking my interest in the Church—when Fr. Mario beamed and said, "Ah! So you've been Catholic all along and you're just now figuring it out." That was it. Checkmate.

Chesterton says the Catholic Church is larger on the inside than on the outside. That is true. I came to see how small I was, how little I knew, how presumptuous I had been, and how arrogant in our ignorance we "educated moderns" really are. Chesterton nails it: "The Catholic Church is the only thing that saves a man from the degrading slavery of being a child of his age."

I was conditionally baptized and confirmed in 2012 and quit drinking in 2014. I've ceased trying to grasp and hold on to a philosophy of life. Rather I have been grasped and am held by the One who created me. Held by God, in Christ, through His Church and in the communion of His saints. And one of those saints is G.K. Chesterton.

THE THREE STEPS

By Theodore Olsen

PROVIDENCE ISN'T ONE OF THOSE THINGS we can see with foresight. In fact, we rarely seem able to understand it much in hindsight. So it is with trepidation, but also with gratitude, that I attempt to tell my conversion story, to relate how, through family, friends, priests, books, and, critically, through G.K. Chesterton, I was, "in the fullness of time," led by God's Providence to the Catholic Church.

When born to Norwegian parents in Minnesota in the latter half of the 20th century, the odds of being baptized and raised Lutheran are fairly high. And so I was. My church attendance was the typical thing: Sunday services, Sunday school, Confirmation. It wasn't like we were fervent Lutherans. But we weren't nominal Lutherans either. So I suppose one could have called us cultural Lutherans. I don't remember ever not believing in the Christian God.

27

But as so often happens, once I graduated from high school, and moved out on my own, I started to drift, physically, emotionally, and spiritually. I moved from apartment to apartment, job to job, and, as for my faith, I simply drifted away.

But in the late 1970s, in order to cut expenses, I moved in a with a friend from high school. Tom, now sadly deceased, was an Evangelical/Fundamentalist Christian. He was brought up in a non-denominational community church that preached a simple Bible-based gospel, built on the twin pillars of Bible alone and faith alone, *Sola Scriptura* and *Sola Fide*.

They also preached Pre-Tribulation Dispensationalism, that apocalyptic teaching that was so-well known through Hal Lindsay's book, *The Late Great Planet Earth*. Pre-Tribulation Dispensationalism, in a simplified nutshell, is the belief that there will be a great seven-year Tribulation near the end of the world, from which all true Christians will be saved by being "raptured" up to heaven just before it starts. All non-Christians will be "left behind." Many will become Christians during the Great Tribulation, but they will either have to suffer or die for their faith. In the end, before the new heavens and the new earth are created, there will be a great final battle: Armageddon. We all know how that ends, of course.

I had never heard any of this before. I knew vaguely that there would be a final judgment, but this was exciting! Cinematic! In fact, it was so cinematic that it was later made into a series of novels and movies called *Left Behind*. Well, not wanting to miss that low-swinging rapture chariot, I bought my ticket and became an Evangelical Fundamentalist. I was a convert.

But my drifting continued, only in a different form, that of searching for the perfect church. *Sola Scriptura* seemed to demand it of me. I needed to be certain that the church where I worshiped had the whole Truth. If it was wrong on one matter,

whether it be on predestination, baptism, faith alone, perseverance of the saints (i.e., "once saved, always saved"), etc. I would
move on to another church, eventually settling for a while with
the Conservative Baptists.

My searching eventually led me to matriculate at a local
Bible college to pursue a degree in Biblical Studies. As much as
I learned there—and I learned a lot—it was also there that my
anti-Catholic biases started to become less vague and more aggressive. In fact, the more focused my Fundamentalism became,
the more aggressive my anti-Catholicism became.

But a degree in Biblical Studies was not in the cards. Finances,
always short in those days, forced me to drop out of college
after two years. What to do? I still wanted that degree. In 1985
I joined the U.S. Army, and after basic and advanced training,
was stationed in what was then West Germany as a Chaplain
Assistant. My best-laid plan was to finish my three-year stint
and then go back home to finish my degree on the G.I. Bill,
possibly even become an Army Chaplain. I discovered early-on
that I was like a fish out of water in the Army, but in those days
I was like a fish out of water anywhere! But I made the best of
it and for the most part enjoyed my tour of duty.

It was in the Army that I met Fr. Raymond J. Guidry, SVD,
the Roman Catholic Chaplain where I was stationed. In fact,
since I was a Chaplain Assistant, he was my boss. Our chapel
had two chaplains, one Protestant (which could be any denomination) and one Roman Catholic. As a Chaplain Assistant, my
job was religious and clerical support, and in war-time I would
be the Chaplain's body guard.

My anti-Catholic biases were about as virulent as ever
in those days, but I didn't allow them to interfere with my
work. So with a little extra time on my hands one afternoon,
Fr. Guidry asked me if I would type out some of his poems.

I didn't know then that he was working on a collection of
poems and short stories for a book, and I only recently discovered that it was published. I could only remember one of
the poems that I typed, and that only partially, but now that
it has been published, I am able to present it here in gratitude
to Fr. Guidry:

Praying Mantis

Clearly I remember, just before September
A Spanish bayonet it leaves
Spire upon spire fell skyward
Its blossoms towered
White, gleaming, cathedral-quiet.
A mantis knelt, prayed
Wimpled in the whited blossoms
An insect strayed, its tilted wings
Swaying, drunk with the summer breeze.
The mantis, hypocrite at prayer.
Spiked, speared, deprived
The insect of all its life
How human-like the mantis.
How mantis-like the human.

I don't think it dawned on me at the time how accurate a
description this poem was of me. But in hindsight I can see
how mantis-like my prayers were. To my mind, the only good
Catholic was a bad Catholic. But despite him being in error (as
I thought), Fr. Guidry was a good and holy man. And though
I didn't think much about it then, he did much to soften my
attitude toward Catholics and Catholicism. I wrote a letter to
Fr. Guidry not long after I became Catholic to thank him and
to tell him about my conversion. He was very kind and called
me on the phone. I think we talked for over an hour. He has
since died. May he rest in peace.

After the Army, my best-laid plan didn't turn out as anticipated. Instead of returning to Bible College, I started settling
down. I was discharged from in the Army in 1988, got married,
and needed to find work. So I went to college part-time for a
degree in Finance, while I worked full-time. In the mid-90s I
went to law school, graduated, welcomed a daughter into the
world, and started my career as a Trust Officer at a major Twin
Cities bank.

That's a decade of my life in one short paragraph. But a
lot more was going on in my spiritual life during that period. For one thing, although I have always been a reader, my
reading picked up and broadened. The topics of my reading
were largely in the areas of philosophy, theology, and literary
and cultural criticism. I found my way back to the Lutheran
Church, but this time it was the more theologically conservative Missouri Synod. And finally, and most importantly, a
friend of mine invited me to a meeting of the Twin Cities
Chesterton Society.

I don't think I can overestimate how crucial Chesterton was
to my conversion to Catholicism. Reading Chesterton was a
major turning point in my thinking, a turning away from what
I've come to identify as heretical thinking. One sees it everywhere in theological and philosophical thought, the tendency
to see one truth, or one aspect of a truth, as the only Truth.
Catholic Apologist and Philosopher Peter Kreeft likes to call it
"nothing buttery." Everything is "nothing but" or only "either/
or," never "both/and." For example, to many Protestants, if we
are saved by faith (and we are), then we are saved by faith alone
(which we aren't). If the Bible is the Word of God (which it
is), then the Bible alone is sufficient (which it isn't). If God is
omnipotent and omniscient (which is true), then our wills can't
be really free (which isn't true).

These are only a few of the many "clean and well-lit" heretical prisons of one idea I had locked myself into. I had begun to question some of my "either/or" presumptions a few years before reading Chesterton, but for the most part, I was just giving up on them in frustration. I knew God was omnipotent and knew the end from the beginning. I also knew in my bones that my will was free—that I made decisions and acted on them. I finally just gave up trying the reconcile them.

But it was in reading Chesterton's book, *Orthodoxy*, that I was finally able to see positively, rather than negatively, that they were both true. Instead of just accepting the contradiction because I couldn't understand it, I was able to embrace both truths because they were both true. For the first time I was beginning to see that a chessboard could be both black on white and white on black. It was like seeing something for the first time, despite the fact that it was right in front of me the whole time. Reading Chesterton was altering my vision. As Chesterton described it, my spiritual sight was becoming stereoscopic. It was a great mystery, but in embracing that mystery, my spiritual insight was becoming more lucid. And it was thrilling to finally see that the spiritual instinct I had held in abeyance for so many years as unreasonable was actually evidence of spiritual health.

So why should this be the major turning point in my conversion to Catholicism? Chesterton wasn't a Catholic when he wrote *Orthodoxy*. By his own admission, he left the question of Church authority unaddressed. Maybe it was the opening of my eyes, or that I was beginning to see with two spiritual eyes rather than one. Maybe it was because I knew that Catholicism was the one big elephant in the room of my mind that I had been avoiding addressing all these years.

In any case, I was beginning to see that I needed to reevaluate some (many!) of my old, longstanding biases against the

Catholic Church. Until this time, almost everything I had read about Catholicism has been from an anti-Catholic perspective. I had been poisoning my own well. But not only did I have to stop poisoning the well, I also had to get out of the well. In other words, I needed to stop seeing only the small circle of sky from deep inside the well and start seeing the entire sky from outside the well. So, in Chesterton's words from *The Catholic Church and Conversion*, I decided to patronize the Catholic Church. I would look at the Church from the Church's own perspective. I would investigate Catholicism's claims to Truth from a consciously unbiased perspective.

But patronizing the Church, deciding to investigate her claims honestly and fairly, according to Chesterton, is only the first stage of conversion. And the first stage leads quickly to the second stage, which is discovering the Church. This stage of discovering the Church usually, as it was for me, is the most enjoyable stage. I read voraciously, ancient and modern; prayed a lot; went to Chesterton Society meetings and conferences; and engaged in many a late-night discussion.

I took on the Church's claims one-by-one: the Eucharist, Confession, the priesthood, praying to Mary and the saints, veneration and praying before images and statues, and on and on. It was exciting and exhilarating, which seems to be why Chesterton also calls this stage "running towards the Church." But it also seemed a never-ending run. To say that the Church is bigger on the inside than it is on the outside is an understatement. The problem was, although I was taking an honest and forthright approach, I hadn't changed my method. I was still trying to satisfy myself on every doctrine, and it seemed like it was going to take forever. Fortunately, I finally got around to investigating what turned out to be the linchpin question: the Papacy, the Primacy of Peter, Apostolic Succession, and the Magisterium. These were all pretty much one multi-part question in my mind.

My point is not to examine this question too closely. Many have done so quite convincingly. Just a few of the authors I found extremely helpful were Msgr. Ronald Knox's *What Catholics Believe*, Scott Hahn's *Rome Sweet Home*, Joseph Pearce's *Literary Converts*, Cardinal Newman's *Apologia Pro Vita Sua*, and Mark Shea's *By What Authority?* The title of Mark Shea's slim volume puts the question quite succinctly. When answering any question of doctrine, one needs to ask what one's authority is. If your authority is not the Church through her Magisterium, then ultimately your authority is you, yourself. I saw no alternative. It's no good to say the Bible is the final authority (*Sola Scriptura*). Someone has to interpret it. And if you say the Bible says of itself that it is the final authority (which it doesn't), that's just circular reasoning.

During this time, I was involved in a scene that almost sounds like a joke. Four men walked into a bar, two Lutherans, a Baptist, and a Catholic. While sitting around a table, one of the Lutherans (in fact, a Lutheran Pastor—now a Catholic) said to the other Lutheran (a Lutheran faithful—myself—now Catholic) while firmly rapping the table-top: "There is no authentic magisterium outside the Catholic Church." The Baptist (now Catholic), listened and seemed to be nodding in agreement. The lone Catholic, being wise, stayed out of the argument.

I did not expect that when I came to the conclusion that the final teaching authority in matters of the Faith and Morals was the Church herself, everything else I had been questioning would start to make sense. I don't mean that I just put on my blinders, fell in line, and followed lock-step what the Church taught. I mean that when I embraced that one mystery that Chesterton talked about in *Orthodoxy*, in this case the teaching authority of the Church, everything else started to become more lucid. I believed the Church's teachings on the Eucharist, Mary, and Confession, not because I had to, but because they made sense.

So there I was, enjoying this wonderful second stage of conversion, open vistas before me, exploring the vast expanses of the Faith—even defending the Faith!—when it slowly started to dawn on me: This is serious business. Does this mean conversion? With that, I had reached Chesterton's third stage of conversion, running from the Church.

For me, conversion—actual reception into the Catholic Church—filled me with apprehension. I was satisfied that the Catholic Church was the one True Church. But I also knew that entering the Church was irrevocable. It wasn't like being Protestant, where I could hop from church to church, denomination to denomination. Once Catholic, always Catholic. There was no turning back. Its finality was like death. But "unless a grain of wheat falls into the earth and dies, it remains alone; but if it dies, it bears much fruit." Yes, I was contemplating conversion because I believed the Catholic Church was the One True Church, but also because—as it was for Chesterton—I wanted to get rid of my sins.

Which brings me to Confession. Confession filled me with dread, to kneel before a priest and reveal the most secret, and not so secret, sins of my life. Maybe that was the nub of it. Yes, that was the nub of it. Or, more precisely, that was the crux of it. I understood that if our Lord and Savior, Jesus Christ, was willing to suffer and die on the cross to save me from my sins— all of which He already knew—and if the Church He instituted on earth provided for the forgiveness of my sins through the Sacrament of Confession, how much sense did it make for me to try to conceal those sins? If I were truly kneeling before

Christ, would I be fool enough to attempt to conceal my sins? Any sins? Well, that's what it is in the Confessional. When we kneel before the priest, who is there *in persona Christi*, we are kneeling before Christ. I knew, as I later came to experience, that there is no grace or mercy in this life as there is in the Confessional.

But despite my knowledge and understanding of these truths, I dithered, I put off the final decision. I was in a desperate way. There had to be a loophole. I knew that there was no salvation outside the Catholic Church, but properly understood, I also knew that there was hope for salvation for those who, through no fault of their own and living by their best lights (the "invincibly ignorant"), were not formally received into the Catholic Church. But it didn't take me long to see the flaw in my logic, and therefore to pull the rug out from under myself: if I agreed with the Church on this provision, then, logically, I had to be received into the Church—I knew where salvation lay, and therefore could not claim invincible ignorance for something of which I was simply not ignorant!

My mind was made up, so while attending the 2000 American Chesterton Society Conference, I asked Fr. James Reidy, also a member of the Twin Cities Chesterton Society, to instruct me in the Faith. On Sunday, November 19, in the Jubilee Year of 2000, in the Cathedral of St. Paul in St. Paul, Minnesota, with Deacon Nathan Allen as my Sponsor, I was received and confirmed by Fr. James Reidy into the Catholic Church.

While the above only scratches the surface (I have left much unsaid), it might seem, looking back, as though I brought myself into the Church one logical step at a time. It would be more accurate to say that I entered the Church only after tripping over a long series of thresholds, each one landing me flat on my face in a larger and brighter room than the one before, until finally, after my own great resistance, I dragged myself through the final door into that great and glorious house of many mansions that is the Catholic Church.

When we look back on certain periods or events in our lives, it often seems as though things couldn't have turned out any other way. The complexity of it all makes it seem foreordained. And yet, at the same time, I have free will. I make choices. And so does everyone else. That's the great mystery of Providence. So if, as Chesterton says, my free will enables me to say "if you please" to the housemaid, it also enables me to say thank you to God and to all those in my life who, in cooperation with God's Providence, helped prepare and lead me as I tripped—sometimes merrily and sometimes anxiously—into the great Universal Household of Faith that is the Catholic Church. But two dear friends I have especially to thank: Deacon Nathan Allen, who invited me to that early Twin Cities Chesterton Society meeting so many years ago; and Dale Ahlquist, President of the American Chesterton Society and "Acting Czar" of the Twin Cities Chesterton Society. With G.K. Chesterton, it is their friendship, patient support, and prayers, through all my questions and arguments, for which I am most grateful. I can't imagine myself being Catholic today without them.

TEN THOUSAND REASONS

By Brandon Vogt

I WAS IN COLLEGE THE FIRST TIME SOMEONE RECOMMEND-
ED G.K. CHESTERTON'S ORTHODOXY TO ME. And to my
endless shame, I dismissed the suggestion. I was a young,
20-year-old Protestant, who had recently encountered Jesus,
was excited about my faith, and was deeply involved with a
Methodist campus ministry. Like many newly energized
Christians, I was hungry to read and learn. I devoured books
by contemporary Protestant writers like Philip Yancey, Rick
Warren, and Rob Bell. But I wasn't interested in my friend's
suggestion because I had never heard of Chesterton and "orthodoxy" sounded dusty and outdated. So even though my friend
recommended the book enthusiastically, I ignored it.

Yet Chesterton hovered in the background. It was hard to
avoid him completely. Even as a Protestant, I began seeing
his name popping up everywhere. It was strange how nearly
everyone I read quoted him. This witty Catholic was one of

the few points of commonality, other than Jesus Christ, who seemed to bind Protestant writers from every persuasion, from senior pastors to the "new monastics" living with the poor to high-minded theologians to hipster Christian bloggers. They all quoted Chesterton, and I found that alluring. Who was this man who seemed equally loved by everyone?

Around the same time, another friend turned me on to C.S. Lewis. That suggestion I accepted. I had never read Lewis' Narnia stories as a child, so it was as a college student that I moved through the wardrobe. Lewis did for me as he's done for so many: he baptized my imagination, sacramentalizing it, confirming that the world bubbles and ripples with meaning and that everything around us can be read as a signpost to something deeper. He gave me wonder and wisdom, and I thought nobody better embodied those traits.

I devoured everything Lewis wrote. *Mere Christianity, Screwtape Letters, The Problem of Pain, The Great Divorce*—they all worked on me. I read Lewis' letters and diaries and all of his novels. I just couldn't get enough. Lewis was the clearest and smartest Christian I knew. He made it seem so reasonable to be Christian. He gave me confidence, and delivered a more thoughtful and substantial faith than the inspirational, therapeutic Christian books I had cut my teeth on.

Little did I know his greatest gift would be paving the way for Chesterton. It was while reading Lewis' memoir, *Surprised By Joy*, that I learned of his appreciation for Chesterton. There Lewis wrote:

> I had never heard of [Chesterton] and had no idea of what he stood for; nor can I quite understand why he made such an immediate conquest of me... His humour was of the kind I like best—not 'jokes' imbedded in the page like currants in a cake, still less (what I cannot endure), a general tone of flippancy and

jocularity, but the humour which is not in any way separable from the argument but is rather (as Aristotle would say) the "bloom" on dialectic itself. The sword glitters not because the swordsman set out to make it glitter but because he is fighting for his life and therefore moving it very quickly. For the critics who think Chesterton frivolous or 'paradoxical' I have to work hard to feel even pity; sympathy is out of the question. Moreover, strange as it may seem, I liked him for his goodness.

The more I read Lewis, the more often I saw him praise and recommend Chesterton. To his friend Sheldon Vanauken, author of *A Severe Mercy*, Lewis asked, "Have you ever tried Chesterton's *The Everlasting Man*? The best popular apologetic I know." In Lewis' famous BBC Broadcast Talks, which were later compiled into the classic book *Mere Christianity*, he said he was inspired by Chesterton's own case for Christianity. So the fact that my greatest Christian hero gave so much deference to G.K. Chesterton finally convinced me that I must read him, too.

I finally did. I tracked down my old copy of *Orthodoxy*, the one I dismissed earlier, and started reading. It was like touching an electric wire. *Orthodoxy* was different than any religious book I had ever read. The prose sparkled and glittered, and yet there was something substantial beneath all that shimmer. He made doctrine dance and theology sing. He made orthodoxy compelling.

From there I read a short profile of Chesterton himself (from Yancey's book, *Soul Survivor: How Thirteen Unlikely Mentors Helped My Faith Survive the Church*.) And from there I was totally hooked. Chesterton's writing is enough to captivate most people. But Chesterton the man is irresistible.

He quickly became my favorite writer. I hunted used book stores for Chesterton titles. I downloaded public domain eBooks. I read *The Everlasting Man*, then his essays, then his novels, and then his mystery stories and poetry. My wife and I even named our sixth child Gilbert after him. Few people have shaped my mind, or influenced my faith, more than G.K. Chesterton.

But how did he help convert me? How did he lead me to become Catholic? Well, to paraphrase the witty master himself, the difficulty of answering that question is that there are ten thousand reasons all amounting to one reason: he showed me that it is true.

Each of Chesterton's writings, in all their different genres, were like converging arrows that seemed to point to this single fact: Catholicism is true. All roads lead to Rome, and so does all of Chesterton.

But there were three specific ways Chesterton guided me to the Church. First, he taught me the value of Tradition. In the best chapter of his best book—"The Ethics of Elfland," in *Orthodoxy*—Chesterton notes, "Tradition means giving a vote to the most obscure of all classes, our ancestors. It is the democracy of the dead." In other words, Tradition is merely democracy extended through time.

As a Protestant, I thought Tradition referred to those antiquated and arbitrary practices that have no meaning and which nobody understands, but which we continue doing simply because our fathers and grandfathers did them, too—likely also without good reason. And on this view, Tradition was a dirty word because Tradition obscured the real practice of faith, encumbering people with pointless rites and rituals.

I also presumed Faith was like science: knowledge building upon knowledge, like a snowball, which meant newer must be bigger and better, the more recent, the truer. This is another reason I thought Tradition was dismissible. Just as we've moved on from the physics of ancient Greece, so we've transcended Tradition.

But in just one chapter, Chesterton knocked down all my arguments and changed my mind. His "democracy of the dead" idea disabused me of what C.S. Lewis diagnosed as "chronological snobbery," determining truth by our calendars or watches. Newer is not always better, and older is not always off. But Chesterton understood this decades before Lewis, and his insights suggested that if I wanted to know the truth about God or the Church, I should give equal voice to Christians from every century—not just the twenty-first. And when I listened to that democracy, I saw it spoke quite clearly. To my surprise I found that Christians for the first thousand years were nearly unanimous in their beliefs. They celebrated the Mass and believed in the Real Presence of the Eucharist. The overwhelming majority prayed to saints, devoted themselves to Mary, and recognized the offices of priest, bishop, and pope. In other words, the democracy was Catholic.

If the truths of faith are gauged not by the "small and arrogant oligarchy of those who merely happen to be walking about," but by the vote of all Christians throughout the last two thousand years, the conclusion seemed unavoidable: in a landslide election, the democracy of the dead has emphatically voted "Yes!" to the Catholic Church. I don't think anything swung my inner pendulum more toward the Church than this one insight.

But there was more. A second way Chesterton helped me become Catholic was introducing me to a compelling priest. The Methodist campus ministry I was part of in college boasted a smart, hip pastor with tattoos and engaging sermons. I deeply admired him. He was someone I wanted to follow and imitate. Yet when I started looking into the Catholic Church, I didn't know any priests like that. In fact, I didn't know any priests. Everything I knew about the priesthood came from TV and movies, which meant the word "priest" connoted old men, disconnected from real life.

Until I discovered Father Brown. He was different. Chesterton's Father Brown showed me the glory of the priesthood, of what it could be—of what it should be. Of course Father Brown was fictional (though I later learned, he was based on a real priest, Father John O'Connor, one of Chesterton's good friends.) Yet still, Chesterton's priest changed my own view of the priesthood. He burst the stereotypes. He was spiritually alert. Though physically small and unassuming, he was magnanimous, large-souled. Nobody hated sin more, yet nobody loved sinners more intensely. And what affected me most was Chesterton's assertion that all of this flowed from Father Brown's time in the confessional. Today, few people take priests seriously, thinking them out of touch with the grittiness of the real world. But for Chesterton, it's a priest's close proximity to sinners in the confessional that actually gives them the most insight into the deepest truths of humanity, including the darkest recesses of the human soul. From Father Brown I learned how priests can be soul doctors, or "experts in humanity" to use a favorite phrase of John Paul II, because they are experts in listening to sinners. And that helped me to love priests, or at least love the priesthood, which was another major step toward Rome.

The next step was similar. Just as Chesterton provided my first compelling image of a priest, he also gave me the first thrilling depiction of a Catholic, and it was Chesterton himself. I didn't know any Protestants like Chesterton. His childlike wonder at ordinary things, his staunch defense of the family (which for him also meant a staunch rejection of contraception and divorce), his overflowing sense of gratitude, his ability to take all things lightly as if this life was just a passing pilgrimage—all of that drew me to Chesterton. It's no exaggeration to say he was the most compelling Christian I had ever encountered.

I lacked the vocabulary at the time, but now, having converted to Catholicism, I see what was happening: I was meeting a saint. Saints always provoke this reaction. They're fascinating and beguiling, other-worldly, and strangely attractive. They cause us to wonder at what inspires them, at what gives them such joy and sanity.

And according to Chesterton, it was his Catholicism. Though early in life he dabbled in the occult and flirted with nihilism, both periods darkly described in his autobiography, he eventually found his way to the Catholic Church. It was a long journey, taking several decades. But when he did finally convert, his life and marriage exuded the fruits of the Holy Spirit. In fact, that's probably the best way to describe what attracted me most about him: he exhibited the fruits of the Spirit unlike anyone I've encountered—love, joy, peace, patience, kindness, generosity, faithfulness, gentleness, self-control. They each sum up Gilbert Keith Chesterton, and explain why he's been such an attractive usher into the Church.

Those are but three of the tens of thousands of ways Chesterton led me into the Church, and once inside, even deeper within. There's so much more to be said. I could have mentioned his Distributism, his marriage, or his mysticism. I could have celebrated his wit, his genius, or his romanticism.

Friends ask me how often I read Chesterton, and the true answer is that I really never stop. I'm now the President of the Central Florida Chesterton Society, where we meet monthly to discuss books by or about Chesterton, which means I'm always in the middle of some Chestertonian title. In fact, our local Chesterton Society is a microcosm of his greater effect on the world. Two people in our group have recently converted to

Catholicism via Chesterton and at least two more have joined R.C.I.A., starting the conversion process. I personally know at least a half-dozen others who, as Protestants, went from reading C.S. Lewis to G.K. Chesterton to Catholicism. It's one of the most consistently effective routes of conversion to the Catholic Church. In fact, Chesterton Society groups may be better described as "conversion incubators."

One day, God willing, the Church will recognize G.K. Chesterton as a saint, ideally alongside his equally holy wife, Frances. And when that happens, I hope the Church immediately designates him the patron saint of converts (and beer, and blogging, among other things.) Because that's what Chesterton is at his best: a convert maker. Most people who read him want what he has. And what he has is Christ, who is found most fully and clearly in the Catholic Church.

A mother once wrote to C.S. Lewis lamenting that her little boy loved Aslan, the lion from The Chronicles of Narnia, more than Jesus. Lewis told her not to worry because Aslan is simply Christ in a different world, and everything her son loved about Aslan he would come to love about Christ.

We might say something similar about Chesterton. So many people love Chesterton, from Catholics to Protestants to atheists. And that's a good thing, because everything they love about Chesterton they will ultimately find in the Church.

That was my story. I wanted what Chesterton had, and I found it where he did.

SURPRISED BY THE JOY OF CHESTERTON

By Joseph Pearce

O N MAY 28, 1982, POPE JOHN PAUL II became the first ever Roman Pontiff to visit the British Isles. As a member of the anti-Catholic Orange Order, I opposed the Pope's visit, arguing that Britain had liberated herself from popery during the Reformation and that the Pope was not welcome in the UK. My militant anti-Catholicism was being compromised, however, by an emerging sympathy with some aspects of Catholicism. I rejoiced at the role that John Paul II was playing in bringing down communist tyranny. His visit to Poland in 1979 had sown the seeds for the founding of the Solidarity trade union in the following year, the rise of which I supported passionately. I had also become an admirer

This essay is adapted from parts of chapters 15 and 16 of Joseph Pearce's book, *Race with the Devil: My Journey from Racial Hatred to Rational Love* (Saint Benedict Press, 2013).

of a number of Catholic writers and intellectuals, including G.K. Chesterton and Hilaire Belloc. I did not approve of their Catholicism, at least not at first, but was enamored of their political and social vision.

I was originally attracted to the radical ideas of Chesterton and Belloc because they represented a genuine alternative to the big government of the socialists and the big business of the multinational capitalists. Although I despised communism and its softer Siamese twin, socialism, I was also opposed to the rise of plutocratic globalism in which organizations such as the World Bank and the International Monetary Fund used their wealth to mold global politics and economics in accordance with their own self-interested agenda. Increasingly I perceived myself as being neither on the left nor the right but as believing in a distinct "third position," mistrustful of big government of whatever political hue, which I perceived in the Orwellian sense as being Big Brother, the crusher of freedom. I came to see that Big Brother was essentially the same whether he wore a swastika or a hammer and sickle. I was, therefore, looking for an alternative to these equally erroneous alternatives to the status quo and was ripe for the ideas of Chesterton and Belloc.

I believe that the person who was most responsible for leading me in the direction of these two great Catholic writers was a friend who, at the time, was a professor of politics at Harrogate College in Yorkshire. It was he who suggested that I should study their Distributist ideas. Specifically, he suggested that I read Chesterton's book, *The Outline of Sanity*, and also an essay entitled "Reflections on a Rotten Apple" in another Chesterton book, *The Well and the Shallows*. Since these volumes were both out of print he directed me to Aidan Mackey, a dealer in used books who specialized in Chesterton and Belloc. Aidan would later become a good friend who helped greatly with the research for my biography of Chesterton.

I devoured *The Outline of Sanity*, agreeing with almost everything that Chesterton said and loving the way that he said it. His personality, full of a vigorous *joie de vivre*, seemed to leap from the page into the intimate presence of the reader. More than thirty years later, I can still remember the thrill that I received when reading Chesterton's political philosophy for the first time. This passage from *The Outline of Sanity*, evoking an idealized once and future England, resonates with me now as it resonated then:

> I should maintain that there is a very large element still in England that would like a return to this simpler sort of England. Some of them understand it better than others, some of them understand themselves better than others; some would be prepared for it as a revolution; some only cling to it very blindly as a tradition; some have never thought of it as anything but a hobby; some have never heard of it and feel it only as a want. But the number of people who would like to get out of the tangle of mere ramifications and communications in the town, and get back nearer to the roots of things, where things are made directly out of nature, I believe to be very large.

In Chesterton, I had found a new friend who would become the most powerful influence (under grace) on my personal and intellectual development over the following years. Having read *The Outline of Sanity* I began to call myself a "Distributist."

Distributism, the new creed to which I subscribed, is rooted in the principle that the possession of productive property, i.e. land and capital, is an essential guarantor of economic and political freedom. As such, a society in which many people possess such property is more just and more free than a society in which fewer people possess it. In practical terms, this means that an economy comprised of many small businesses is better than an economy comprised of few big businesses. The same principle applied to politics means that a society comprised of many small governments, i.e. revitalized local governments, is more just than a society comprised of one big government, the latter of which is separated from the needs of local people by its size and its geographical distance from them.

Whereas capitalism concentrated the ownership of property into the hands of a few businessmen, socialism sought to concentrate its ownership into the hands of the State, which meant, in practical terms, handing over the ownership of property from a few businessmen to a few politicians. In both scenarios the people are deprived of the productive property which is the guarantor of their economic and political liberty. Choosing between socialism and capitalism, Chesterton wrote, "is like saying we must choose between all men going into monasteries and a few men having harems":

> There is less difference than many suppose between the ideal Socialist system, in which the big businesses are run by the State, and the present Capitalist system, in which the State is run by the big businesses. They are much nearer to each other than either is to my own ideal—of breaking up the big businesses into a multitude of small businesses.

Little did I know it at the time but the "kernel" of Distributism is to be found in what the Catholic Church has called subsidiarity and in the Church's understanding of the inviolable sanctity of the family. This connection between Distributism and the family was highlighted by Chesterton in an article from *G.K.'s Weekly*:

> The recognition of the family as the unit of the State is the kernel of Distributism. The insistence on ownership to protect its liberty is the shell. We that are Christians believe that the

family has a divine sanction. But any reasonable pagan, if he will work it out, will discover that the family existed before the State and has prior rights; that the State exists only as a collection of families, and that its sole function is to safeguard the rights of each and all of them.

Without being a Christian myself, I had no difficulty agreeing with Chesterton's words. I had learned to despise Big Brother in all his manifestations and was enough of a cultural traditionalist to value the role of the family in society. The idea of strengthening the family by weakening the State was very appealing.

Although *The Outline of Sanity* had been easy to read, in the sense that it dealt with political and economic issues with which I could sympathize, my reading of *The Well and the Shallows* would prove more of a challenge to my political pride and religious prejudice. I had bought it for the solitary essay, "Reflections on a Rotten Apple," which was on page 220 of the book, but I decided to read the book from cover to cover.

The Well and the Shallows was one of Chesterton's last books, published in 1935, the year before he died, and much of the book was a defense of the author's Catholic faith. There were six separate essays at the beginning of the book, entitled collectively "My Six Conversions," which outlined the various reasons for Chesterton's embrace of Catholicism. For whatever reason, I devoured these essays with the same enthusiasm with which I devoured Chesterton's political essays. I didn't necessarily agree with everything that Chesterton said but I couldn't help liking the way that he said it. Even more unsettling to my own religious prejudices was the uncomfortable feeling that I wanted to like what Chesterton liked, even if I had always believed that I didn't like it. I have no better way of explaining this strange bond that I had formed with Chesterton than to quote C.S. Lewis' brilliant description (from *Surprised by Joy*)

of Chesterton's immediate impact upon him when, as a young
atheist, he had first read one of Chesterton's books:

> I had never heard of him and had no idea of what he stood for;
> nor can I quite understand why he made such an immediate
> conquest of me. It might have been expected that my pessi-
> mism, my atheism, and my hatred of sentiment would have
> made him to me the least congenial of all authors. It would
> almost seem that Providence, or some 'second cause' of a very
> obscure kind, quite over-rules our previous tastes when It de-
> cides to bring two minds together. Liking an author may be
> as involuntary and improbable as falling in love. I was by now
> a sufficiently experienced reader to distinguish liking from
> agreement. I did not need to accept what Chesterton said in
> order to enjoy it. His humour was of the kind which I like
> best ... the humour which is not in any way separable from
> the argument but is rather (as Aristotle would say) the 'bloom'
> on dialectic itself ... Moreover, strange as it may seem, I liked
> him for his goodness. I can attribute this taste to myself freely
> (even at that age) because it was a liking for goodness which
> had nothing to do with any attempt to be good myself ... It
> was a matter of taste: I felt the 'charm' of goodness as a man
> feels the charm of a woman he has no intention of marrying
> ... In reading Chesterton ... I did not know what I was letting
> myself in for. A young man who wishes to remain a sound
> Atheist cannot be too careful of his reading.

Lewis was nineteen-years-old when he first read Chesterton,
about the same age that I was when I read *The Outline of Sanity*
and *The Well and the Shallows*, and I can testify that his reaction
to Chesterton was exactly the same as mine. I was as mystified
as Lewis at the way that Chesterton had made an immediate
conquest of me. Like Lewis, it might have been expected that my
own anti-Catholicism would have made Chesterton the least
congenial of authors. Yet, as with Lewis, it was almost as though
something mystical or providential had brought together our

two minds in friendship. It was indeed like falling in love. I had fallen in love with the wit and wisdom of Chesterton and had fallen under the charm of his humour and humility. Like Lewis, I did not know what I was letting myself in for. A young atheist cannot be too careful of his reading but neither can a young agnostic anti-Catholic. In reading Chesterton I was undermining my own most dearly held prejudices. Lewis believed that "Chesterton had more sense than all the other moderns put together"—except, of course, his Christianity. I believed that Chesterton had more common sense than anyone else—except, of course, his Catholicism.

I realize now what I had no way of realizing then, that it was the combination of Chesterton's eminently rational mind and his transparently virtuous heart that had captured and captivated me. It was the presence of goodness, the light of sanctity shining forth in the darkness, the life of love that can kill all hatred.

Shortly after I finished reading Chesterton's *The Well and the Shallows* a Jehovah's Witness knocked on the door of the house in which I was living in south London. Normally I would simply do whatever was necessary to induce these intrusive proselytizers to leave. On this occasion, however, I decided to indulge in an enjoyable intellectual exercise. I decided to pretend that I was a Catholic and set about using Chesterton's arguments for the Faith in my discussion with the visitor on my doorstep. I had great fun putting myself in the shoes of a papist and was convinced by the end of our discussion that I had won the argument. The Jehovah's Witness was, however, not convinced, thereby depriving me of the strange satisfaction of converting someone to a creed in which I did not myself believe. Looking back on this episode, I nurture the quixotic hope that I had perhaps sowed a few seeds of doubt in my interlocutor's mind about the false creed in which he believed so fervently;

more importantly, I hope that I had also planted seeds of faith in the ancient creed which he had argued against.

I had paid the princely sum of £12 for my copy of *The Well and the Shallows* due to its being a first edition with its original dust jacket. It was, however, very easy in those days to pick up Chesterton books in used bookstores for around 20 pence. Chesterton's star had faded in the culture of liberalism that prevailed in the wake of the Second Vatican Council and few people seemed interested in his robust apologetics. Although times have changed and Chesterton is once again very much *en vogue*, I am happy in hindsight to have built my extensive library of Chesterton titles at so little cost. I had very little money and I doubt that I could have indulged my Chesterton habit so liberally had the cost of his books been much higher.

I spent many happy hours trawling through used bookstores, of which there were many in those more literate times, buying anything by Chesterton and also anything by his great friend and comrade in arms, Hilaire Belloc. Chesterton acknowledged that Belloc was the founder of Distributism, of whom Chesterton considered himself a disciple, and Belloc's *Servile State* and his *Essay on the Restoration of Property* were seminal works which demanded a place in any self-respecting Distributist's library. I devoured these books with the same devotion with which I devoured the works of Chesterton. Furthermore, I developed a literary friendship and ideological affinity with Belloc, which was second only to my love of Chesterton in intensity. I read many books by Belloc during this period and his *Four Men* became and has remained one of my all-time favorite works, transporting me into a Shire every bit as arcane and Arcadian as that to be found in Middle-earth.

And speaking of the Shire, my reading of Chesterton and Belloc caused me to reconsider the nature of my love for my own country and, more radically, to ask fundamental questions about which country it was to which I owed allegiance. I had been brought up by my father to love Britain and the British Empire and to rejoice in great British military victories, such as Trafalgar, Waterloo, Rorke's Drift and the Battle of Britain. No real distinction was made between "Britain" and "England," the two words being used synonymously, so that the English victory at Agincourt was mentioned in the same breath as the aforementioned British victories. England and Britain were certainly not synonymous in Chesterton's eyes. On the contrary, Chesterton seemed to owe his allegiance to the one and not particularly to the other. He was an Englishman who looked upon the Scots, Irish and Welsh as being distinctly different peoples, no more English than were the French or the Germans. He taught me the difference between being a Little Englander and a Great Britisher, the former of which rejoices in the small-ness of his country and its uniqueness, whilst the latter rejoices in its greatness and the extent to which it had expanded and implanted its influence around the world. A Little Englander was a nationalist, in the diminutive sense of the word; he merely wished for autonomy for England in the same way that a Welsh, Irish or Scottish nationalist sought autonomy for their respec-tive nations. A Great Britisher was not a nationalist in this healthy sense of the word but was an imperialist who sought to impose his will on other nations. Far from being a nation-alist, a Great Britisher was an internationalist who sought to bring other nations under the British imperial yoke. In coming to understand and sympathize with Belloc's and Chesterton's opposition to the Boer War, I came to see that the power of the British Empire was that of a big bully, fighting at the behest of plutocratic mining interests to subjugate the legitimate aspi-rations of the Afrikaans farmers. Slowly but surely, under the

benign influence of Chesterton and Belloc, I metamorphosed
from being a Great Britisher to being a Little Englander. Many
years later, I endeavored to summarize the difference between
the two in a short poem:

> When Britain had an Empire
> The sun would never set,
> But the sun set over England
> And Englishmen forget
> That greater than the Empire
> Are the rolling Yorkshire Moors,
> And more glorious the Dales
> Than all the Empire's wars.

As I delved deeper into Distributism I became increasingly aware that it was a manifestation of the social teaching of
the Catholic Church. Belloc and Chesterton were merely the
propagators and popularizers of the Church's social doctrine
as expounded by Pope Leo XIII in *Rerum novarum* (1891), a
doctrine that would later be re-stated, re-confirmed and rein-
forced by Pope Pius XI in *Quadragesimo anno* (1931), by John
Paul II in *Centesimus annus* (1991), and by Benedict XVI in
Caritas in veritate (2009). It was from *Rerum novarum* that
Belloc had drawn the ideas and inspiration for his writing on
political and economic issues, although his later writings, most
particularly his *Essay on the Restoration of Property* (1936),
would have been able to draw inspiration from *Quadragesimo
anno* also. Aware of this connection between the Distributism
that I now espoused and the teaching of the Catholic Church,
I made a point of reading *Rerum novarum* and *Quadragesimo
anno*, which I very much enjoyed. I was also pleased, whilst
browsing in a used bookstore in Streatham in south London,
to come across Pius XI's encyclical *Divini redemptoris* (1937),

his famous attack "on atheistic communism." Almost against my will, I found myself being attracted to the papacy as a clear voice of wisdom in a muddled world, further stimulating my embryonic attraction to the Church.

If I had to pick only one moment from the many marvelous moments I have spent with Chesterton over the years, it would have to be that moment when, for the first time, I opened the pages of *The Well and the Shallows*, and with the opening of the pages discovered the opening of a whole new world before my awakened eyes. Without such a meeting with the rational mind and faithful heart of Chesterton, I might never have been received into the salvific arms of Holy Mother Church. This is why I thank God for introducing me to the wit and wisdom of G.K. Chesterton.

THE CRESCENT AND THE CROSS

By Zubair Simonson

K HALID AND I STOOD ON THE SIDEWALK CORNER, staring down at the flyer in my hands: free admission to a strip club. Our eyes looked up, and met. We were both grinning.

Having just moved to New York, in 2005, I had gotten in touch with Khalid, a friend of mine from the Muslim Student Association (MSA) at the University of Michigan, who lived in the city. By this point I was a lousy Muslim. I had grown up to understand Allah as an objective "out there" to be obeyed or, when the need arose, blamed. To me, Islam, submission to God, was an endless list of arbitrary rules, deeds that were labeled as *halal* (pleasing to God) or *haram* (displeasing to God). For a good number of years, I was motivated by the belief that by being a "good boy," God would bless me with what I wanted; a family, wealth, and a political career down the line. An adequate fear of hell likewise motivated me to stay fairly clear from *haram*. But having grown up in the United States, with mostly non-Muslim friends, I also developed doubt that many of these rules (such as prohibiting alcohol and pork), had anything to do with being a decent person at heart. I found some of the punishments prescribed by *Sharia* law, such as the capital punishment for apostates, to be retrograde and barbaric, a stark contrast to Common Law. But I had never shared such sentiments with Khalid up to this point.

"I'll go if you go," I said.

"Okay," Khalid enthusiastically replied.

The gentleman who had handed us the flyers pointed south-ward. Khalid and I began walking down the vibrant Manhattan streets. Soon enough, we were in the strip club. Our eyes, like the eyes of the other patrons, were hypnotically staring at the voluptuous fake breasts of the topless woman dancing on the stage. We suddenly realized that we were standing right in front of the bar. Again, our eyes met.

"I'll have a beer if you have a beer," Khalid said.

I shrugged my shoulders. "Sure."

And we proceeded with our drink order.

Khalid and I would laugh about this for years afterward. I always went to MSA events whenever free food was advertised, and always saw Khalid there. Khalid always went to MSA events whenever free food was advertised, and always saw me there. We each assumed that the other was pious. We were re-ally both tourists, but neither of us desired to be found out, for fear that our fellow Muslims would rescind the invitations to events with free food. I knew of other nominal Muslims while in college, who drank or even used drugs, but never suspected Khalid of being nominal. We had to pick and choose who to be open with about such matters, or risk alienation from the local community. This was how we found out about each other.

I was walking through Times Square, in February 2006. My eyes caught the news, scrolling on the ticker on the side of the building: the Al-Askari Shrine, a holy site to Shia Muslims, had been bombed by Sunni terrorists in Iraq. The Sunni-Shia split occurred during the 7th Century, over a dispute regarding Muhammad's proper successor, leading to the tragic death of Muhammad's grandson during the Battle of Karbala. But that was almost 1400 years ago!

Memories began to flood into my mind: of September 11 and the weeks that followed, of a *khutba* (Friday sermon) in which the speaker complained that the American government was "wrongfully" preventing young American Muslims from serving *jihad* in Iraq, of so many fellow Muslims casting blame for failed Muslim-majority states on "the Jews" or "the West" and casually throwing around conspiracy theories, of witnessing a friend get struck by a Sunday school instructor, of listening to a debate amongst Muslim-American college students over whether apostates should be executed, of a Sunday school instructor explaining that it is *haram* to yawn and *halal* to sneeze, of being lectured about the "sin" of getting my ear pierced in college, and so on. Those who gave in to violence and superstition could cite verses from the *Quran* or a *hadith* (sayings of Muhammad) to support their claims.

My mother's family (a mixture of practicing and nominal Muslims) tended toward moderation and were integrated in the countries that adopted them. Because of that, for years I accepted the idea that violence done in the name of Islam was not in accord with real Islam. I also had a deep fascination with Sufism, Islam's inward-looking mystical tradition. Those who stressed that Islam was a religion of peace could likewise cite verses from the *Quran* or a *hadith* to support their positions.

Which of these was the real Islam? I wondered.

I reflected upon Muhammad, a man who, according to what I had been taught, lived as a perfect model to follow. Under his guidance, monotheism replaced the barbaric paganism of the Arabian Peninsula. Orphaned at an early age, having grown up in a backwater, he founded an empire. He spoke many words of peace during the early years of his mission, when he had a handful of followers. And he died a warlord, when he had many followers. He suddenly seemed akin to a Shakespearean tragic figure; a man of great integrity corrupted by great power.

I knew that violence committed by a Buddhist or Christian could not fairly be thrown at the feet of Buddha or Jesus Christ. Neither of them commanded armies. Siddhartha Gautama even renounced his princely title. But the armies under Muhammad had conquered the Arabian Peninsula by the time of his death, and continued expanding for centuries afterward.

Why was it that so many of Muhammad's actions, such as orders to execute (or even mass execute), or his having nine wives (when Islam only allows four), needed to be clarified? If a person lived perfectly, would his words and deeds need to be explained away? Muhammad certainly lived an impressive life. But a perfect life is a different matter.

The news scrolling on the ticker was far from the first report I had heard of violence done in the name of Islam. But it was the last straw. I vowed never to call myself a Muslim again.

It was a Saturday in January 2007. I was walking along the Hudson River, wondering if it made sense to hurl myself into the water. In retrospect, I think I was depressed.

I was working in a marketing company, under a boss who helped me realize that evil does, in fact, exist. There are people who lie, to themselves and others, so routinely that all bearing of truth gets lost, and evil is the fitting description for such a state.

I had caught my boss routinely lying to clients, to me and my co-workers, to his superiors, to his boyfriend, and above all, to himself. He remarkably seemed convinced of so many of his lies. Being immersed in such an environment, and telling myself it was acceptable to look the other way, took its toll. Circumstances easily crush a person who looks outward for meaning.

I had subscribed to the sentiment that all religions were equally useless. The nearest thing I had to any religion was a mild interest in New Age. Being spiritually rudderless, I knew of no way to contextualize these circumstances.

Is this what life is like? I thought to myself.

And as I continued along the Hudson River, wallowing in depression, a thought occurred on me: to be born again.

Having grown up in North Carolina, the born again message was, culturally, always near. Many of my friends were (nominal) Christians. Some of my relatives were (mostly nominal) Christians. I had heard reports that a former acquaintance had recently "given his life to Jesus" after being arrested, and began turning his own life around.

Much Christian teaching did not make sense to me. Equating the Trinity with monotheism seemed like bad math. I preferred a more "coherent," meaning simpler, theology. Why an omnipresent, omniscient, and omnipotent God would ever have a son seemed preposterous. I had even less clue of what a "Holy Spirit" was. The little I knew about Original Sin impressed me as overly cynical. And I had more than once passed by a street preacher, or spoken with a well-meaning friend, whose presentation of the Christian faith came across as far from inclusive. For several years, I had been at peace with the popular notion that Christians—believing Christians—were dense.

But above all, I just wanted a fresh start. So I walked to the nearest Barnes & Noble to pick up a book. And that book was...

The Purpose Driven Life, by Rick Warren.

Rick Warren's book was alright. It was enough to convince me to read the Bible. This made sense from a secular standpoint, given the Bible's influence. I began attending Mass at St. Patrick's Cathedral (and partaking in the Eucharist when I was not supposed to), despite my conditioned discomfort with statues in the church.

A desire to learn the basics of Christianity led me to read the works of C.S. Lewis, starting with *Mere Christianity*. As a trained Muslim, the greatest shock for me was to read the claim that Jesus Christ was, in fact, God. It never previously occurred to me that "Son of God" meant just that. My knee-jerk reaction was to think "blasphemy." But determined as I was to resist this claim, much else of what Lewis wrote about made a great deal of sense. Perhaps, I thought, I can be a Christian without believing Jesus was God.

The internet informed me that Lewis had been profoundly impacted by a book titled *The Everlasting Man,* a historical outline with Christ as the turning point. It was by a guy named G.K. Chesterton. So I resolved to read it. Although I had long been at peace with the notion that believing Christians were dumb, the words of G.K. Chesterton challenged this notion in only the first few sentences: he was clearly more intelligent than me, yet he was a believing Christian.

It was this book, more than any other, that helped me realize that the Incarnation and the Resurrection of our Lord were plausible.

That is how I met Mr. Chesterton.

By May of 2007, I had been reading the works of Lewis, Chesterton, and the Bible in its entirety for several months. I suddenly realized something odd: that I believed in Jesus Christ's divinity. In fact, I had believed this for several weeks, but could not pinpoint a moment when any "switch" happened. So I began looking around for a church that would baptize me with minimal-to-no preparation.

In June 2007, I was baptized in a non-denominational church. I swiftly involved myself at the Haven, a weekly worship gathering of Christian artists, and joined a Presbyterian church in 2008. I also left the marketing company, on very hostile terms with my former boss, and it would be more than a year until I would know financial stability again.

My Christian infancy was a clumsy period, years of learning and incertitude. Whereas I had previously viewed sin as an act, something objectively done "out there," I began understanding sin as a condition, something subjective, that our misdeeds are an outpouring of sin, from which we cannot save ourselves from just by "being nice." This revelation helped me spend a lot of time guilt-tripping myself (and likewise becoming cynical about all of humanity), and helped me spend a little bit of time dwelling on grace. I was taught that, as a Christian, I had the Holy Spirit, but was almost as perplexed about what that meant as before. To sing in worship was refreshing. A lack of political discourse during sermons was even more refreshing!

Prayer became a source of frustration. Having been taught how and when to formally pray, it was disorienting to informally speak at God with my own words (and in English rather than Arabic), and to arrange a schedule. I spent many hours worrying whether I was "doing it right." Being told what to do seemed so convenient! Freedom can feel frightening, and servitude safe.

It delighted me much that Jesus Christ's harshest words were directed at men obsessed with observing religious laws and customs, as my imagination made such men out to be surrogates of my Sunday school instructors. It never dawned on me that, like those Pharisees, I compulsively worried about "doing it right." Since I drank beer and used profanity more often than most of my Christian friends, I naïvely assumed that I was in no way Pharisaical.

The Gospel records showed that Jesus Christ's understanding of morality and ethics often bewildered his contemporaries in Roman Judea, as though His understanding came from another world altogether. His words and His deeds could baffle, or seem cryptic, but they never needed to be explained away. This is an earmark of someone who lived perfectly.

There were a few, and far between, cases when I met a fellow Christian with a Muslim background. When I would introduce myself, and explain to him or her my similar background, it always came as a shock, as though they wanted to say "I thought I was the only one." In all of these cases, the former Muslim was eager for knowledge about his or her conversion not to be in the public domain. A fear of alienation, from family or the community, culturally carries great weight for many Muslims. The result is that many Muslims will not express the doubts about Islam that rise up in their hearts, much less suspicions that another faith is better-suited for their spiritual journeys. In all of the silence, of never speaking and never hearing what others hold in their hearts, a doubting Muslim can be in great danger of concluding that he or she is utterly alone.

Between my Presbyterian church and the Haven, a few fellow Christians had explained to me that Catholics clung to certain doctrines that were "out there," such as transubstantiation, the Sacrament of Confession, Purgatory, beliefs and practices surrounding the Virgin Mary, the intercession of saints, and the Magisterium. Being a new Christian, I hardly had any idea what they spoke of. The majority of my fellow Christians considered

Catholics to be Christians. But some did not, which came to me as both a surprise and a turn off.

Being an avid reader, and eager to learn more about the faith I had impulsively embraced, I continued in my readings. G.K. Chesterton quickly became one of my favorite authors. I read (and re-read) more of his apologetics, as well as his fiction. The reading of Chesterton's works was a mental gymnastics of sorts. When a person's mind absorbs a paradox, or an insight, it silently acknowledges that there was something to learn, something not already known. But when a person's mind encounters the works of the "Prince of Paradox," absorbing many paradoxes and insights in one sitting, that mind learns much, and simultaneously begins fathoming just how much it never understood. The expansion of one's understanding is a humbling experience, and also the beginning of wisdom—or perhaps more accurately, common sense. The world around all of us, and the world within each of us, is incredibly complex.

Chesterton's writings did much to help me view history less in terms of the content of events, and more in terms of a movement of ideas. By giving consideration to context, rather than merely content, he pointed out how often it is, and has always been, the case that many of the ideas we call "new" are really just recycled heresies. His works illuminate the extent to which the Gospels have positively impacted Western culture, that I finally made the connection that high art, modern notions about political liberty and the individual, Common Law, and much else of what I took pride in as a Westerner (even before I was a Christian) are the implications of Christian teaching. He helped lead me to suspect a very odd notion that truth and humor go hand-in-hand, that every moment can be an adventure, and that there may well be an intimate bond between sainthood and sanity.

G.K. Chesterton's words, through the fields of reason, all point toward a much greater truth beyond the edge of reason: toward a world full of mysteries, a world of spirit that gives life to our ideas. When a person follows the paths of reason long enough, he may discern that reason itself will only help him understand so much.

With Chesterton's help, even the Holy Trinity, elusive to me for so many years, would eventually make sense.

Christ, the Son, gives all of Creation much richer meaning through His Incarnation; God participating in our world by being one of us. By this great Mystery Saint Francis could declare that the sun and the moon, and all of Creation, were his brothers and sisters. By this Mystery Saint Teresa of Calcutta could see "Jesus in His most distressing disguise" in the face of each slum-dweller. Our divinity, our sin, and our salvation, are all summed up in the Gospel accounts of Christ's Incarnation, Crucifixion, and Resurrection.

We are all so hopelessly lost and confused that only the Holy Spirit, God dwelling in our very hearts, can guide us toward God. It is by the Spirit, and only by the Spirit, that we may subjectively experience the Presence of God. My teenage fascination with Sufism was much the result of reading Sufi poetry, in which the Holy Spirit is strongly implied. But the Spirit implied in mystical Islam is standard teaching throughout Christianity.

It is through Christ, and through the Spirit, that we may recognize divinity in one another, and in ourselves.

The Holy Trinity was not a replacement, but a completion of the vision of God!

And as much as Chesterton's works impacted me, there was also one glaring mystery about his life that I had come across several times: he was a convert to the Catholic Church, an apologist for so many of those "out there" matters.

By 2011, my own Christian journey was wanting for some sort of change. New York is a very transient city, and many of my church friends had moved on, whether to another city, or to another congregation.

My Presbyterian church was outstanding at teaching a truth; it was the right church for me in my Christian infancy. But I began wondering if others truths were being neglected in its teaching, if there was perhaps some balance of truths. I had listened to the same message during sermons, about being a terrible sinner desperately in need of God's gift of grace which I did not deserve, so many times that it seemed like a monomania. I could no longer sit near the front pews, or the pastor would catch me sleeping. Though I could acknowledge that I am a sinner, part of the problem, how could I move forward from there, be part of the solution?

The black-and-white categorizing of people as either "believers" going to Heaven or "unbelievers" going to Hell seemed oversimplified; we come in many shades of grey. Even if this particular church molded its members into solid theological Christians, my confidence in its ability to mold psychological Christians was wavering. Though I had learned much, I had learned all I ever would from this church. And so the question arose: where shall I go from here?

On several occasions I had unwittingly run into G.K. Chesterton's explanations on some of those "out there" Catholic matters, most especially the Sacraments, and found myself thinking: "Well, that actually makes a great deal of sense." The Catholic Church is very catholic, absorbing complexity as handily as simplicity.

Of course, coming to a decision of finding a home in the Catholic Church takes much more than books, or art. My decision needed to be emotional as much as it needed to be cerebral, and I was most blessed to have experiences and (living) people to help along the way. But it was the works of G.K. Chesterton that, almost singlehandedly, satisfied me that such was a reasonable decision.

By the summer of 2011, I made the firm decision to join the Catholic Church, and soon began the months-long process of Rite of Christian Initiation for Adults (RCIA). One gesture that meant much to me was what I did not have to do: my impulsive baptism was already valid in the eyes of the Church. During the Easter Vigil of 2012, I was confirmed.

That Saturday night remains one of my most cherished memories to this day.

Never say never: some bro at a strip club this very moment might be much closer to becoming a practicing Catholic than he would allow himself to imagine.

When I reflect upon my own spiritual journey, with the benefit of retrospect, I see that having taken many (sometimes reluctant) steps, I have traveled many miles. And upon solemn reflection, I understand that I still have many miles ahead of me, that many of my old attitudes and beliefs still need to be fully surrendered and purged. I do wonder about Muslims that are like my friend Khalid. Islam is not a monolith. I know plenty of practicing Muslims who are very decent people. I have met many Muslims who tragically give in to the belief that the world is divided into an "us" and a "them" to be conquered, and this happens at rates far greater than what politically correct paradigms will allow for. And I have met many nominal Muslims, such as Khalid.

Nominal Muslims are wary of arbitrary rules, wary of violence or reports of violence (globalization and the internet do much to exacerbate such wariness), wary at a cruel vision of God, unpleasant experiences, et cetera. Many of them have sought refuge in atheism or agnosticism, as both are growing throughout the Muslim world. Their faith has not satisfied them. How many feel like they are spiritually suffocating? How often is it the case that a Muslim is curious about another faith, but does not inquire, out of fear, engaging in a great silence that makes him or her feel so lonely? Or what would a well-meaning Christian be willing to do to help?

These are important questions to ask, though God alone knows the answer.

SURPRISE

By Victoria Darkey

PARADOXICALLY, G.K. CHESTERTON'S INVOLVEMENT in my conversion was something that I didn't realize until after I had become a Catholic. He was a person who kept popping up, especially during the final years, when I was consciously cooperative in the process of conversion. I'd be reading Catholic convert authors, Catholic apologetics, or listening to an audio presentation. Suddenly a little quotation from G.K. Chesterton would be there, often casually or even carelessly tossed out as an aside, or ornamentation by the speaker or the author of the material I was working through. The quote would usually startle me… like a jovial, innocent prankster having some fun by jumping out from behind a doorway. I would find myself musing and pondering it, even returning to it for weeks to come. Usually Chesterton's quote would feed my sanity, or nudge my curiosity. Often, it challenged me to humble up, step back, and enjoy the paradoxical nature of things. The words of this funny, wise, unseen friend reminded me to not to take my faith-journeying self too seriously. In the midst of what sometimes was an intense, and even frightening process, he helped me to take a deep breath, smile, and let go. Chesterton's quotes were a vehicle of grace. They helped me to trust the truth that was unfolding before me. The healing effect of this was essential in order for me to navigate the shift in my spiritual world and embrace Catholicism. This Chestertonian thread of grace wove itself through the tapestry of my conversion process with enough regularity, that after having entered the Church I knew the next step was to look up this guy and find out more about who he was. Again, I was startled and surprised to find that when this English journalist from my great-grandparent's generation described his conversion, he articulated what I had experienced in my own conversion process. He described the convert just before conversion as someone looking through a leper's window, or a small crack that seems to get smaller the longer he looks at it. But, Chesterton said, this little crooked hole is an opening that looks toward the Altar, and only once inside the Catholic Church does the convert find that the Church is bigger on the inside than it is on the outside. With insight like this, G.K. Chesterton met me as I stepped awestruck over the threshold of the Narthex, and with avuncular wit and wisdom, joyfully offered me his arm and ushered me into the Nave of the Church, where we've knelt together ever since.

I was born in the summer of 1961, sixteen months after my mom and dad married. A brother followed in 1962, and another brother in 1972. My parents were devout evangelical Christians and there was a sense of God's constant presence in our home. Love for Christ, love for each other, and a strong Christian identity were integral with our family life. I remember "asking Jesus into my heart" at age 4, with the belief that at that moment I became a Christian and was saved. I now could be assured that I would go to heaven when I died. I understood that to be a Christian meant that I had a personal relationship with Jesus, and would live my life in obedience to Him.

Sunday school and church involvement, daily bible reading and prayer, bible stories, memorizing scripture, church activities, VBS, reading Christian books, and listening to Christian recordings of hymns, gospel singing, and stories predominate my early childhood memories. The first word I learned to spell was B-I-B-L-E. In Sunday school we sang a little song "The B-I-B-L-E. Yes, that's the book for me. I stand alone on the Word of God, The B-I-B-L-E." At age ten I was baptized at a regular Sunday evening service. I understood baptism not as having any spiritual effect on me or in me, but as simply serving as a public profession of my commitment to Jesus.

Up to this point, the Christianity I'd been steeped in was soft Calvinism, colored with Rationalism. In its simplest form, with the belief in the utter depravity of Man and fallen nature of Creation, it reasoned that humanity could be divided into two groups: the 'saved' and the 'unsaved.' Of course, the Christian always assumed the unsaved were someone other than himself or the folks from his home congregation. This divide presented those on the 'saved' side with the grave Christian responsibility to convince the unsaved to get saved. The definition of 'saved' varied between churches. This created a kind of sub-culture within each one, and contributed to a sense of congregational unity. There was often an unspoken elitism between groups, with each sub-culture believing itself to be superior. Church shopping and the subsequent church hopping was an expected part of the churchgoers' lifestyle. A believer would look for, and hopefully find a church that offered what they needed or wanted. In joining the church the believer would become part of that group's sub-culture, and stay as long as the group continued to meet their needs, or until it split apart over doctrinal or devotional differences.

During my Middle School years, I attended Bible camp in the summers. There, in addition to bible study and prayer, I received instruction in how to evangelize, or witness to "unsaved" friends. That often meant Catholics. Throughout high school I regularly participated in the youth groups at our church.

At age 16, I saw Mother Teresa of Calcutta in person at a speaking event at the University of Pittsburgh. She radiated Christ in a way that was new to me. I'd known Protestant believers whose inner spiritual life had reflected Jesus in powerful and attractive ways, but this remarkable little nun was different. She recognized Christ in every other human being, not just in the "saved" ones... not just those who were righteous, not just those who had the right doctrine, or those who were fellow members of her Christian sub-culture. Instead of reacting to the taint of sin with evangelistic fervor, she saw the incarnate Christ in the lowliest of the lowly, and responded with self-giving love. She could love any and every creature in Creation because in complete humility, she lived in Christ's love. She was radically free of any form of cultural elitism. Although I didn't know what to call it, I was seeing the Incarnational reality of a sacramental life, and I knew I was drawn to it.

Fascinated with the art and history of Western Civilization, and with a particular interest in the Middle Ages and in classical music, I went to college with an undecided major, intent on exploring the Humanities to see if a vocational direction might emerge. During the summers I worked as a nursing assistant in a large Catholic nursing home. I enjoyed a connection with elderly people I cared for, and often found inspiration pondering what I'd seen and heard from Mother Teresa. I also saw a similarity between Mother Teresa and the religious and philosophical outlook of the Vincentian Sisters of Charity who ran the place. Over the summers working there, some of them would occasionally make comments suggesting that I consider religious life. I always would politely decline, and say something to the effect that "That's not likely, since I'm not a Catholic." Once, one of the feistier nuns responded with a shrug, "Well…so, become a Catholic." Inwardly, I was equally scandalized and intrigued by the suggestion.

Meanwhile, the Humanities courses I was taking in college were increasingly frustrating and disappointing. The underlying nihilistic worldview prevalent at the university failed to provide the truth-based context for human history and culture for which I hungered. The philosophy being offered was a shattered window. It was philosophical homelessness. To me it mocked all the Good, Beautiful, and True that I knew existed. I knew there must be a cosmology that would integrate me with Creation, not just pronounce the meaninglessness of it all. I was looking for an authentically Christian anthropology. I knew that it would have to be a seamless garment with a universal Christianity, and not likely to be found in the secular academic world.

I had a number of Catholic friends with whom I would occasionally attend Mass. Confident in my Protestant view of righteousness, and since none of my friends were catechized enough to satisfactorily explain why I should do otherwise, I would receive communion. I was surprised by a palpable presence of Christ in the Mass and in the Eucharist.

After struggling in a serious involvement with an atheist-leaning agnostic boyfriend, I ended the relationship, and re-affirmed

my Christian identity. I also transferred to the University of
Pittsburgh, and began the pursuit of a degree in Nursing.

Once settled back in Pittsburgh, I met and fell in love with
an "ex-Catholic," born-again man attending my non-denominational, charismatic, pseudo-mega church. Bob and I married a
year and a half after we met. Early on in the dating relationship,
I told him that I believed that eventually he would need to deal
with his issues with the Catholic Church and make some kind
of reconciliation with his Catholic upbringing. Even though
I believed it was inevitable and must be tolerated, Protestant
denominationalism bothered me. Though I saw Catholicism
as just another of the many denominations, Jesus' prayer at the
Last Supper in the Gospel of John spurred my "intuition" that
something was seriously wrong with the picture of post-ref-
ormation Christianity. Though unsure of what it would look
like, I held the belief that unity in Christendom seemed like the
original intention. Somehow, I didn't think that Jesus founded his Church to be a fragmented assortment of sub-cultures,
each vying for allegiance of the believer, like the competition
between shops in some kind of spiritual retail mall.

Early in our marriage, our home church in Pittsburgh sent
us as missionaries to South Bronx. There we were part of a
small neighborhood mission church led by people who had
played a significant evangelistic role in Bob's decision to
leave non-practicing Catholicism and become a born-again
Christian. In the Bronx we organized and conducted a door-
to-door prayer ministry, learned much about the importance
of cross-cultural communication in relationships, and began
to gain some objectivity in regard to our own cultural biases.

We spent the next twelve years living and working in the
five boroughs of New York City. We became familiar with the
harshness of urban reality, and a variety of human responses to

it. Early in 1989, in labor after a challenging first pregnancy, we were surprised by the discovery of two babies when everybody thought there'd only been one. Six months later, when the shock and upheaval of instantaneously going from married couple to family-of-four was just beginning to wane, we lost our home and most of our belongings in a 5-alarm fire. Although that year was clearly marked by feelings of deep gratitude for God's generosity and His infinite mercy, I realized that I needed something that our middle-class protestant background was missing. I needed a church that knew what to do with suffering.

One sunny, New York autumn afternoon in 1990, as our 22-month-old twins napped in the next room, I stood in the tiny kitchen of our tiny apartment, determined to empty the sink of the ever-present pile of dirty dishes. With my hands in the soapy water I began to place before God the grief, loneliness, and spiritual isolation that I was experiencing at the time. Out of nowhere an interior but almost audible voice said, "Go to the Catholic Church." With hardly a thought, and in a totally audible voice I answered, "OK Lord, ...someday, after I bury my mom and dad." At this I was shocked. The surprise was not that I had experienced an internal locution. These had happened to me a couple of times before. And I wasn't completely surprised by the content of the message. After all, God is a God of surprises. What astonished me was the poverty of my reply. It had sprung from a nakedly honest place in my heart, but I'd heard of someone who once responded to the Lord in a similar way, and the Scriptures say he went away empty. I knew that my answer wouldn't suffice. As the grey water disappeared down the drain, I put the entire affair into God's hands and gave my fiat to His leading in the matter.

Over the next 3 years, like a champion fisherman, God gave us ample play on the line. By 1993, I was pregnant with

our next child, and surprised myself with the awareness that
I wished we could baptize this baby when he came. We were
part of a small evangelical, Anabaptist congregation, and infant
baptism was not something even remotely considered in that
tradition. I had developed some friendships with neo-pagans
and at the same time I had begun reading some Anglo-Catholic
authors. When I realized that a Christian sacramental system is
the best answer to paganism, a sacramental seed was planted.
Reading Anglo-Catholics developed into dialogue with Anglo-
Catholics, and though I had long been familiar with C.S. Lewis,
our Anglican friends took him to a new level. Although we
continued attending the Anabaptist church, a hunger for the
Sacraments was rapidly developing in both Bob's and my heart.

It was around this time that I was introduced to G.K.
Chesterton. First I heard him vaguely referenced. I was already
familiar with him as the author of the Father Brown stories, but
knew nothing else about him. Then, just as the journey started
to intensify, he started jumping out from around the corners
with his quotations.

One area where the Anglo-Catholics were more Anglo than
Catholic, was when it came to the Virgin Mary. The Holy Spirit
knew He'd have to take care of this one without them. At one
point in 1996, I was having my daily prayer time. This day, I
brought before the Lord some struggles I was having in my
life as I realized the effects of some of the misogyny I had
encountered as a woman and as a mother. After pouring out
my heart before the Lord, I quieted myself, focusing on Him
in my heart's eye. I saw Him looking very much like what I
later came to recognize as the image of the Divine Mercy. As I
gazed, He extended His hand to me and in a sweeping gesture
much like the perfect host making an introduction said, "I'd
like you to meet my mother." At that moment, much to my

surprise, He stepped to the side and there behind Him was the Blessed Virgin Mary. She said nothing. She just looked straight into my eyes with unfathomable love and healing.

From this point Catholic resources and Catholic people began flooding our lives. We found a local Catholic bookstore and began reading Catholic apologists and converts. We started frequenting a local Perpetual Adoration Chapel. It wasn't long before we started double dipping on Sunday mornings, attending both protestant church services and the Mass. Soon, Bob made his reconciliation with the Church. Now expecting our fourth child, I began attending a weekly Rosary prayer group for mothers. I joined the RCIA classes at a local parish. Finally, we validated our marriage and had our children baptized in the Church all on one February Sunday in 1999, just a few weeks before the Easter Vigil where I was received into the Church.

In the heart of the Church, through the voice of G.K. Chesterton, I've found the Christian cosmology and anthropology that I'd long hungered for. In the years since becoming a Catholic, Chesterton has played a significant role in my devotional life. I regularly read him, and ask for his and his wife Frances' intercession. Especially at times when I need insight or deeper understanding of an issue or situation, or at times when I am in need of creative inspiration, Gilbert and Frances come through with effectual prayers for me. Consistently, G.K. Chesterton points the way to Christ and His Church. I've found his spirituality to be enlightening and integrating. Gaining a Chestertonian appreciation for paradox has consoled me in times of suffering. In a modern world that appears to be rapidly deteriorating into chaotic darkness, Chesterton's spiritual lens is shaped by faith and joy. Learning to see through it has given me a heartfelt sense of wonder, gratitude, and peace.

During the years of my journey toward Catholicism, the Communion of Saints was operating in my life whether I believed in it or not. St. Teresa of Calcutta, St. Faustina, St. Therese of Lisieux, St. Louis de Montfort, St. John Paul II, and St. Elizabeth Ann Seton each showed up in significant ways along the path. And of course, the Queen of all the Saints, the Virgin Mary led the throng. But the appearances of G.K. Chesterton hold a unique place in the heart of my story. His little game of surprise helped me to not shy away from the leper's window, that little crooked crack that could seem to get smaller. Those playful peeks of Chesterton in his quotes were enough to get things turned upside down, or back from the front, so that I could see the truth. Then I could step into that place that is bigger on the inside than it is on the outside. In the end, it's really no surprise that he was there to greet me.

You Can Have It All

An Interview with Peter Kreeft by Dale Ahlquist

DA: Is it safe to say that Chesterton has been one of your inspirations?

PK: Yes. GKC has made more of a difference to me, my thought, style, and career than anyone else in the 20th century except, I think, C.S. Lewis. I've been especially influenced by *Orthodoxy* and *The Everlasting Man*. *Orthodoxy* showed me the Catholic mind and worldview. He wrote it before he became a Catholic, and I read it before I became a Catholic, but it was a Catholic book from one Catholic to another. *The Everlasting Man*, for which many readers used history to put Christ ("The Everlasting Man") into perspective, for me used Christ to put the rest of history into perspective—like Augustine's *City of God*, but more fun to read!

Editor's note: this interview first appeared in the December, 1997, issue of *Gilbert!* magazine.

DA: You have made quoting Chesterton one of your literary devices.

PK: Quoting Chesterton is not a literary device. It's a habit. Can't help it. Like potato chips—can't eat just one.

DA: I was thinking of one of your books, *The Best Things in Life*, a modern Socratic dialogue in which you have one character who keeps quoting Chesterton to drive home his points, much to the irritation of his professor and fellow students.

PK: Students get irritated at GKC because they can't answer him. He backs them into a corner and parries all their thrusts, and thrusts all their parries. Wouldn't you get irritated at a Marxist Deconstructionist Positivist Secularist Abortionist who was cleverer, funnier, profounder, and more logical than you were?

DA: Professor, I'm supposed to ask the questions. You have played a role similar to Chesterton in making difficult concepts very comprehensible. Just as Chesterton made St. Thomas Aquinas accessible to the layman, you went one step further and made the very daunting *Summa Theologica* approachable for folks like me who are still learning to read.

PK: The only way I have played a role similar to Chesterton's is in the same sense as a kid with colored chalk on a sidewalk plays a role similar to Michelangelo's. My best books are the piggyback ones, on Aquinas, Pascal, and three books of the Bible (*Job, Song of Songs,* and *Ecclesiastes*). When dwarfs stand on the shoulders of giants, they see far. I have the advantage over many Thomist scholars that allows me to introduce Aquinas to beginners: I'm one. I never wrote a scholarly book. Chesterton was wise because he *didn't* go to University. I wrote *Making Sense Out of Suffering* only when Servant Publications answered my objections to writing such a book. I said, "No, I can't write a book on suffering; C.S. Lewis wrote the best one ever. I can't approach that." They said: "We don't want you to. We need a second rate book on suffering." Okay. A book for simpletons should be written by one.

DA: Do you bring Chesterton into your philosophy courses at Boston College?

PK: GKC is like a spastic neck muscle, or an Alabama accent— you can't *help* bringing him into your teaching, consciously or (more often) unconsciously. Often I find myself discovering an idea that I explained in class—for instance Hume on causality, or the contingency of the world—discovering that idea in Chesterton and realizing, *that* is where I first understood it. Not in Hume, or Aquinas, or whoever. In Chesterton. And so I have been happily plagiarizing him all along.

DA: How do you suppose we could get Chesterton back into the curriculum?

PK: "Ask and (eventually) it will be given you." Even by an unjust judge. Pester. It works with God. It'll work with department chairmen, administrators, and committees.

DA: We have put Chesterton on the Internet, but how else do you think we can bring him to the electronic age?

PK: I fancy Chesterton's heart, like mine, had a soft spot for the Luddites. Wendell Berry's classic essay, "Why I Will Not Buy a Computer," could have been ghostwritten by Chesterton's ghost.

DA: But don't you use a word processor?

PK: My favorite word processor is a pen. Cheap, portable, trouble free, easy to learn, and obedient. I do not have E-mail. Why should I? Only saints and fools do, just as only saints and fools risk being elected President.

DA: You have my vote.

PK: Flattery.

DA: You mentioned your conversion to Catholicism. Chesterton was also a convert. This is obviously a profound experience to share with someone. At what point did you find yourself connecting with Chesterton?

PK: Kierkegaard almost kept me Protestant. He was the profoundest Protestant who ever wrote. Chesterton showed me all the central insights of Existentialism in a thoroughly Catholic world view. Chesterton answered all the questions that Kierkegaard asks.

DA: And if you were to sum up Chesterton?

PK: "You can have it all." The best text for this is *Orthodoxy*. And even though *The Thing* and *The Catholic Church and Conversion* helped, more than any of his arguments, it was his *example* that moved me. "How come those Catholic philosophers are better? Why do I, a Protestant, long to be like GKC more than like Calvin or Luther?" In judging writers and thinkers, as well as lovers, the heart has its reasons which the reason does not know of.

DA: You said that *Orthodoxy*, written by Chesterton before his conversion, profoundly spoke to you before your own conversion. I don't think there is a great deal of difference between Chesterton's pre-conversion writings and his post-conversion writings. Do you think that may be one of the reasons he appeals to Catholics and non-Catholics alike?

PK: Chesterton's writings are a seamless garment, or a jointless waterslide. True Anglicans follow GKC into the Tiber. The genius of Catholicism is its catholicism, its universality. Be true to, and follow, the truth in your partial tradition, like following a river, and you'll end in the Catholic Sea.

AN ATHEIST ACTOR MEETS
G.K. CHESTERTON

By Kevin O'Brien

WHEN THE PRIEST FOUND OUT I was a reader, he brought out his copy of *Brideshead Revisited.* He read a scene from it aloud to my wife Karen and me and he laughed and laughed as we sat there in his office. This was not what we had been expecting when we began to receive private instruction in the Catholic Faith. But Fr. John Jay Hughes—who was giving us private instruction—was an Evelyn Waugh fan, so he knew a Chestertonian like me would appreciate Waugh's humor.

After a few more weeks of Karen and me asking questions and Fr. Hughes answering them, and of Fr. Hughes occasionally waxing poetic on one of his favorite authors, he said, "I think the two of you are ready to be received into the Catholic Church. I will contact the pastor of your geographic parish

and he will arrange a date to receive you during an upcoming
Sunday Mass."

This date happened to be July 30, 2000, the next convenient
Sunday for our pastor—a date which is significant for a reason
I will explain in a moment.

As we drove home from our final session of private instruction with Fr. Hughes, I wondered how in the heck did I get
here? Clearly G.K. Chesterton had been the primary influence
on my conversion, but how did this all begin?

After all, I was an atheist at the age of nine.

I became an atheist when I saw Madeline Murray O'Hair on
TV. She was an evangelizing anti-God crusader who pushed
hard to get prayer out of public school—and succeeded. The
studio audience at the television show I saw her on, in 1969,
were aghast and shocked at the things she was saying. This was
long before atheism became a trendy fad and someone who
publicly professed disbelief in God, in those days, was a kind
of monster.

But she made perfect sense to me. Christianity was just another myth, O'Hair pointed out, and religion has always been
used so that one class of people could control and dominate
another class. Faith was a scam for suckers.

This assertion was only confirmed when I saw Christians
on TV, who were (in those days) televangelists—"Television
preachers with bad hair and dimples," as Jimmy Buffett describes them, snake oil salesman and faith healers whose cred-
ulous victims were as much to blame for attending their dog
and pony show as they were for staging it. Faith, apparently,
required the sacrifice of reason. And this was a sacrifice I was
not prepared to make.

For, whatever the strange psychology of a child atheist may
be, as I grew older my own quest was (as I understood more

and more) a quest for the Truth. I was an atheist because I thought that "no God" was the truth. More than that, if Christ is a liar, we must burn down all the churches. On the other hand, if Christ is God and died for people's sins, then you can't worship Him by taking gullible people's money and pretending to offer cheesy televised fake-healing services. Either way, if Christ was right about anything, it was this: "The Truth will make you free."

And I thought I was free. I was a glib and successful student in high school, never really challenged by anything, and I thought I could skim my way through life—until I met my mentor, Jiman Duncan, an acting teacher/stage director who showed me how challenging the performing arts could be. I had always loved acting, but Jiman Duncan showed me how serious and consuming it was, and how it was an activity that was somehow plugged in to the transcendent. Duncan demanded a level of energy and emotional intensity and authenticity from his cast that you couldn't fake. Faith healers could fake "faith healing," but I couldn't fake this. Suddenly I had found something that challenged me—that challenged me at every level … physical, intellectual, emotional and spiritual. Yes, spiritual.

Because I learned that there was something bigger than me and my efforts. No matter how well I learned my lines, researched my character, prepared for my role, my performance would be perhaps technically perfect but sterile and lifeless. My own efforts were not enough to make a performance engaging. My fellow actors and I had to lose our lives to find them; we had to lose our performance to gain it. If I abandoned my preparation and hard work when I made my entrance, and if, once on stage, I opened myself up to something I could not fully control—to a kind of inspiration, to something that was beyond me—then and only then would my character come to

life. Then and only then would my performance be sponta-
neous and compelling to an audience.

But what was this "something that was beyond me" that I
depended on in my art? Whatever it was, when I stopped trying
to control it and when I let it inspire me, it facilitated a kind
of communion—a communion of actor with audience and a
communion of both actor and audience with something that
broke the bounds of the theater itself—which was what? God?
Whatever it was, we actors, apparently, were bridge builders,
in a sense: we were priests, after a fashion, whose job it was to
lead the audience to something beyond them—to something
beyond us all.

I suddenly realized I was no longer an atheist. I was spiritual
but not religious.

I liked the plays of George Bernard Shaw, and I liked his essays even better, many of which mentioned something he called
the Life Force, this *elan vitale* that was the source of motion,
desire and creativity. I liked the Life Force a lot because it was
exciting but impersonal. The Life Force would never observe
Lent, for instance; it would never ask for self-sacrifice. It wanted
Life and more of it! If the Life Force wanted what you wanted,
well then, you grabbed whatever you and the Life Force wanted
and you both enjoyed it—Life enjoyed by Force!

C.G. Jung was into this, too. Jung was a disciple of Sigmund
Freud, and Jung was very big on this quasi-spiritual aspect of
our souls, which were engaged in a process he called "individ-
uation," which was a fancy word for the god of our belly—what
I would call "deified desire." But I didn't analyze Jung, I simply read everything he ever wrote—30 or so volumes, mostly
translated from the German. Jung was likewise spiritual but
not religious, and that, I found, was a very handy thing to be.

But I augmented my reading of Shaw and Jung with people

like Evelyn Waugh, Eric Hoffer, Joseph Campbell, William Shakespeare—and Scripture. The Gospels, at least, were fascinating, and Jung was adamant that Christ symbolized something—namely the Self, the Self fully individuated and doing exactly what the Self wanted to do … which, apparently, in Christ's self's case included crucifixion, which didn't make much sense. Still, Jung was my hero and he was at least a scholar at a level far higher than the anti-intellectual Christians in the media I occasionally bumped into.

But then I got married and had kids and had some troubles in my life, amidst all the blessings. And then my kids would say, "Daddy, who is God?" And I would answer, "Well, nobody really knows, honey."

Then one day I found this book. Or this book found me. It was a book I stumbled upon at the library, *God in the Dock,* an anthology of writing by C.S. Lewis. And I was floored! Here was a Christian who was a great writer—and who did not sacrifice his intellect in order to believe! Everything Lewis wrote was a cogent and compelling rational case for the Faith! How could this be? I decided the only way to find out the key to Lewis' worldview was to do with him what I had done with Shaw and Jung, to read everything he ever wrote.

And so I did. And I kept noticing something—or someone. Lewis kept mentioning this guy Chesterton. G.K. Chesterton. I assumed he was a contemporary of Lewis, and since he made such an impression on Lewis, I decided to check him out—literally, from the library.

The library nearest to my house had a few books by Chesterton, mostly detective stories about a priest who solved mysteries—but I had no interest in mysteries and even less in priests. They had one non-fiction work, *What's Wrong with the World.* I checked it out and commenced to reading.

"This guy is better than Lewis!" I exclaimed after a few chapters. Lewis could write, but Chesterton could *really write!* "And
What's Wrong with the World is so up-to-date!" I said to myself.
"This book must have been written around C.S. Lewis' time, in
the 50s or 60s—and yet it's all about stuff we're dealing with
today, in the 90s! Divorce, feminism, insipid fads and fashions,
a basic irrationality at the heart of our society. How amazing
that this book, a book that must have been written thirty or
forty years ago, is so relevant today!"

I turned to the title page. 1910. *What's Wrong with the World*
was written in 1910.

"This man is not just a great writer," I said to myself, "This
man is a prophet." And so I dived into Chesterton—into all the
books I could find.

The very second Chesterton book I read was his book on my
other favorite author, George Bernard Shaw. And Chesterton
nailed Shaw! He clearly loved Shaw and understood the man
and his philosophy (such as it was) at a very deep level—and
yet these two were obviously polar opposites: great friends, but
opposites in every way. I didn't agree with Chesterton's assessment of all of Shaw's plays, but I could see that Chesterton was
on to something, that he perceived not only something deeply
true about Shaw and Shaw's "shavian" limitations, but in the
process, he perceived something deeply true about reality itself.
I later learned that this is what GKC does in all his books. Even
seemingly slight works that are supposed to be about literary
criticism are really and truly about man and God. Here was not
a writer to be taken lightly.

So I read more and more. And I discovered the humor, the
humility, and the astonishing and penetrating insight. I discovered the greatest writer and the deepest thinker of the 20th
century.

Chesterton kept mentioning this guy Hilaire Belloc. And if you follow that thread—Lewis to Chesterton to Belloc—you will find a Mere Christian, a Joyful convert Catholic and a Militant cradle Catholic—and that's exactly the order I discovered them in, a Providential order, for each author has something I could receive only at certain stages of my conversion. Lewis, for all his brilliance and style, is a bit diffident and occasionally unreal. Chesterton is like fireworks. Belloc is straightforward, utterly fearless, and deep and even sad at times … not really sad, but somber and serious the way the Latin Mass is somber and serious; the way the Mass is profound, devout, aware of death, and never silly—though Belloc could be silly, in his own way, and with a sense of humor that was very different from Chesterton's.

I loved these three writers. I loved these three men.

But Chesterton was bigger than them all—physically and intellectually and spiritually. Chesterton's great wit was never glib. His profound gratitude for existence itself was born out of a darkness and suffering, out of an encounter with evil and despair early in his adult life that made him understand the book of Job and the cross of Christ in a way that informed everything he said and did from then on. And his humor was never cheap, never facile or shallow. His humor was always philosophical (while still being funny). It was borne of humility, the greatest of God's gifts, the biggest virtue that is happy to bow down and appear as the smallest.

Chesterton was, among these three writers, my patron. He led me into the Catholic Church—almost by hand. He was certainly at my side the whole time.

There's much I'm leaving out, including my conversion experience itself, which is rather remarkable and includes a kind of miracle. There's my journey with my wife Karen, after my conversion, into a few other waysides before coming Home. I went (in my own life) from atheism to vague spirituality and then (with Karen) to the Lutheran Church Missouri Synod (the far right) to the Episcopalian church (the far left) before finding the great balancing point that is is the center of all things. We even overcame Karen's memorable last words, "I will be ANYTHING BUT CATHOLIC!" which she uttered about six weeks before signing up for private instruction.

If I'm ever tempted to wonder about this Church, the Body of Christ, and how sinners like me and saints like Chesterton are both somehow part of it, if I'm tempted to doubt the graces it conveys and the communion of saints it joins us with, if and when I'm tempted to that kind of despondency, I think of that date, July 30, 2000, the date that my wife Karen and I were received into the Catholic Church and took our first communion. It was an unusual date to be received, since most converts today come into the Church via RCIA and are received at the Easter Vigil. But we came in through private instruction, and we came in on that unusual date—Sunday, July 30, 2000.

I did not know it at the time, but I later learned that we were received 78 years to the day after G.K. Chesterton, who came in on Sunday, July 30, 1922. We shared his reception date … "by chance."

G.K. Chesterton not only led me by the hand—but by the heart and mind. He was, and he remains, my dearest friend in heaven. And he was clearly by our side the day we were received, and the day we received (in Holy Communion) Our Lord and Savior.

G.K. Chesterton, pray for us.

A Jewish Convert Because of Chesterton

An Interview with Robert Asch by Dale Ahlquist

DA: Please tell us about your background.

RA: I was born in London, England, in 1968, of first-generation Canadians, both of them opera singers. My ethnic background is Jewish and English, and the cultural background of my Jewish ancestry is English, Spanish, Rumanian, Dutch, Austro-Hungarian and Ukrainian. I was sent to a French primary school, and then to St. Paul's School in London—Chesterton's alma mater, as it happens.

My parents were both practising Reform Jews, and I was brought up a practising Reform Jew: regular attendance at the

Editor's note: this interview first appeared in the September/October, 2008, issue of *Gilbert!* magazine.

Sabbath Service; Bar Mitzvah at thirteen; celebration of the major festivals, and so on. I have never been an atheist or an agnostic.

On the other hand, we were very much a culturally assimilated family—more so, I would say, than most practising Jews. Also, as I said, my parents were classical musicians, and our house was full of music: my parents' work, but also lessons (my mother taught and had a studio at home), concerts and records. My parents had a cultivated circle of friends, and my younger brother and I were made very welcome in the discussions that went on in the household. We were good readers early (my parents frowned on TV culture, and though television wasn't banned our access to it was restricted), and often taken to concerts, plays, exhibitions, museums. Now most of what we assimilated in this environment was of Christian—and usually Catholic—provenance.

We moved to Toronto in 1984 and I went to the University of Toronto, graduating with a B.A. in English and French Literature in 1990. Early in 1991 I moved to Czechoslovakia, and taught English language, literature and history in Prague until 1998. During this time I'd holiday in London. When I made up my mind to become a Catholic, in 1994, I went to Farm Street Church for instruction every six months or so till my reception in 1996.

I moved back to London in 1998 and began to work as an editor with the Saint Austin Press in 1999, since when I have been involved in Catholic publishing and education.

DA: How were you first exposed to Chesterton?

RA: I was aware of who he was at St. Paul's (there was a bust of him at the school), but I didn't read any Chesterton until I was sixteen. I had just finished Oscar Wilde's *Picture of Dorian Gray*, which I relished, and went in search of something similar—something *fin de siècle* and rich in verbal swordplay. I found *The Man Who Was Thursday*, which seemed to me just the ticket, as it proved to be. I was struck with the distinctiveness of Chesterton's wit, and that it seemed, uniquely in recent English literature, to dazzle as brightly as Wilde's. But, as I say, it was distinctive: the style was not the same, nor was the substance. I didn't read any more Chesterton until, I think, my last year at university; but *Thursday* had planted a seed, and when I found P.J. Kavanagh's *A G.K. Chesterton Anthology* at a bargain price, I bought it. That book exposed me to a fairly broad range of Chesterton's work.

DA: What effect would you say Chesterton had on you?

RA: Chesterton very quickly became a great favourite with me, and ultimately exercised a profound influence on my life. Humanly speaking, I probably owe more to Chesterton in the matter of my conversion than to anybody else. He wasn't working on a tabula rasa, though.

DA: Go ahead and tell us the other influences.

RA: God, as the Portuguese proverb has it, writes straight with crooked lines. Looking back now on the slow and often submerged process of my conversion, I can discern many influences—Plato, Sophocles, Bede, Pascal, Dr. Johnson, Newman, J.R.R. Tolkien, C.S. Lewis, T.S. Eliot, Hawthorne, George Herbert, Dickens. There were artists, like Raphael, Giotto, Botticelli and Mantegna. There were the great architects of the Gothic and the Baroque. Above all, perhaps, there were the musicians: Mozart, Haydn, Purcell, Handel, Tallis, Schubert, Berlioz (yes, Berlioz!). I couldn't possibly minimize the importance of Mozart and Haydn as influences, for example, particularly in their liturgical and quasi-liturgical music (I know some will raise an eyebrow at this, but I have no patience whatever with people who dismiss Mozart and Haydn Masses as "operatic")—the Requiem, the Credo Mass, the Heiligmesse, the Seven Last Words of Christ, and the Creation. Also, *The Magic Flute*, which, despite its Masonic associations, had an influence of a wholly Catholic tendency on my sensibility.

DA: It's interesting what an effect music had in bringing you to the Catholic Church.

RA: Yes, music can condition one's sensibility, but it can only address ideas obliquely. In Chesterton, however, I was confronted with the specific implications of what was attracting, influencing and nourishing me. I devoured anything of Chesterton's I could lay my hands on (no easy task in Prague in the days before the internet): *The Man Who Was Thursday* was already one of my golden books; now came *St. Thomas Aquinas*; some of the journalism and writings on Dickens; the comic poems; *The Napoleon of Notting Hill*—particularly the last chapter, which made a profound impression on me; above all, *Orthodoxy*. I can still see exactly where I was (a café in Salzburg) when I read it right through for the first time. Reading Chesterton accelerated my progress towards the Church more rapidly and consistently than any other repeated experience I can recall.

DA: How did you feel as a Jew becoming a Catholic?

RA: I still fondly remember the rather racy pleasure of being a Jewish admirer and defender of things Catholic. But all of this was certainly not to me merely a matter of belonging to a group (I have a constitutional distaste for groups) nor even of identifying with a cause or causes. It was a much deeper and dearer thing: the character and the quality of perceptions of life—of my life, and of Life in general—perceptions with which I was profoundly in sympathy. It was my patrimony, it was home, in a sense, and yet I was an alien—I was looking in from outside. Coming into the Church was, for me, very like Chesterton's description in *Orthodoxy* of the discovery that this ostensibly strange country is actually your native land.

There were, of course, creedal issues, which I should be obliged to accept, and which I came in God's good time to accept fully. Had I not done so, I suppose I should have had to face the melancholy prospect of feeling dislocated from all that was dearest to me; but you can't lie to yourself about things like that—I can't, at any rate. How I came to accept the dogmas of the faith is a long story, and probably best told elsewhere.

DA: Did Chesterton strike you as anti-Semitic?

RA: That is a difficult question to answer with a straightforward "yes" or "no." Let me say straight off that I do not think Chesterton was an anti-Semite. But in my personal experience the cards were, so to speak, stacked somewhat unfairly against him, at least initially. You will remember that, after *The Man Who Was Thursday*, the first considerable exposure I had to Chesterton's work was Kavanagh's *Chesterton Anthology*. In the introduction to that book, Kavanagh asserts that, uniquely in the case of anti-Semitism, Chesterton breathed the air of his time too freely. So in a sense, I never had the opportunity of approaching Chesterton entirely without preconceptions—at least, never after *Thursday*. Jews are (unsurprisingly) very sensitive to anti-Semitism and perceived anti-Semitism, and I assumed that there was at least a fairly generally held perception that Chesterton was anti-Semitic.

Perhaps this was a blessing in disguise, as it made me more conscious of anything in Chesterton redolent of anti-Semitism.

Had he been a Germanophile too, that might have been a bit much for me at the time; happily, he and Belloc were Francophiles, which suited me down to the ground. I know these are suasions rather than arguments, but you must remember I was a lad of sixteen-seventeen when I began to read Chesterton in earnest, and suasions counted for a good deal. In any case, I never felt uncomfortable as a Jew in Chesterton's company. I never felt, "Well, I'll put up with this nasty business, because there is some real sense in him, and, after all, he writes so well." That would have taxed my powers a good deal at that age. And one must remember that much of this material was polemical, the sort of writing where one would expect to find a bias if the author was a bigot. Sometimes—though this was rare—I'd come across a remark which gave me pain: I remember, for example, his referring, in *Orthodoxy*, to Oscar Levy as a "non-European alien" —though the reference is ultimately complimentary (he calls him "the only intelligent Nietzscheite"). There is an aspect of Chesterton's thought I am not entirely in agreement with here (and which I'll come to later), but, even when I first read it, I couldn't call it anti-Semitic as it contained an element of truth I was already only too familiar with—although I should put it differently.

DA: You say you've run across rare passages in Chesterton that gave you pain because you did not agree with his assessment of the situation, but have you ever run across anything that could be labeled anti-Semitic?

RA: In all the hundreds of pages of Chesterton I've read, I can think of perhaps six or seven instances which a Jew today would be likely to construe—incorrectly, as I believe—as anti-Semitic. There were many more provocative references to Muslims and to Germans in his work than there were to Jews.

My abiding impression was that Chesterton was a very good friend—something I should never have felt had I considered him to be anti-Semitic.

DA: What do you say to people who say that Chesterton was anti-Semitic?

RA: It depends on whom I'm talking to, and whether they care to listen. Chesterton is very much a late-Victorian/Edwardian writer, in style, sensibility and, obviously, in his frame of reference. It is one of the things that first drew me to him, just as it is perhaps the major reason that some readers are insensible to his stature. I am very much at home in the world of 19th century letters: it is my chosen field; and it is a *canard* (and an increasingly common one) to think that any figure—no matter how far-sighted or prophetic—can be taken wholly out of context. Let us take a couple of cases of changing cultural contexts: Gustav Mahler was a German-speaking Jewish convert to Catholicism, born in what is now the Czech Republic. He was, of course an Austro-Hungarian composer, but Austria-Hungary no longer exists. What would we call him today? A German? A Czech? A Jew? An Austrian—with all that that now fails to imply? Or suppose Quebec should separate from Canada: would that make an English Canadian born in 19th century Montreal a Quebecois? A French Canadian? The same is true of intellectual contexts. As circumstances change, the conditions of discourse are altered. We must be sensitive to these changes or we shall simply end by talking about nothing but projections of ourselves. Now, this is nowhere more evident than in matters of language. The meanings and inflections of words change. William Magee, for example, the Anglican Bishop of Peterborough, referred to Wilfred Ward as a pervert, by which he meant that he had left the Church of

England for that of Rome. So the term was understood. But I can easily imagine some modern clown declaring "We can trace the Church's pedophile problems right back to the Victorian age. Why, even reputable contemporaries described Ward as a notorious pervert!" In this sense, should Chesterton have written today some handful amongst the millions of things he wrote ninety years ago, he would probably be called anti-Semitic. But we must ask ourselves two simple questions: would he have phrased them thus today, knowing how they would be construed? And are they, in fact, what we understand by anti-Semitism? The two points are connected, obviously. Did Chesterton hate the Jews—racially, socially or ethnically—and are his comparatively few "anti-Semitic" remarks an expression of such hatred? That, to me, is the real question; and my answer is an emphatic and confident "No."

DA: Can the charges against Chesterton be dismissed?

RA: Yes, but I don't think it is helpful to dismiss the accusations out of hand as merely cynical, stupid or dishonest. On the contrary, it is worth looking into why Chesterton made the few remarks on which the charge of anti-Semitism has been based. To the best of my knowledge, there is, as I indicated above, only one area where his attitudes are substantially at variance with mine, and that is the extent of the relationship between cultural identity and political autonomy: Chesterton tended to identify nations with political states—at least ideally; as is evident in his support, in World War I, for the cause of Polish independence (in which I agree with him, incidentally) and Bohemian (i.e. Czech) independence (in which I don't). Now, between, say, the 1830s and 1945 Nationalism tended to be anti-Semitic, culturally, racially, or both. Also, the identification of nation and race was nearly universal. While the hatred of other peoples is as old as the hills, we tend to forget that genetic racism is a relatively recent phenomenon.

If we turn to the Jews in this period, we find them to be everywhere a cultural and racial minority in environments of growing nationalist activism: an activism which tended to understand itself in racist terms. This was not necessarily or invariably an anti-Semitic phenomenon, nor were Jews themselves free from the tendency. The most famous theorist of race was Joseph Arthur, Comte de Gobineau (1816-1882), whose magnum opus on the subject was *The Inequality of Human Races*. Because of his racism and influence on Wagner, Gobineau is usually thought of as an anti-Semite, but he wasn't: he believed the Jews to be one of the superior races. The same was true of Benjamin Disraeli, a great hero to most Jews, who declared in *Conningsby* that "Race is everything; there is no other truth." Indeed, *Conningsby*—an enormously stimulating political novel—is somewhat marred for me by the author's occasional (pro-Semitic) emphasis on the importance of race. Ironically, our old friend Oscar Levy was both an admirer of Disraeli's (he translated him into German) and much influenced by Gobineau's racist theories: he wrote the introduction to the English edition of *The Inequality of Human Races*.

The reaction of assimilated Jews to the hostility of their environment tended to be of two kinds: a determination to succeed in defiance of every barrier erected against them, or a wholesale rejection of the establishment. In other words, one tends to find a high proportion, among assimilated Jews, both of conservative supporters of "The Establishment" and revolutionaries. This is tragic, particularly as this attitude was the fruit of centuries of proscription and abuse. In any case, it is, with the new racism, one of the two main reasons for the anti-Semitism of 19th century Nationalism: more often than not, assimilated

Jews supported the Austrian, Russian or German imperial governments against which the Nationalist Poles, Czechs,
Hungarians, etc. were struggling. After all, to the extent that the
Jews had succeeded in attaining any measure of security and
success, it had been in the established order the Nationalists
were seeking to overthrow; nor could the Jews expect better
treatment at the hands of (often) racist ideologues: insofar as
the Austrians, Germans and Russians governed multinational
empires, they had (particularly in Austria) to tolerate—at least
to a limited degree—ethnic groups other than their own; the
Nationalists did not. And in Chesterton's beloved France, with
its aggressive political factions and endless social upheavals,
anti-Semitic sentiment was rife: representatives of all parties,
whether Republicans like Barrès, Royalists like Maurras and
Léon Daudet, or Leftists like Clémenceau, were often coarse
or violent in their anti-Semitic language. (In fairness, I should
add that Daudet and Barrès both renounced anti-Semitism well
before the advent of Nazism, while Maurras and Clémenceau
were Germanophobes.)

DA: What about Chesterton's use of the term "The Jewish
Problem"?

RA: To those who are intimately familiar with this era, the so-
called "Jewish Problem" was not mere anti-Semitic rhetoric
(though the tag might make us wince today with the advantage
of hindsight). Indeed, there were many prominent Jews who
felt the same way—it was, in fact, one of the presuppositions
of the Zionist movement.

Now, as regards GKC, I should say that three things here are
of particular relevance:

On the debit side, I believe that he exaggerated the continuity of Nation State, and that consequently he doubted the extent

to which Jews could become fully and happily integrated into a predominantly Gentile *Patria*. He could see, as a matter of daily fact, the strife that existed between the Jewish communities and the Gentile majorities; and that where national sentiment was strongest, this friction was most intense. He also disapproved of the cosmopolitanism of many secular Jews, which he tended to see (and here I agree with him) as antipathetic to patriotism.

To his credit, however, one must add two very important points: In the first place, Chesterton's Nation Statism didn't translate into anything like the fundamentally anti-Semitic position of most Nationalists. On the contrary, in accordance with his principles, it led him to espouse the cause of a sovereign state for the Jews in the Holy Land. Chesterton was, in fact, a Zionist, and said as much, frequently. I'm not sure that any Jew of my acquaintance is aware of this fact, but fact it is. Secondly—and perhaps more remarkably—Chesterton was one of the few men of his time who utterly rejected the tenets of race identity. It is impossible to read Chesterton in any depth without being confronted over and again with his contempt for the racist interpretation of culture. He is forever ridiculing "Celtic" culture, "Teutonic" culture, "Anglo-Saxon" culture, "Arian" culture. It led him to be—with Churchill—one of the few Englishmen to be utterly, unremittingly, hostile to Hitler and Nazism from the first. And in his anti-Nazi diatribes, we find GKC coming explicitly to the defense of the Jews. Again, this is a fact sadly unknown to most Jews.

DA: This makes your point about the historical context all the more significant. Those who accuse Chesterton of anti-Semitism never seem to look at what else was going on during Chesterton's time.

RA: Yes, that's true. And one could ask: Is it irrelevant to the question of Chesterton's supposed anti-Semitism that he excoriated Hitler as a racist in his weekly journalism when figures—still respectable in Jewish circles—such as Shaw and Lloyd George were praising Hitler as the greatest thing to come out of Germany since the Reformation?

Again, I wonder how many Jews are aware, today, of the pervasiveness of racial assumptions before World War II. Unless their attention is drawn to it, most people tend to assume that any writer not identified with anti-Semitism was probably fairly "sound" by modern P.C. standards—especially if they were "progressives," like H.G. Wells. It is widely assumed (by Jews among others) that Wells (an author whose fictions I greatly admire) wasn't anti-Semitic because he was a "progressive." But he was very anti-Semitic.

Finally, people simply weren't as sensitive to these issues—as hypersensitive, one might sometimes feel—as they have been since the War. One finds anti-Semitic gibes in the correspondence of Byron, for example, and Byron was unusually sympathetic to Jews by the standards of his society. And it was Browning, a poet Jews regard (rightly) as pro-Semitic, who quipped:

> We don't want to fight,
> By Jingo, if we do,
> The head I'd like to punch
> Is Beaconsfield the Jew.

DA: A reference to Disraeli, who was known as Lord Beaconsfield. But that little rhyme is never brought up about Browning the same way "I am fond of Jews" is brought up about Chesterton.

RA: Another man without a shred of vulgar anti-Semitism, Lord Rosebery, whose blissful marriage to Hannah Rothschild led to grumbles of Jewish political interference, has been accused of anti-Semitism because of a few casual witticisms.

Chesterton was probably the most prolific major author of the last century, and he was a religious, political, and cultural polemicist, a journalist with a daily column for decades: it's simply not plausible that an author answering to that description could be anti-Semitic without leaving a large trail behind him, particularly in the late 19th-early 20th century. It must, I think, be conceded that Chesterton does not display any interest in the deep and ongoing relationship of the Jews to the Church and Cosmic History that we find in the writings of writers like Bloy, Péguy, Pascal, Solovyov or Mickiewicz—but then, attitudes such as these have always been rare, and the same could be said of scores of authors never accused of anti-Semitism. But had Chesterton lived through the Second World War, I should not, for my part, be surprised if he had turned his attention to this phenomenon. And when Chesterton wrote, in response to the early Nazi persecutions, that he and Belloc were prepared to die defending the last Jew in Europe, I am quite prepared to believe him. There is nothing of bitterness in his tone, let alone hatred; I have always found him the very best company, the most lovable, as well as the most engaging, of writers.

DA: As a Jewish convert to Catholicism, you must have some interesting things to say to people on both sides of the aisle.

RA: Well, actually, the only anti-Semitic experiences I had before my conversion were at the hands of Protestants and agnostics. Perhaps that was mere coincidence, but in any case, I never associated anti-Semitism with the Catholic Church particularly. I certainly never remember my parents saying anything of the kind. As a child I had learned something of the pogroms in Eastern Europe, but though the Poles were Catholic, the Russians weren't; again, the Holocaust tended to be seen as a German crime, rather than a Christian one; certainly not a specifically Catholic one. At university, when I began to be more aware of Catholicism, I read Pascal—who is an admirer of Judaism—before I read Kavanagh, and then, in Central Europe, I found that it was the practising Catholics I met who were most friendly to Judaism—much more so than the Secularists. Again, I was aware, at least from my university days, of John Paul II's very warm relationship with the Jews, which made an impression. And I have never forgotten a remark made by one of my parents' friends in a particularly interesting conversation from this time, that Luther was the first anti-Semite. I don't believe it influenced me, but it certainly didn't incline me towards a belief that the Catholic Church had a monopoly on anti-Semitism. And since becoming a Catholic (except where long-standing ethnic frictions are concerned—among the Poles or Irish-Americans, for example), I have not found anti-Semitism in Catholic circles at all.

I did harbor the suspicion, as a Jew—which I am persuaded I shared with most Jews (certainly most of my acquaintance)—that Christians generally were anti-Semitic, and, vaguely, a sense that perhaps all non-Jews were—at least in Europe, the Americas and the Middle East. And I'm afraid I don't believe that most Jews who feel this way try very hard to rationalize (responsibly, at least) what would appear to be such an extraordinary conviction.

Jews tend to be extremely sensitive to any perceived hostility or criticism, and this is, after all, only to be expected. What Christians must try to realize—if they are going to reach Jews—is the extent to which centuries of persecution, extending well into this century, have branded these insecurities into the Jewish psyche. I suppose this is a truism, but it is one which cannot be repeated often enough. It has led to a warping of Jewish objectivity. For example, 19th century England and Austria-Hungary, where opportunities for Jews and acceptance of Jews were much more widespread than elsewhere, have nevertheless been characterized by Jews as fundamentally anti-Semitic cultures. While there is an element of truth in this (and sometimes more than an element), it also involves a considerable distortion of perspective.

DA: And this distortion of perspective has led to what?

RA: The saddest aspect of this is that it has led to an attitude of cultural solipsism among Jews: nothing is fully real, or at least important, outside the circle of Jewish concerns. In this sense, the creation of Israel is perhaps the best thing that has happened to Judaism in centuries, if only because of they have had to shoulder the responsibility of governing other peoples. And this is the key to much historical anti-Semitism. Anyone with a knowledge of history is aware of the cruelty which nations visit on one another, and particularly on weaker cultures, vanquished nations or ethnic minorities. And minority cultures—or former minorities—are jealous of suffering: the attitude tends to be "*No one* has ever suffered as *we* have suffered." The Poles complain of the Germans and the Russians, the Jews complain of the Poles; the Irish were abused under English rule, yet Irish-Americans have been notorious in their treatment of Jews and Blacks; the French Canadians also complain of abuse at the hands of the English, yet the Jews and Indians could tell you a thing or two about the French-Canadians; the Czechs were mistreated by the Austrians, the Slovaks and Gipsies by the Czechs; while the Slovaks, in their turn, have a very poor track record with Gipsies, Jews and ethnic Hungarians…and on and on it goes. And now it is the Jews themselves, in Israel, who stand accused of the same crime.

Something which was apparent to me some time before my conversion was the inconsistency of the charge of anti-Semitism against specifically Christian culture: Islam is quite as anti-Semitic as the West, and both pagan Rome and Macedonian Greece persecuted the Jews. If anything, it tended to confirm two things in my mind: the peculiar history and identity of the Jews, and the reality of fallen human nature. Perhaps, in a generation or two, conditions will be more propitious for a more magnanimous exchange of perspectives.

FOUND DIFFICULT AND
LEFT UNTRIED

By Tod Worner

AVE YOU EVER READ THIS?"
He looked at me intently as we were standing in the basement of a peanut bar in Minneapolis' Uptown district. The sticky floor underneath us was littered with peanut shells and popcorn. The waitress had just taken our orders and scurried off to gather our pints of beer. We were here to tell stories, to tease each other, to celebrate the conclusion of a difficult internal medicine rotation. Scott was a third-year medical student assigned to my team for six weeks of early morning rounding, late night calls, critically ill patients, countless conferences and bedside teaching points. Over six weeks of being overtired, underfed, overworked and underappreciated, you would be surprised how well you get to know people who were once complete strangers. And so tonight, on

my dime, Scott, his fellow medical student, my junior resident and I would feast (or rather, would eat bar food and find ourselves a touch overserved).

"Have you ever read this?" he asked.

It was an unexpected question and an unfamiliar book that was held in Scott's outstretched hand that night. *Orthodoxy.* A blue, beaten-up, $1.95 Image Books edition of G.K. Chesterton's self-described "slovenly autobiography." He pressed it into my hand.

"No, I can't say that I have," I answered.

"You should. I think you'll like it."

After thanking him and enjoying our evening's subsequent lightheartedness, I found myself driving home with *Orthodoxy* resting on my passenger seat. Glancing over at it, I asked myself, "*Where have I heard the name G.K. Chesterton before? And why did Scott, a bright but otherwise reserved medical student, think I would like this book so much?*" During the rotation, our only conversation that seemed to touch on matters of faith was related to the book I was reading one call night: *Hitler's Pope* by John Cornwell. At the time, *Hitler's Pope* was a New York Times bestseller and a delicious character assassination of Eugenio Pacelli (the future Pope Pius XII). As a Lutheran with haughty misgivings about the Catholic Church, *Hitler's Pope* was red meat as well as a shoddy hit job which satisfied my poorly considered, thinly-veiled biases. I remember Scott raising his eyebrows (skeptically and for good reason) as I was describing some of the "unsettling facts" I was discovering in the book. Perhaps G.K. Chesterton was his delayed, but well-thought-out response. So that evening, *Orthodoxy* came home with me where I set it on my shelf. There it rested untouched for years.

My next encounter with Chesterton was at the invitation of a physician mentor and good friend, Mike. Mike is the lead physician of a well-respected Twin Cities internal medicine practice. A winsome and devout Catholic, he is a graduate of St. John's University in Collegeville, Minnesota. Upon first meeting Mike as my attending physician during residency, I found his intuition striking, his mind endlessly inquisitive and his wit razor-sharp. Before long we were engaged in debates and discussions about history, culture and religion while simultaneously peppering our conversation with towel-snapping humor. And so, it was one late Spring day that Mike invited me to a G.K. Chesterton conference (at the University of St. Thomas) sponsored by Dale Ahlquist and the American Chesterton Society. "*Hmmm,*" I thought, "*A conference on a long-dead, unfamiliar British guy? Why not?*" And so we went.

If you have ever been to an American Chesterton Society conference, you are immediately struck by the eclectic mix of folks in attendance (from college students to nuns in habits, from esteemed lawyers to Catholic housewives), the soaring quality of the intellectual and theological sparring, and the pure mirth of those who enjoy the wit and wisdom of G.K. Chesterton. The first lecture I ever attended had to do with Chesterton and hagiography. I was in awe and overwhelmed. I couldn't believe the depths to which these people considered such an issue. After leaving the conference, I had to look up the word *hagiography.*

But as I walked away from that conference—a little dizzy and carrying a sack full of new and used books—I was struck by the Catholic intellectual subculture that I had happened upon. The quotes of G.K. Chesterton were so succinct, so pithy, but so utterly penetrating to the core of my wandering, uncertain soul that I couldn't help but reckon with him. In the days to follow I turned some of this newly discovered wisdom over and over again in my hungry mind.

The Christian ideal has not been tried and found wanting; it has been found difficult and left untried.

The act of defending any of the cardinal virtues has to-day all the exhilaration of a vice.

To have a right to do a thing is not at all the same as to be right in doing it.

When I arrived home, I felt compelled to go to my bookshelf. Once there, I pulled down a much-loved book of quotes that I remember reading in high school. I recalled perusing it while lifting weights and circling my favorites. And what should I find? On page after page, quote after quote was circled, starred and underlined from none other than G.K. Chesterton.

The Lutheran in me was in trouble.

By this time, I was married to my wife (a cradle Catholic) and we were alternating weekends between Mass at the Catholic Church and services at the Lutheran Church. Early in our dating relationship, I had argued and sputtered about my discomfort with prayers to Mary, the exclusivity of Communion for Catholics, the need for Confession to priests and the hierarchy of the Church. My wife listened patiently (but also argued fiercely). *"I'm Catholic, Tod. It is who I have always been and always will be."* Desperately, I tried to reason, *"But how about becoming Episcopalian? Or non-denominational? Perhaps there is a compromise church we can agree on?"* She stared at me blankly.

But as I continued to attend Mass every other week and talked with our priest, as I prayed and read the story and writings of Pope (now St.) John Paul II and Pope Benedict XVI, and as I had more open conversations with my wife and with my friend and colleague, Mike Cummings, something in me began to change. Imperceptibly, but inexorably I was drawn to the

Catholic Church. It wouldn't be until later when I read Evelyn Waugh's masterful Catholic novel, *Brideshead Revisited,* that Chesterton's words (spoken through his sleuthing character, Father Brown) would describe what was, in fact, happening to me. God and his Church,

> [Had caught me] with an unseen hook and an invisible line which is long enough to let [me] wander to the ends of the world and still to bring [me] back with a twitch upon the thread.

And so, laying on a beach chair during a Spring Break trip to Mexico, I decided to pull that blue, beaten-up, Image Books paperback out of my satchel and read it. I read it rather quickly (only 160 pages long) and when I closed it, I took a deep breath, turned to my wife and said, *"I have no idea what Chesterton is talking about."* A little dismayed, I put the book away and wondered if this was another overrated thinker with an incomprehensible classic. *Sigh*

But I wouldn't give up. Chesterton had sunk his hooks into me. So, I read more of his quotes (stunning). I attended more of the American Chesterton Society conferences (brilliant). I devoured Joseph Pearce's *Wisdom and Innocence* and Maisie Ward's *Gilbert Keith Chesterton* biographies (extraordinary). I watched Dale Ahlquist's *Apostle of Common Sense* and read his books which vividly distilled Chesterton's thinking (insightful). And then I began to read essay after essay, poem after poem, and book after book written by Chesterton himself. After four years had passed since my first attempt, I felt it was time for me to re-approach *Orthodoxy.* Fingering through the books in my increasingly sizable and sprawling library, I came across the dog-eared copy Scott gave me. And I read it again. Only this time, I turned to my wife and said, *"This is one of the most brilliant books I have ever read."*

I discovered that upon my first endeavor to read *Orthodoxy*, I wasn't ready. The fault rested not with G.K. Chesterton, but with me. I realized, to paraphrase G.K. himself, that, *"Chesterton has not been tried and found wanting; he has been found difficult and left untried."* And to quote the late Supreme Court Justice Antonin Scalia upon the similar merits of struggling through Shakespeare, *"When you're reading Shakespeare, Shakespeare's not on trial—you are."*

G.K. Chesterton was (and is) an indispensable friend on my journey to the Catholic Faith, along with my wife, my friend Mike, my priest, my children and my many friends. One Sunday, my wife and I awoke and she reminded me that it was my turn to select church services that weekend. Almost reflexively, I responded, *"Let's go to Mass today."* Increasingly (unconsciously and inexplicably), I felt the need to kneel, to smell incense, to crave the Eucharist, to get lost in the mystery of the miracle that would unfold before my eyes every time I was in the Catholic Church.

In his book, *The Catholic Church and Conversion*, Chesterton observed,

> It is impossible to be just to the Catholic Church. The moment men cease to pull against it, they feel a tug toward it. The moment they cease to shout it down, they begin to listen to it with pleasure. The moment they try to be fair to it, they begin to be fond of it.

I was beginning to be fair to the Catholic Church. Its ineffable mysteries remained mysteries, but its motives no longer seemed suspect. Its exaltation of Christ, its veneration of Mary and the Saints, its insistence on a prayerful, mystical interiority and its mandate for a just and merciful mission, its embodiment of artistic beauty and realization of unsurpassed intellectual richness was now becoming clear to me. And it was utterly beautiful in its holiness. Only days after Chesterton was received into the Catholic Church, Hilaire Belloc poignantly and fervently wrote,

> The thing I have to say is this (I could not have said it before your step: I can say so now. Before it would have been like selected pleading). The Catholic Church is the exponent of Reality. It is true. Its doctrines in matters large and small are statements of what is…My conclusion—and that of all men who have ever once seen it—is the faith. Corporate, organized, a personality, teaching. A thing, not a theory. It.

Belloc could just as well have been writing to me…for the centrality of Catholic Truth is what I have discovered as well.

As I found myself being "drawn to ground" by the "twitch upon the thread," I was helped by Chesterton's words,

> The convert often feels as if he were looking through a leper's window. He is looking through a little crack or crooked hole that seems to grow smaller as he stares at it; but it is an opening that looks toward the Altar. Only when he has entered the Church, he finds that the Church is much larger inside than it is outside. He has left behind him the lop-sidedness of lepers' windows and even in a sense the narrowness of Gothic doors; and he is under vast domes as open as the Renaissance and as universal as the Republic of the world. He can say in a sense unknown to all modern men certain ancient and serene words: Romanus civis sum; ["I am a citizen of Rome."] I am not a slave.

The more time I spent in Mass, in prayer, in the company of my wife and friend, and in the exhilarating pages of G.K. Chesterton and Hilaire Belloc, Georges Bernanos and Flannery O'Connor, the Saints and the Popes, the more I encountered the spacious, sublime, tried and true Catholic Church. My conversion was not the experience of St. Paul, blinded and knocked off his horse. No, mine was different. As Chesterton said, "*The Church is a house with a hundred gates; and no two men enter at exactly the same angle.*"

Instead, mine was a portrait being painted. Each truth understood and each prejudice relinquished served as one of a thousand brushstrokes…until, in the end, I saw myself restored to original wholeness resting in the arms of Christ.

There came a day in 2009 when I told my wife that I was going to look into RCIA (the Rite of Christian Initiation of Adults). She smiled but said little. And as I signed up and attended Sunday after Sunday, leaving home early for lectures and Mass early for discussion with fellow candidates, my wife never fussed over the extra burden of childcare and organization that I left on her shoulders. She made it easy. Years after my conversion, I reflected on the scant discussion we had during my RCIA process. When I asked her why she didn't want to discuss it more, she answered, "*I didn't want to trample on new grass.*" She knew my pride and, instead, deferred to the Holy Spirit.

I have been a Catholic for eight years now, but feel I have been one forever. To borrow from Fr. Richard John Neuhaus, I feel I became the Catholic I always was deep inside. Along with marrying my wife and having our children, becoming Catholic is the greatest call I have ever answered. And to this very day, I can vividly remember standing by the altar on that Easter Vigil. As the censer swung toward me and the sweet incense filled my nostrils while wafting to the heights of the sanctuary, I closed my eyes. And a voice seemed to be whispering in my ear, "Tonight, Tod. Tonight, *you* are the offering."

But it is also G.K. Chesterton's own words that echo in my mind as I reflect upon my conversion. Penned as a poem shortly after arriving home from his own conversion ceremony in

1922, Chesterton's *The Convert* seems to say it all: "*My name is Lazarus and I live.*"

I became Catholic because of the Holy Spirit, my wife and my good friend, Mike. And G.K. Chesterton.

I still remember it: Scott looking at me earnestly and handing me that beat-up copy of *Orthodoxy.*

"Have you ever read this? You should. I think you'll like it."

Thanks, Scott. I really did.

GILBERT CHESTERTON, MD

By Stuart J. Kolner, MD

IN THE VENERABLE PRACTICE OF THE CATHOLIC CHURCH, the recognition of sainthood requires heroic virtue, a rigorous vetting of one's life and writings, and at least two confirmed miracles. With equal parts of humility and cheek, I propose that my unthinkable conversion to Catholicism should see G.K. Chesterton at least halfway home.

Can a highly unlikely convert serve as a saint-maker? Consider the requirements of a miracle. There have been roughly 10,000 saints canonized in 2,000 years of Church history and some 95% of these involved miracles of bodily healing, thus leaving at least 500 saints who qualified through other sorts of supernatural events. My conversion miracle is of the latter type.

Saint-making miracles must be: 1) *miraculous*, that is, unexplainable by any other means; 2) instantaneous; 3) comprehensive; and 4) permanent. I will argue that the miracle of my conversion, precipitated by my reading of G.K. Chesterton, satisfies all of these criteria.

---

1) A CANONIZING MIRACLE MUST BE OTHERWISE UNEXPLAINABLE

My lineage is a melding of my father's Lutheran upbringing and my mother's Southern Methodist beliefs. While indelibly Christian, my father found the particulars of denomination unimportant. For example, after my Catholic conversion he told me that Lutherans also believe in transubstantiation; the distinctions between that and Lutheran consubstantiation weren't on his radar.

Mother had difficulty speaking of her own strong beliefs but could clearly articulate her anti-Catholic prejudices. She believed that Catholicism succeeded only through "tyranny over the mind of man." Although an otherwise well-educated and worldly woman, she had an inexplicable emotional block against calm, rational discussion of religion, and pressing such matters would only lead her to anger and tears. As a result, I spent an anxious year before sufficiently steeling my courage in order to share the news of my conversion with her.

In a spirit of compromise, my parents' disparate faith traditions led them to espouse a third denomination, and the Presbyterian Church became the first church of my catechumenate.

These roots were planted in northeastern Oklahoma in a town of chemists, engineers and businessmen, a town surprisingly diverse in everything but religion. In our nine years there, I never met a single Catholic. There was only one small "parochial school" as it was called at the time, a place veiled in mystery to me.

Presbyterian communicants' classes, Sunday school, and sermons interested me superficially but left me unenthusiastic, and religion seemed merely a thing to be memorized. We had no home discussions of religion or philosophy. My well-read parents, who taught me the joy of learning and the utility of science, were mute on these weightier subjects, perhaps due to a combination of my mother's emotional barricades and my father's disinterest in abstract things. A combat veteran of World War II, he believed the paramount principal to be freedom, and would grumble after church about the trendy, 1960s-steeped sermons: "Peace, peace, and more peace. What about freedom?" I could see his point. Although we prayed together at meals and at bedtime, the only traditional prayer I was taught was the Lord's Prayer, complete with the Protestant gloss about the power and the glory. Formal religion was confined to church.

In eighth grade I was on the football team, played guitar in a rock and roll band, belonged to the Boy Scouts, owned a dog, had a large circle of friends, and enjoyed a comfortable, middle-class, self-assured, all-American life. And then everything changed.

One day my parents called a rare family meeting, and my sister and I apprehensively joined them in the living room. My father's company had offered him a job in Belgium, so our family had the opportunity to move to Europe for at least two years. My sister, three years my senior with only one year left at home before college, was immediately thrilled. But all I could see was the end of everything that made life worth living. I lost the family vote 3-to-1.

Belgium: cold, wet, smelling of *pommes frites* (French fries) and diesel exhaust. You could, and needed to, wear wool 300 days out of the year. Antwerp: a busy, industrialized harbor city where I knew no one. My new high school: the International

School of Brussels, run like a British public school—we wore coats and ties to class and answered to a headmaster.

Classmates and teachers, while largely American and British, hailed from all over the world. Not only were there Catholics, there were Buddhists, Jews, Muslims and others I had not encountered in Oklahoma. American traditions and taboos were ignored, even flung down and danced upon. Upperclassmen would go the village pub on Thursday after class to drink beer with the faculty ("The Thirsty Thursdays Club"). Our class trips were to such places as Moscow, Greece, and Tunisia. We learned to be immigrant visitors in a foreign place, and our school buses would drive past graffiti that read "Yanquis Go Home." Through no fault of our own, we were "Yanquis," distrusted, disliked, and displaced. Having no choice, we struggled to adapt.

The rigorous school curriculum opened new doors to me in European history, the French language, philosophy, and Western traditions from an Anglo-European perspective, clashing abruptly (and sometimes hilariously) with my pedestrian American frame of reference. Instead of Civics, we were required to take "Problems in American Democracy," taught by an Englishman who referred to the USA as "the colonies." We playfully put a sign over his door: "Abandon Democracy, All Ye Who Enter Here."

After high school, I returned stateside to college and was again disenfranchised from everything familiar. High school friends who were British, Canadian, European, Indian, and African likewise returned home in a wide diaspora. Some American friends remained and became Europeans. In a real sense, my own citizenship changed as well: while I will always bleed red, white, and blue, in Belgium I became a citizen of the wider world.

Through these experiences, I grew to be a child of the 1960s whose "miracles" were space exploration, organ transplants, and polio vaccinations. I trusted only the priesthood of science, dogmas concerning the indomitability of the human mind and spirit, and the ultimate goal of freedom. The world was a vast machine, its parts connected into a coherent, interdependent, and ultimately knowable whole. Despite my broadened European perspective, I remained at best a lukewarm and primitive Protestant, and at worst, a skeptical, lazy, hedonistic agnostic, content that truth was sufficiently contained within a sensible, measurable, "provable" realm. In short, my credo had become "seeing is believing," and my patron saint, Doubting Thomas. Mathematical likelihood of Catholic conversion? Zero percent.

2) A CANONIZING MIRACLE
MUST BE INSTANTANEOUS

My unconventional path next led me to Williamsburg, Virginia. The College of William and Mary was held in high academic regard, but I chose it just as much for its convenient East Coast location.

It was a fine and fortunate choice for many reasons: beautiful, historic surroundings; lifelong friendships; a stimulating curriculum; and best of all, it was there that I met my future wife. But its secular environment only fortified my humanistic formation.

Drawn to the sciences as a biology/pre-medicine student, I was soon disappointed to discover a worm in the apple. The sciences do not just lead to unanswered questions, but to *unanswerable* ones, paradoxes that lie outside the measurable and sensible world and thus outside of the scope of science itself.

But instead of respecting their own limits, scientists fill the void with what must be described as fables. It has been said that nature abhors a vacuum, but in truth, the universe is *mostly* vacuum; it is the mind of man that abhors a vacuum.

Like simple shepherds who saw mythic figures in the starry sky, scientists dream up elaborate explanations for science's unknowables and immeasurables. But unlike simple shepherds, they fervently believe their myths. It is doubtful that ancient star gazers tried to feed The Swan or weigh their grain in Libra. Yet the scientific community too often plunges headlong into a sea of mythology rather than admit that their tools are powerless to penetrate some things. In the rarified atmosphere of science's cutting edge, it is easy to forget the crucial distinction between theory and proof.

This fundamental dissatisfaction, as well as the pressing need to make a living, led me from the pursuit of science to a more immediate and practical field: medical librarianship. I moved to Cleveland for further education, and from there to Chicago in pursuit of both a career and the girl I had met in college whom I was determined to make my wife. She was Catholic.

Although raised in the Faith, Barbara, like so many, had succumbed to the vapid diversions of the 1960s and had let her faith stagnate. However, our re-acquaintance in Cleveland coincided with her Catholic re-awakening. From the very beginning of our relationship, we talked. And talked. And talked some more. The scene: newly re-committed Catholic meets cynical, arrogant agnostic with no Catholic database except for a few trite prejudices. I was accustomed to winning dorm and classroom debates, but had never met such a worthy opponent. Sparks flew. I tried every gambit, and was in turn haughty, coldly scientific, or witheringly sarcastic. And I was utterly frustrated because my every volley against the Faith was effortlessly and patiently swatted back, and I remained scoreless.

As is so often the case, my fascination with this woman and her impenetrable citadel of Faith (St. Barbara comes to mind) attracted me all the more. I faced two irreconcilable conclusions: I could not live without her and I could not live with Catholicism.

We began to discuss, as young couples do, the ways and means of our joining. Despite prevailing trends, we understood the dangers of simply living together. What about marriage? Barbara's principal condition was simple but non-negotiable: she intended to continue to live as a Catholic, with all the expectations and obligations thereunto.

This dilemma led to my first instantaneous, impossible metamorphosis. The skeptical humanist I had become could simply not concede to Catholic dogma. And yet, in that moment, grace won the day. With disbelief but with no other choice, I put out into the deep and made my first marriage vow: although I could not promise to convert (an impossibility, I was sure), I swore that I would remain always open to the Faith. A man so certain of his own map had mysteriously and suddenly tossed it aside, closed his eyes, and stepped into the unknown. This satisfied Barbara and her Church, although a dispensation was required for our "mixed marriage" in 1978. To my growing astonishment, this was to be only the first untying of the long ribbon of Gordian knots I had fashioned.

Months before this transformation, Barbara's parents had unaccountably accepted me, an absurdity for at least two reasons: not only was I an unappealing work-in-progress with meager means of support, but their default position toward her suitors had become dismissive, based on prior disappointments. Either they saw something of promise in me or were merely resigned, but they opened their home to me, fed me in body and spirit, even took me to Tridentine Mass with them and patiently helped me follow along in the Latin/English missal.

And they made me laugh. As I struggled to keep up with a tedious and complex Latin choral sequence, Barbara's mother leaned over to me and whispered, "Now you know what they mean by the 'never-ending hymn of praise!'" When the possibility of my conversion arose, she promised me a portrait of Jesus whose eyes would follow me around the room. A convert herself, she was a refreshing drink in an arid desert of catechism. Her favorite jokes were Catholic jokes. I was introduced to Father Cletus Healy, SJ, an Irish leprechaun farm boy from Iowa with an infectious giggle, an encyclopedic grasp of the faith, and a living demonstration of heroic virtue. Father Healy would eventually instruct and receive me into the Church, marry us, and baptize all of our children.

While still a bachelor in Chicago, I was invited to Barbara's family home in Milwaukee on weekends. Barbara's father would sit with me at the kitchen table long after the evening meal, smoking cigarettes and sharing his bottomless bottle of red wine and his observations on life. Most importantly, he shared his faith with me. Somehow sensing that I would have run from pressure, he simply answered my questions, reasonably and gently countering my objections. Through his patience, quick mind, impish wit, and invincible faith, I first began to thrill to the image of a novel and authentic religion, one that was robustly coherent, engaging and finding meaning in paradox, and thoroughly satisfying to the intellect. It was nothing like the vague Protestantism of my youth nor the sciences that were blind to their own fables.

And he introduced me to G.K. Chesterton. Widely read, he suggested many authors to supplement our kitchen table discussions, from Archbishop Fulton Sheen to British journalist and improbable Christian convert Malcolm Muggeridge. But it was Chesterton who most delighted, enlightened, and eventually overthrew me. And led directly to another tectonic shift in my conversion.

I commuted daily on the elevated trains from our Evanston apartment to my library workplace in Chicago, and it was my habit to pass the time reading. One fateful day, engrossed in Chesterton's *The Everlasting Man*, I suddenly looked up from the page to the faces of those around me. And in an instantaneous, mysterious epiphany, I could see in those faces that it was all *true*, just as it had been handed down: the Gospel stories and the Old Testament, as preserved, interpreted, and insisted upon by none other than the Roman Catholic Church.

3) A CANONIZING MIRACLE MUST BE COMPREHENSIVE

I soon began to sense a hunger for the Eucharist. One blessed day, I realized that, despite my energetic efforts to repel the Faith, I was out of ammunition. In a Chestertonian paradox, however, I surrendered in victory. Through God's unfathomable mercy, I was conditionally re-baptized, confirmed, and received my first Holy Communion from the hands of Father Healy on Pentecost Sunday in the year of Our Lord 1983.

These movements were accompanied by a slow toppling of other "immovable objects" that collapsed like dominos (*Dominus*) and reformed every part of me. When we married, I had grudgingly agreed to Church rules on natural family planning, something I had initially dismissed as unscientific but came to cherish as central to an authentic marriage. I agreed to raise our children Catholic, only to find that they raised *me* Catholic. I dutifully followed Church rules on such things as abstaining from meat on Fridays, and discovered therein a source of spiritual health and grace.

After years of denying it, my calling to medicine reawakened. Despite some lackluster undergraduate grades, intense competition for medical school openings, and seemingly impossible odds against me, I again acted on faith. Taking three grueling months to refresh my knowledge of basic sciences, I took the Medical College Admissions Test at age thirty-three, and then did the unthinkable: I applied to only one medical school. Miraculously admitted and even more surprisingly successful, I eventually secured the rare prize of a dermatology residency. Moreover, my medical training and practice succeeded without a single contraceptive prescription or other transgression of Catholic medical ethics, an outcome that I would have thought unattainable until the complete transformation that was my conversion.

4) A canonizing miracle must be permanent

I have now been a Catholic for thirty-five years, well over half of my life. My forty-year marriage is stronger than ever. Our three children are in Catholic marriages, and our ten (and counting) grandchildren are being raised in the Faith.

In 2016, I founded a local Chesterton society in Des Moines, and currently serve on the board of directors of the American Chesterton Society, thereby making small installment payments on the great debt I owe to Chesterton, one I could never truly satisfy.

Only in retrospect could I appreciate the many other seeds of conversion scattered along my wandering way. It was years later when I learned that my maternal grandfather, an otherwise devout Methodist, refused to partake of Communion, considering it cannibalism. This simple, uneducated man somehow perceived the body of Our Lord in a Methodist cracker that made no such claims about itself! Belgium's central location had allowed us easy access to diverse weekend destinations, and we often visited churches, cathedrals, and shrines. Out of respect for believers, my anti-Catholic Presbyterian mother wore a mantilla when visiting churches, and taught me to genuflect for the same reason. We toured St. Peter's, the Sistine Chapel, Assisi, and other locales of only historic interest to me at the time, but which I now hold to be very dear. One Sunday in the summer of 1967, I stood in a crowd in St. Peter's Square and received Pope Paul VI's blessing after the Angelus. These robust seeds eventually bore fruit, even in my rocky ground.

By now it is evident, I trust, that my impossible, comprehensive, permanent, and, at times, instantaneous conversion seems the stuff of miracles, what Chesterton called "things that cannot be and that are." He often surprises us by pointing out that the reality of a situation is the precise opposite of what we perceive it to be, and that our first impression is merely an illusion. In this, he is a master disillusionist, revealing that what seems an indisputable fact is in truth a reflection in a fun-house mirror.

I am among the many people gratefully disillusioned by Chesterton. I now realize that "seeing is believing" often leads to illusion; the surer way is "believing is seeing." Clues are everywhere: Our Lord told Martha, "If you would believe, you would see the glory of God" (*John 11:40*); He told Thomas, "Blessed are they who have not seen, and have believed" (*John 20:29*); St. Augustine taught that faith precedes understanding.

We are all prone to illusions. The image that our eye perceives is in fact first projected upside-down onto the seeing surface of the retina—it must then be "converted" to be rendered right-side-up. Thank you, Gilbert Chesterton, MD (Master

Disillusionist), for my corrective lenses. May you one day be acknowledged as a saint, and may I one day be blessed to thank you face-to-face!

It Only Took One Sentence

By Tito Galindo

"I SHARED SOME QUOTES WITH YOU."

That's how it started. My daughter Nicki shared a list of quotes from various poets and writers on Facebook. As I read through the quotes my mind landed on a quote from G.K. Chesterton. Or maybe it was heart. Yes, more my heart than head. But both.

> "Fairy tales are more than true, not because they tell us dragons exist but because they tell us dragons can be beaten."

To me the quote was warm, inviting, and full of meaning. It touched a nerve or awoke something in me that was dormant.

As a young person, I had been brought up in a very strict fundamentalist denomination. It was a twig from Seventh Day Adventism, one or two branches removed. The Church of God Seventh Day in Huntington Beach, California. While the doctrines were a little off, the people were good, sincere seekers of God. They were trying to serve him the best they could. This particular group was highly influenced by Pentecostalism and eventually split from their more buttoned down brethren. There was a desire to be freed from denominational constraints that hindered the work of the Spirit. In time, they shook off the name Church of God Seventh Day and called themselves Rainbow Christian Fellowship.

It was in this church that I was raised. My parents, old school Catholic Hispanics from New Mexico and South Texas were converted into this form of Protestantism shortly after they arrived in Southern California. They weren't exactly catechized very deeply. Catholicism for them was more cultural—like saying you were a Cowboys fan because you live in Dallas. One or two years after they converted I was born and began to learn about God, Jesus and the basics of Christianity—from that perspective. They had found something new and exciting in a Bible-based community and were all in. After a bit of a rebellious streak in my teenage years, I decided to give my life to Jesus. I made a decision to follow him and live according to the Bible as best I could. Those days I was heavily influenced by Keith Green (a Christian pop culture icon who tragically passed away in a plane crash), Billy Graham and, of course, my local pastor.

While working in construction, I would listen to Christian radio on the long rides to and from home. The drive home would afford lots of time to listen to various Christian speakers. There was J. Vernon McGee, Charles Stanley, Chuck Swindoll, David Jeremiah, Dr. James Dobson…the list goes on and on. And then there were the Christian Apologists on the radio. That really got me going. These guys were taking on the cults and false preachers and that was exciting. I wanted to be right and true and there they were, right in the thick of things.

One of my favorites was Hank Hanegraaff, the Bible Answer Man. He wrote a book in the early '90s called *Christianity in Crisis*. Although directed at the prosperity-oriented ministries, the book introduced me to the Creeds. I had never heard of the Nicene Creed, the Apostle's Creed or the Creed of Athanasius. This was new. This was clarity. I had never heard a concise, precise and definitive statement about God. This I found in the Creeds, and it was like a light shining in the darkness. It cut through the feel good, ethereal vagueness that surrounds so much of modern Christianity. With its heavy emphasis on 'personal' relationship, personal interpretation of scripture, and lack of connection to the past, the Christianity I had been raised in seemed small and inadequate. After being convinced that the church we were attending was a cult, my wife and I left that church, looking to become part of the larger body of Christ.

We had started to move toward something. Where we were going was not clearly defined. Only the direction. My poor young wife was horrified and astonished. We were raised as Sabbath-keeping Christians who thought worshipping on Sunday was major compromise. We were taught that 'Sunday worship' was a practice invented by the Roman Catholic whore of Babylon. Under protest she trusted my intuition. We were only married a year or two when I decided to make a major break. We had to leave. This was not an easy decision as we both had family associated with Rainbow Christian Fellowship and affiliated congregations.

This step was the first in a series. Being raised Pentecostal, we joined an Assemblies of God church. It was good to be out of the tiny cult and into something bigger and more exciting. There were plays and musicals, lots of people to interact with and robust children's ministries. The sting of leaving the cult was easing for my wife as she made new friends. We were happy for a while but I soon became disillusioned and disappointed. While the Assemblies of God is a good denomination, it didn't seem like a good fit. I became increasingly interested in the Creeds and a more serious type of Christianity. The high of joining a more mainstream version of evangelical Christianity was wearing off. I became disillusioned with what I thought was sensationalism and emotionalism. I wanted to be serious. I wanted a grown-up type church. That was my thought process. This is not to say there are not serious and good Christians in the Assemblies of God churches, only that for me there was an unmet need.

Once again, the destination was not clear only the direction. I wanted something I couldn't explain. I only knew I wasn't satisfied. We chose to attend Calvary Chapel churches. We weren't really Baptists, Presbyterians or tied to a denomination so a non-denominational church seemed like it would be just fine. I was very impressed by the laid-back style and the 'come as you are, blue jeans are just fine' mentality. Jesus was cool. Then things started to change: starting with the size of our family. One kid, then two. Two turned into three, then three into four. Before long, I was disinterested in church. I would still listen to my favorite radio programs but I was not interested in going to church any more. I would do it to be a good Christian but by now I was more interested in work and the Creedal Church. I was introduced to C.S. Lewis and began reading him in earnest. *Mere Christianity, Screwtape Letters, The Problem with Pain*. I saw that there was another type of church, a more historical church.

One day we decided to leave Calvary Chapel. This time it was my wife. She was unhappy with some elements of Calvary Chapel, and I had no interest in staying. I wanted a more historical church. I was tired of what I considered faddish

Christianity. Flip flops and jeans, coffee-cup-in-hand-while-in-church style of Christianity seemed thin and uninteresting. I wanted a church intimately connected to the Creeds and to the saints who defined the Creeds. I wanted to be in the same church as Sts. Athanasius, Jerome, Polycarp and Justin Martyr. I was reading Church history and it was more interesting that anything I found in the modern books.

I was on a path toward Rome. I didn't realize it or maybe even think of it at the time. While looking for another church, I flirted briefly with the idea of going to a Catholic Church, even though such an idea had always been off limits. Actually, it wasn't flirting. It was one quick thought that was quickly put out. It had a connection to the past but that would be taking things way too far. I was an Evangelical type of Christian and definitely had to stay on the Reformation side of the fence. However attractive the Catholic Church might appear, salvation through works, Mary worship, adding books to the Bible and other practices made joining it an impossibility. My wife's a good sport, being an open-minded person and all, but being Catholic would be unthinkable. Besides we really didn't know any Catholics and all our friends were some type of Protestant Christian. Through church hopping and having kids in Christian schools we had accumulated a small band of friends with diverse backgrounds and theologies. There was always a gentleman's agreement when we were together that we would all play nice. We had friends who were Baptist, Non-Denominationalist, Reformed, etc. As long as you were within the general realm of Bible-oriented Christianity you were fine.

I guess I pushed the envelope a bit when I landed at my next church, the Lutheran Church Missouri Synod. This was definitely the boundary. I wanted to be in the historical church but as a Bible believing and Reformed Christian. The Lutheran

Church provided this mechanism. To use a concept used the LCMS, I could be in the church catholic without being in the Catholic Church. That was it. I got my Creedal Church and got to eat the cake of being an Evangelical. Nice work.

Besides, my kids were multiplying and getting older. Church-hopping would not do. No, I had to put down roots and the Lutheran Church was as good as could be expected: solid, historical, respectable. It also had the Creeds: The Apostle's and Nicene Creed recited on Sundays, and even the Athanasian Creed was read on occasion. Yes, this may not be perfect or even the True Church (I had played nice with my Protestant brethren for years and understood that there probably really is no True Church on earth and that as long as you weren't a Mormon or Jehovah's Witness you were probably in…), but it was just fine.

I hadn't realized how far I had fallen from true religious joy. In my youth, it was all joy and no real theological depth. I loved Jesus with the zeal and innocence of a child. By my mid-forties, that all seemed a little distant and maybe even naïve. I was still deeply interested in church history but I had hit a wall. This was as far as it could go. I was in a branch of the True Church, and that was as good as could be expected. When we joined the Lutheran Church we had to sign that we believed a certain body of teachings—the Augsburg Confession, the Smalcald Articles, the Formula of Concor—that I didn't believe as such, but I didn't disbelieve either. I asked the Pastor if he really thought the Lutheran Church was the True Church. He sort of shrugged and said "so far as can be known." I signed. It didn't matter. Does anyone know or care what the Formula of Concord really says? No Lutheran I knew had ever read the Formula of Concord. How important could it be?

I encountered Chesterton's writings when I was in a world of fog and vagueness. I later learned that he disliked vagueness for that is where the devil lives. When I first heard the quote about fairy tales I thought I would google his name to see if he had written anything else (Laugh here). I was hooked. His writings touched a spiritual nerve. I was able to feel like a kid again. In my quest to find the historic, serious and Creedal Church, my faith had grown stale.

Shortly after reading my first Chesterton quote, I was recalled to active duty for service in Afghanistan. During the mobilization process I spent every free moment reading Chesterton quotes. I couldn't get enough. After I landed in Afghanistan, I asked my wife to send books. She sent *The Everlasting Man* and *Orthodoxy*. I had converted in my heart to Catholicism somewhere along the way. I can't say at what moment because I don't know if it was while reading Chapter 2 of *Orthodoxy* or while reading Chapter 3 of *The Everlasting Man*. I hadn't thought too much about it except that one day I woke out of my readings and realized I had to formally convert. I identified as Catholic while away. The military provides religious services—Protestant and Catholic—during deployment. On Sundays, I would sit in the back of the Catholic services just to be as close as possible to the Catholic Church.

After arriving home I made a decision to come into the Church. It was not an easy thing to endure. For my poor wife, yet another church change. How many moves are we going to make? We were spiritual gypsies and nomads. By this time our family had grown to six children with one more on the way. I promised it would be the last change. I told her there would be no more church changes, we had reached the end of the road. Rome or atheism. It would be a bumpy road. Not everyone in the family was super thrilled. We were in a crisis. We had always been a tight-knit family sharing the same faith but now we would be separated. To me things were not looking very good.

Fortunately, the parish priest was very wise and advised patience. People have to be free to choose. The kids had grown older, I couldn't insist they go with me. I had to face the reality that I couldn't make decisions for my wife and kids, and so I had to face the idea that the family might be religiously divided. The older kids and my wife would have to be free, and I would have to leave it in God's hands. My wife started by reading *Catholicism for Dummies*. To her delight and surprise, the Catholic Church was different than what we were raised believing. She truly fell in love with the Church, maybe even more so than me. It is everything we dreamed of. I know there are problems with it like there are problems in every family but it really is the answer we had been seeking all along.

In May of 2012 we joyfully entered the Church with five of our children. I honestly feel like my daughter Nicki saved my life when she casually introduced me to one sentence by G.K. Chesterton.

THE REPOSE OF REALITY

By Carl E. Olson

Y EARS AGO, not long after having entered the Catholic Church in 1997, I was asked to give a talk on my journey to and into the Catholic Church. Although still fairly young and not prone to humility and moderation, I recognized—thanks in large part to my spiritual director at the time—that conversion accounts can be a tricky business. Put simply, they can be a temptation to pride. But having benefited from reading the testimonies of so many who had journeyed from Evangelicalism to Catholicism, I hoped my story—hardly dramatic or remarkable by any reasonable measure—might be of encouragement. Such accounts really should be invitations to humility, reflection, and, finally, to deeper conversion to faith in Jesus Christ, for the essence of conversion is located in God's love for us and then our cooperation with His grace.

I hit upon a simple approach: to relate my journey from the perspective of "the Communion of Saints in action" (I also couldn't resist subtitling it "Confessions of a Former Anti-Catholic Fundamentalist," just in case the main title proved too vague for some). I began the talk—which I've since given several times–with this quote from Monsignor Ronald Knox:

> A convert was asked why he became a Catholic, and he said he tried all the other places of worship, and everywhere they thrust a hymn-book into his hand, and stood at the door asking him to come again—except the Catholic church, where nobody took any notice of him at all.

That, in fact, was what my wife Heather and I experienced. And, again, it speaks a bit to the relatively mundane nature of our story, which I now see as a long and rather logical arc, even if filled with some necessary emotional bumps, familial tensions, theological clashes, and spiritual agonies.

And there, close to the center, was the sprawling prose and penetrating thought of one Gilbert Keith Chesterton.

I must hasten to explain what I mean by "close to the center." First and foremost, of course, becoming Catholic is a matter of drawing closer to Christ and entering, by God's grace, into full communion with his One, Holy, Catholic, and Apostolic Church. There is a list of seven; seven persons (or pairs of persons) who had pointed me and guided me, in some significant way, toward Christ and his Church. Some of them on the list might be taken aback by the thought that they helped draw me to the Catholic Church, because some of them, including my wonderful parents, who are number one on the list, to this day, remain Fundamentalist Protestants. The rest of the list consists of my favorite poet, T.S. Eliot (#2 and an Anglican); my favorite Bible college professor, Ken Guenter (#3 and an Evangelical); another covert, Walker Percy (#5), the early Church father, St. Ignatius of Antioch (#6), and two popes St. John Paul II and

Benedict XVI (#7; I began reading Cardinal Ratzinger back in 1992).

And right in the middle—at #4—is G.K. Chesterton.

That placement makes sense in many ways. After receiving a two-year degree from Briercrest Bible College (Caronport, Saskatchewan) in 1991, I moved to Portland, Oregon. I soon met Heather, who was attending Bible college, and I also began reading more and more Catholic "stuff," as well as some Church history. Through reading a number of books by Russell Kirk (himself a convert to Catholicism), I was introduced to St. Thomas Aquinas, John Henry Newman, and Chesterton. It is strange, in retrospect, that it took me as long as it did to "discover" Chesterton, as I had read and studied C.S. Lewis, Flannery O'Connor, and Gerard Manley Hopkins while in Bible college. It is, in hindsight, a grace that I was introduced to Chesterton when I was, for he was the bracing thinker, joyful Christian, and exuberant apologist that I needed at that very moment.

Heather and I helped lead a young adults Bible study while we were dating, and I recall telling her about this great book I was reading, titled *Orthodoxy,* while we were driving to one of our studies. As I wrote in my 1998 account for *This Rock* magazine (now *Catholic Answers Magazine*):

> Reading G.K. Chesterton's *Orthodoxy* was the opening of a door I would not have found on my own. This stunning apologetic for Christianity against the errors of modern philosophies made me realize how central "paradox" is to the Christian faith. True Christianity is a radical balance of "both/and" instead of just "either/or." This understanding later became the key to understanding certain Catholic teachings. Soon afterward I read Dorothy Sayer's *Creed or Chaos,* an excellent explanation of the need for creeds and formal statements of belief in maintaining and continuing doctrinal purity. Then I read Chesterton's *The Everlasting Man,* his study of the Incarnation and its effect on human history.

We married soon after and then moved down to Eugene, Oregon, which is Heather's hometown. Things, as they say, were coming to a head—that is, I was growing discontented with Evangelicalism and was increasingly curious about Catholicism, despite having countless questions and an abundance of emotional reactions against such a crazy consideration. In the meantime, we were attending a small "Bible church." One Sunday, the pastor gave a sermon on why the Holy Spirit was "better" than Jesus; he wasn't just trying to compare the work of the Second and Third Persons of the Holy Trinity—he was actively pitting them against one another. As we walked out, I muttered, "I'm done. No more." The problem wasn't just the bad theology—after all, plenty of Evangelicals would dismiss such a poor sermon—but the fragmentary nature of church authority. Who would question the pastor? What would happen? Who had the final authority on such matters? Why should I listen to Pastor Smith rather than Pastor Jones?

In fact, there was much more going on, as I had a long list of questions about matters of history and theology. But that sermon, for me, was the final straw. And so, for nearly a year, we did not attend any church at all; we entered a state of ecclesial limbo, knowing that Evangelicalism was no longer an option but not knowing if the Catholic Church was really any option at all. During that year, I read Chesterton almost every single day. And during that "year of Chesterton" I experienced the first two "stages of conversion" (or "states of mind") described by Chesterton in *The Catholic Church and Conversion*.

The first stage or state, Chesterton wrote, was when the convert "imagines himself to be entirely detached, or even to be entirely indifferent ... The first phase is that of the young philosopher who feels that he ought to be fair to the Church of Rome." I had already worked through the most nonsensical and outlandish of the Jack Chick-ian assaults on the Catholic Church: that she enforced the worship of Mary, practiced pagan-inspired rituals, and hated the Bible. I simply wanted to give the Catholic Church a fair hearing, something I had certainly not experienced in my Fundamentalist upbringing and had only glimpsed briefly in a couple of my courses in Bible college (by an exceptional professor who was Anglican). There was, honestly, a part of me that hoped my studies would conclude with the qualified admission that, yes, the Catholic Church has some good qualities—but it also has plenty of problems and surely isn't The Church.

But I found myself, as so many others have, moving into the second stage, "in which the convert begins to be conscious," explained Chesterton, "not only of the falsehood but the truth and is enormously excited to find that there is far more of it than he would ever have expected." I found that he was quite right in observing this was "not so much a stage as a progress; and it goes on pretty rapidly but often for a long time." It is full of discovery; it is the unraveling of anti-Catholic knots, the opening of previously locked windows, and the washing away of prejudices deeply ingrained but held in place by the most shallow of roots. "This process," wrote Chesterton, "which may be called discovering the Catholic Church, is perhaps the most pleasant and straightforward part of the business; easier than joining the Catholic Church and much easier than trying to live the Catholic life. It is like discovering a new continent full of strange flowers and fantastic animals, which is at once wild and hospitable. To give anything like a full account of that process would simply be to discuss about half a hundred Catholic ideas and institutions in turn."

Over the years, when asked for the one reason why I became Catholic, I have always responded: "The Holy Eucharist."

I believed, as a Fundamentalist, in the Triune God and I confessed, as an Evangelical, the reality of the Incarnation; as a Fundamentalist and Evangelical I had taken part nearly every Sunday in "the Lord's Supper," most often consisting of bread and grape juice, presented as a "reminder" of Christ's saving work on the Cross. Having read St. Ignatius of Antioch on the Eucharist, I recognized the ancient Docetists—gnostics who believed Jesus only appeared to be enfleshed (*dókēsis* = apparition)—as forerunners of American Fundamentalists. As it has for many other Protestants, the sixth chapter of John raised essential, difficult questions.

I am quite certain Chesterton would laugh dismissively at being called a theologian, but he was in fact a very good theologian—especially in his reflections on the relationship between the supernatural and material realms. In *The Thing: Why I Am a Catholic*, he applied his gift to the matter of the Incarnation and the Eucharist. "Heaven has descended into the world of matter;" he wrote, "the supreme spiritual power is now operating by the machinery of matter, dealing miraculously with the bodies and souls of men." This is a pithy commentary on the entire Gospel of John, a deeply sacramental and theological work. Chesterton, responding to a Protestant critic who denied the Eucharist is the true body, blood, soul and divinity of Jesus Christ, stated that he couldn't understand why Protestants do not see "that the Incarnation is as much a part of that idea as the Mass; and that the Mass is as much a part of that idea as the Incarnation." A Puritan "may think it blasphemous that God should become a wafer," but that stance is an illogical prejudice against the notion that "the miraculous should descend to the plane of matter..."

I realized that saying the Eucharist cannot be Jesus Christ is to deny the words of Christ, the tradition of the Church, the power of God to become man, and the goodness of the created world itself. Chesterton emphasized the latter two points: "If it be profane that the miraculous should descend to the plane of matter, then certainly Catholicism is profane; and Protestantism is profane; and Christianity is profane." If God did, in fact, become man and dwell among us—as St. John contemplates in his great Prologue—then heaven has invaded earth with a passionate abandon, a sort of divine recklessness, that changes everything.

This is just one cursory example; I could give dozens and hundreds more. There is my favorite passage of Chestertonian brilliance, the sixth chapter of *Orthodoxy*, titled "Paradoxes of Christianity," in which the young Chesterton described his own journey from paganism to agnosticism to theism, noting that the Church "was attacked on all sides and for all contradictory reasons." There is his rollicking but deeply insightful book on Saint Thomas Aquinas, which the great French Thomist and author Etienne Gilson flatly described "as being without possible comparison the best book ever written on St. Thomas." There is the striking chapter on "The Five Deaths of the Faith" near the end of *The Everlasting Man*, arguably Chesterton's masterpiece, in which he declares that "Christianity has died many times and risen again; for it had a God who knew the way out of the grave." And there is his overlooked travelogue and study *What I Saw in America*, which the historian Glenn W. Olsen has judged to be "the most profound book on America ever written"—even more profound than the Tocqueville's classic *Democracy in America*.

Chesterton, I found, was able to synthesize and summarize what I was already studying or was, in many cases, struggling to fit together, to see aright, to grasp more fully. Paradoxically, Chesterton had the unique ability to both sum up and break open; put another way, in making the Faith accessible, he never made it simple or simplistic—rather, he pointed insistently to the wonders and depths of the Mystery. And he did so with an effusive joy, so palpable that some of his critics mistake it for flippancy or glibness.

Finally, then, came the third stage of conversion. Chesterton described this as "perhaps the truest and the most terrible. It is that in which the man is trying not to be converted. He has come too near to the truth, and has forgotten that truth is a magnet, with the powers of attraction and repulsion." There was a clear sense that a decision was fast approaching, which elicited excitement, fear, and a bit of panic. As I moved further into the deep, I glanced desperately at Anglicanism, Lutheranism, and Eastern Orthodoxy; I tried to find historical reasons to turn my back on Rome; I sought solace in highlighting the faults of Catholics, only to be reminded, first, of my own sins and, secondly, that Christ did not promise that his followers would be sinless, but that "I will build my church, and the powers of death shall not prevail against it" (Matt. 16:18).

The "year of Chesterton" led to a long visit with Fr. Timothy Mockaitis at St. Paul Catholic Church, conveniently located directly across the street from our apartment. A year later, Heather and I entered the Catholic Church on March 29, 1997, at Easter Vigil. It was the culmination of the Christian faith I had been raised in and it was also, in a real way, a conversion— an act of "turning from" and of "turning around." It was, in short, a new and deeper relationship with the One who is the Way, the Truth, and the Life, who is the creator of all things and author of all reality. "The phenomenon of conversion," wrote Chesterton, "apparent in every class, affecting every type of character, is the great modern witness to the truth of the claim of the Faith; to the fact that the Faith is reality, and that in it alone is the repose of reality to be found."

COMING HOME WITH
G.K. CHESTERTON

By Peter Wilson

IT WAS THOMAS WOLFE who told us that we "can't go home again." I'm not sure just how true that is because it wasn't true for me. And it was Gilbert Keith Chesterton who proved it could be otherwise.

My early years in this life were somewhat sheltered and lonely; friendships couldn't seem to get off the ground. So I would take refuge in the world of the imagination, being especially fascinated with historical biographies and classical music. I enjoyed the Narnia series long before the movies came around and before I had ever heard of C.S. Lewis. I took up the violin in grade school but had to put up with considerable teasing from my peers who didn't think the violin was a suitable instrument for the male persona. So my father brought home an old trombone case, which successfully hid the identity of my would-be Stradivarius and saved me from repeated after-school ambushes. This was my first experience with the world's bullies—and I couldn't understand how others of my age could look down upon something that could create such beauty. My brother took piano lessons and since he didn't have to carry a piano around, there was no problem with bullies. He was also the star pitcher on my father's junior baseball team, winning considerable fame around the neighborhood and much praise from his parent-coach. I didn't much care for organized kiddy athletics and the wild adult ranting and cheering that always seemed to spoil a good time. Parents are usually not very sportsmanlike when it comes to their children's sport teams. Even though I was, ironically, a better pitcher than my brother (which he admitted) I settled on being sort of an unofficial towel-boy, shagging foul bowls and packing up game equipment when it was time to leave Mudville. I didn't feel any need to prove my manhood—boyhood was enough of a challenge. I don't recall Chesterton's view on athletic valor, but I've certainly never pictured him as an Olympian.

My folks had a respect for religion and forced it on us siblings—just not on themselves. Every Sunday we dutifully marched ourselves to Mass with our family pet, a beagle with a penchant for incense. Our most embarrassing moment was when he insisted on accompanying us kids up to the altar rail for communion. It's impossible to pretend you don't know a certain dog when he's kneeling beside you in church. Catechism class was conducted for public school students on Monday afternoons after our secular classes had finished for the day. And here I was introduced to that perennial favorite of Catholic liberals everywhere, the Baltimore Catechism, a succinct presentation of the faith for all ages, which could never find an equal match in the hippie-church. Unfortunately, however, the reputation of many of the nuns preceded them. In 4th grade I was assigned to Sister Osmond's First Communion class and all hell broke out. Shrouded in black with only a mean countenance showing its presence, Sister Osmond was the quintessence of tyranny. Every week she would take a poll on Mass attendance for the preceding Sunday. One Monday afternoon I neglected to raise my hand to indicate I had faithfully done my Sunday duty. My mother had exempted me from Mass that morning since I was cursed with an obstinate cough. The good sister said I should inform my mother that I would suffer a far worse cough in Hell! I bolted out of the classroom. I won't say that Sister caused me to lose my faith. I'm not sure I had any at this point. After the angst passed, I resolved to stick to the public schools—unlike my "famous" brother who elected to attend Catholic high school with its uniforms and bizarre discipline.

But one of the most seminal experiences in my young life happened on a rainy Sunday afternoon when I was about 11 or 12. It was one of the few times I defied my father and completely disregarded the probable consequences for my disobedience. I was thoroughly captivated by a Sunday afternoon rained-out baseball movie that had earned a golden palm nomination at the Cannes Film Festival in 1955. *The Miracle of Marcelino*, a Spanish film that earned widespread success in America and touched many a doubtful heart, is a story about an orphan boy who is adopted by a poor Franciscan monastery. The brothers raise him and become as a family to him. Like all boys he likes to explore his surroundings and is a little too fond of mischief. One day Brother Cookie discovers that little bits of his scanty food supply are missing and decides to follow Marcelino up to the storage attic. He hears conversation and, peering through the peephole, witnesses an improbable miracle. Marcelino has brought food and wine to Christ who is hanging from an antiquated crucifix abandoned in the attic. Our Lord and Marcelino share thoughts about their mothers and Jesus asks him if he would like to see his mother again. Marcelino excitedly accepts the invitation. Meanwhile, Brother Cookie runs frantically to the other monks to get them to come and witness the miracle taking place in the attic. The film ends with Marcelino peacefully asleep in the shadow of the Cross and no doubt also in the arms of his mother... After the curtain fell, I couldn't move an inch from the living room sofa and had already ignored repeated calls to come to the Sunday dinner table. I knew what awaited me—but curiously there was no shouting or hair-raising rebuke. I went to bed that night without supper but fully convinced that miracles can and do happen and serve to nourish our doubting souls. The wonder of God's miracles and His preference for the innocent wisdom of a child's heart has remained with me all these years because of this extraordinary, grace-filled film. G.K. Chesterton had that same kind of fierce wonder and innocent wisdom both of which poured forth on his pages. Paradoxically, one might say that he had the mind of a genius and the heart of a little child in a physical frame almost too big to believe. Once he crawled out from underneath the world, his life became an almost perpetual *joie-de-vivre* full of appreciation and gratitude for his fortuitous and redeemed existence—and for the resurrected life of the world to come.

During my adolescent years something of a domestic miracle interrupted my hermit-like existence and directed my life in a way I could never have imagined. An orthodox Jewish family moved into the neighborhood and totally won my heart. They were not like others and lived apart from the world in some special sacred space—and they also seemed to possess a secure identity that I was unfamiliar with. We engaged in all kinds of activities together—from making music in our rather rustic quintet, filming clichéd good guys vs. bad guys dramas, playing sandlot baseball for fun instead of for league standings, big-hill sledding in winter, chess and Monopoly tournaments on Saturdays because the Sabbath forbade much physical activity. I remember how they used to walk to and from shul 5 or 6 times during the duration of the Sabbath. Occasionally, on special occasions, I witnessed the ritual of candle-lighting especially joyous during the Hanukkah festival. While the rest of the neighborhood was putting up Christmas lights and dressing up spruces, my friends were remembering the miracle of the oil. "HEAR, O ISRAEL THE LORD OUR GOD, THE LORD IS ONE...." is a haunting and holy refrain going all the way back to Abraham's call. The earnestness of their faith was not severe but rather binding and no doubt kept me in touch with my own embryonic and struggling Catholic faith not yet awakened. Sadly for me, the family eventually moved to New York and took with them a big part of my life—for they had helped me appreciate, if not fully understand, what faithful religious observance is all about and how it reflects the order God intended for the days and seasons of our lives—a faith lived from a transcendent perspective and through a divinely-inspired moral universe. I shall never forget them and the emptiness they helped fill in my own dysfunctional experience of family. Chesterton was never so right as when he said, "The world owes God to the Jews." And he was right again when he reminded us: "The way to love anything is to realize it might be lost."

My senior year in high school advanced a growing interest in the fine arts. Drama was my chief focus and our little low-budget drama club staged an unforgettable production of *The Diary of Anne Frank*, which brought me face-to-face with the horrors of the Holocaust. In my senior year we chose an almost un-known one-act drama by Eugene O'Neill to enter in the state high school drama championship. Every year the big schools with big bucks would assemble fabulous and high-tech perfor-mances with all kinds of special effects and walk away with all the top prizes. In contrast, whatever scraps we could gather up from that year's leftover football budget were barely enough to rent a bus for the trip down to the competition. Against all odds, we won both the best actor and best drama awards and were invited to perform our obscure one-act at the recently opened Eugene O'Neill Theatre in nearby Waterford, Connecticut. Hardly a congratulatory word was to be heard from school or city officials. It was not an important enough feat to celebrate. Not like winning a state football championship. And here I was to experience another false value embedded in the ways of the world. I was starting to ask my own questions about "what was wrong with the world" or perhaps even "what was wrong with the Church." It's best to ask these questions early on before one is poisoned by the rampant cynicism of middle-age.

As I began my first year of college (we used to call this the freshman year but some have now contrived to be offended by the term), my world was at peace. The academic world lay before me with all its intellectual treasure and future promise. Bowdoin was an exceptional school to attend and boasted such distinguished graduates as Hawthorne, Longfellow, Joshua Lawrence Chamberlain and Admiral Peary—and, dare I say, President Franklin Pierce. These heroes of literature, explora-tion, poetry, military and political campaigns cast a bright light of scholarly excellence over the tiny college. But...something changed radically by my junior year when the "counter-cul-ture" came to Bowdoin. Vietnam was making more and more demands on the public's attention, especially on the young men destined for a lottery-draft. This was like no other lottery (except perhaps for Shirley Jackson's) since it included the very real possibility of face-to-face combat and death. In addition to the war, the sexual liberation craze and the marijuana boom (together with their allies in the rock subculture) was open for business on campus seven days a week. Nothing seemed stable any more—daily SDS protests on the steps of the student union (complete with Marxist tracts and angry petitions), sit-ins at the ROTC building, strikes throughout the nation's campuses, and political assassinations—and then there was Kent State. Tradition became not just an ugly word but also a subversive activity that served to undercut the "transformation of America"—as someone in recent years arrogantly identified it. To many of the sane, it seemed as if Yeats had been dead right when he prophesied that the center could not hold. It looked like everything was coming apart. Many graduating students left academia not so much with hope for a bright future but with a whole lot of confusion and uncertainty.

That "anarchy" Yeats spoke of unleashed itself on my own family during those same years of campus chaos, 1968-70. My father heard the clarion call of the good life in California, a state where Disneyland doesn't stop at the gates. He abandoned the family home and a mother with five children, some of whom still suffer from the slings and arrows of no-fault divorce. In that day wives and children were on the losing end of divorce settlements, and soon the remainder of the family plunged into a de-facto poverty. The youngest children got tangled up in the budding drug culture while their mother nurtured what appeared to be an almost irreversible depression. My nearest brother was serving as "the man of the family" but this was a burden too heavy for a college freshman. My spicy Italian grandmother was too old and crippled to fill the void and died soon after the divorce was finalized, probably of a broken heart. Children never really recover from the ravages of divorce—they just limp on into a wounded adulthood as best as they can. Meantime, the family physician even advised my mother to make the two youngest children wards of the state, which at long last forced her to overcome her stagnation.

I think Chesterton knew better than most of the social engineers of his time that the family was the bulwark of civilization and that without it civilization would crumble. No new trendy social arrangements or so-called "paradigms" could ever substitute for the traditional family. The permanent nature of marriage is guaranteed by the very sacred words of the Savior Himself. It is in the family that men learn how to love—and that life is given as a gift and must be lived as such. Family life must also be lived and shared from a transcendent reference point and grow into a mutuality of self-giving that helps us to overcome our innate preference for self: "What you have seen me do, do also." Without family we are but orphans in a cold and indifferent universe. Our only anchor becomes the State, which can never replace the warmth and unity of family life. Chesterton condemned the growing scourge of an anti-family materialism in the 20th century. Today he would surely note the great paradox to be found in the "smart phone"—instant electronic communication with anyone anywhere in the world yet experienced from within a social isolation so profound that it threatens the very sanity of humankind. He also understood that "homelessness" was more than a physical state and that in this respect we are all homeless until we begin to entertain the possibility that this world is too small for the human heart: "Only where He was homeless are you and I at home."

Graduate school kept me away from the endless turmoil at home and allowed me to pursue additional studies in the fine arts. I attended a more intellectually stimulating Unitarian church in Northampton, Massachusetts. The Maine church I frequented was more Universalist in tone, more people-oriented. Early on in my Northampton tenure I became serious about the possibility of studying for the ministry. In fact, while completing an MFA degree at Smith College, I applied and was accepted to both Yale and Harvard Divinity Schools—but without any financial assistance. And that was a divinely engineered outcome. During my graduate school years, I read countless Unitarian and Christian authors and was especially fond of the New England utopian-transcendentalists though I was never inclined to set-up shop at Walden Pond. My Unitarian pastor also gave me well-known Christian works such as Lewis' *Mere Christianity*, Thomas Merton's *Seven Storey Mountain*, and a small unfamiliar volume called *Orthodoxy* by an English journalist who also had been Unitarian in his youth. (It's true!) The work of the French Christian existentialist, Gabriel Marcel, introduced me to the "mystery of being" and the French personalists. The little flame of faith began to flicker. I also spent some time in a Catholic Worker style soup kitchen where I became acquainted with the corporal works of mercy as lived out by the co-founders of that movement, Dorothy Day and Peter Maurin. Later on my impression of the workers sullied as they seemed to become more and more like "social justice" warriors rather than the humble servants portrayed in Matthew 24. In my final year of study, I traveled to a small college in Vermont to attend a performance of Bach's most dynamic, eloquent work, the Mass in B minor. The sublime beauty of this music had always struck me but never so much as in this live performance. For the first time I realized I was not just hearing a magnificent masterpiece, I was also hearing a call to me personally from "that beauty ever ancient, ever new." My longing for God had come to its fruition in the mysterious reality of the Incarnation—the transcendent creator God taking on our humanity so that we might someday participate in His Trinitarian divinity. In Chesterton's theological imagination the Incarnation has to be the paradox of all paradoxes. So one Sunday morning I sheepishly edged my way down to the local Catholic parish at the foot of the campus and attended my first Mass since pre-college days. To be sure, it was a very prodigal moment. I felt like a fish-out-of-water for some time and even attempted to toss myself out of the ark and back into the tumult of the worldly seas. I dabbled a bit with the Theosophists and found an interest in something called the Enneagram, both of which probably should have qualified me for an exorcism. But, as Thomas Wolfe also wrote, "Sometimes you have to see a thing a thousand times before you see it once." (He probably got the idea from Chesterton who said practically the same thing.) And that was how my reversion to the faith slowly began and long-continued and how I ceased to be enslaved as "a child of my age."

I found very little in the post-Vatican II Church that inspired or deepened my faith. Where had all the "Mystery" gone (with apologies to Joan Baez)? I needed to be confirmed in my nascent commitment to the Church, and all I kept getting were folk masses and charismatic prayer meetings and modernist homilies. It was like the Council had opened the windows... and thrown the baby out with the baptismal water. I became sorely confused, which gave rise to persistent doubts about my Catholic reversion. The Fathers of the Church gave me support, as did some of the Eastern Rite Churches in my neighborhood, which offered a more traditional and reverent liturgy. Ah, but then I turned—long overdue—to a second great apologetic work by Chesterton and one which has no other contemporary equal: *The Everlasting Man*. With *The Everlasting Man* I became utterly convinced of Chesterton's genius. His explanation of the unfolding of the Christian faith over the centuries is unique and could persuade even the most stubborn of atheists, like C.S. Lewis. In "The God in the Cave," we see an originality and theological freshness rarely seen in the 20th century. He illumines the faith as something more than a sterile ancient creed, and he portrays it in a way that makes it inescapable. Chesterton demonstrates that Christianity is not only reasonable and utterly sane but that it is preferable to all other religion and "revelations" of the divine. His poignant picture of the Nativity rivals that of St. Francis' popular medieval version of Midnight Mass. With the angels, the shepherds and kings, the star, the evil rival, the man and woman and child—we have something greater than a fairy-tale or myth. Chesterton shows us that what we actually see in Bethlehem is the ultimate reality, the dream come true. The cast of characters huddled together in the cave have come to witness the birth of a new creation and a new humanity. Chesterton's insight into this stupendous event in man's history makes it clear that, after Bethlehem, nothing will ever be same again: "The hopes and fears of all the years are met in thee tonight." Each of us is called to find that place, to "follow the feet where all souls meet at the Inn at the end of the world."

What is it about this man Chesterton that is so compelling and so enriching? Is it his uncanny ability to turn an unlikely, contradictory juxtaposition into a monumental truth? Is it his lively wit and common-sense wisdom? Is it the overflowing generosity we witness in his friendships and even toward his enemies? Or is it his incredible largesse or massive intellect? And what about his supremely child-like and almost playful heart that surely must qualify him for the heavenly ranks? Yes to all of these. And much more. Chesterton had the mystic's unique intuitive vision that is able to see beyond surface realities to deeper truths. As the great poet William Blake explained, the mystic is the one who can see "a world in a grain of sand, heaven in a wildflower and eternity in an hour." In my own journey of faith, I have never encountered a more "alive" person than G.K. Chesterton. He radiated life and shared his gratitude for existence with the whole world. He is living proof of St. Irenaeus' famous declaration: "The glory of God is Man (fully) Alive!" Chesterton's was a life that could have come about only from a profound humility born of truth. And for Chesterton this truth is a Person. And so in his own powerful personalism, so vivid in his fiction, no one and nothing is unimportant. He could turn the most ordinary event into a revelation of extraordinary, even supernatural significance. In Father Brown, for example, we have a most memorable character, who without a doubt could put Sherlock Holmes and perhaps even Miss Marple (who owes her own creation to the priest detective) to shame.

Chesterton was also relentless in his condemnation of the materialistic conception of man. His philosophy of Distributism offers acute criticism both of the socialist and capitalist systems and their attempts to reduce humanity to mere economic beings. He also rebuked the pretentious, absolutist unbelief of his age and those who scorned the time-tested traditions of civilization. And he was a tireless defender of the family. In brief, it was his writing, more than any other, that allowed me to discover for the first time the unfathomable humility of the Incarnation—Jesus, the Suffering Servant who loved us until there was nothing more for him to give except His very life—so that we ourselves might have an abundant, eternal life. No earthly paradise could ever make such an offer.

In November of 1979, while still in the infancy of my faith renewal, a sudden and devastating disaster propelled my life into radical uncertainty. A car struck mine from behind and sent me flying over to the emergency lane and then straight down a 60-foot drop. A missing piece of the state's guardrail ensured that I would not escape uninjured. The diagnosis was that of a spinal cord injury and the prognosis indicated a lifetime of paralysis and immobility. Most of my days were occupied with extensive therapies (water therapy was invaluable in my recovery) and learning how to negotiate life from a wheelchair. It was all too primitive and made me easily susceptible to the "black dog" (as Churchill called it) of depression. Even the simplest functions of daily life were difficult—I could not discharge the normal bodily functions without special equipment or humiliating assistance. The loss of income, physical control and everyday freedoms were such overwhelming losses that it seemed my life had been conquered by a random, undeserved fate. Worse, my search for some form of vocation was put on permanent hold since most religious communities do not accept people who aren't "vertical." When I finally did achieve a standing stature and could once again drive, I returned to teaching at a small college in my hometown and began as well to take regular short stays at a nearby Benedictine monastery with an outstanding reputation for both its orthodoxy and fraternal hospitality. At the local college, I taught English classes to an ever-growing number of ill-prepared young people struggling to overcome functional illiteracy. I kept on reading and delighting in Chesterton's perceptive paradoxes and introduced myself to his poignant poetic imagery. I'm not exactly sure just how this grand figure of a human being kept me balanced and hopeful through these dark times, but I think it had to do with the role of suffering in our lives and how it gradually begins to make sense to us through the prism of God's love and His desire to make us holy as He is holy. But Chesterton also helped me to see the life-saving humor that underlies much of the regret and personal failures in our lives.

I'm sure I don't exaggerate when I call G.K. Chesterton the greatest communicator of the faith in the last—or even present—century. His great gifts of mind and imagination, his genuine and overflowing goodness and his apologetic genius are sure to have a lasting effect on those who believe and on those still looking to believe and still hoping to return "home." In the prophet Daniel's stirring words we surely see the most definitive Scriptural image of the great Chesterton: "...and those who lead the many to justice will shine like the stars for all eternity." (Daniel 12:3) May the Universal Church soon acknowledge his sanctity and claim his intercession.

How Chesterton
Converted my Conversion

By Noel Culbertson

THE CATHOLIC CHURCH was never on my radar. I had no hatred or malice for the Church, more of an American ignorance and apathy toward it. But like many a road that leads to Rome, I was on it long before I knew it. We were happy in our Baptist congregation, involved in ministry, studying the Bible, and surrounded by wonderful Christian friends, but along the way we were wooed by the great Bride of Christ. As G.K. Chesterton puts it, "He has come too near to the truth, and has forgotten that truth is a magnet, with the powers of attraction and repulsion."

I grew up the second of four kids in a wonderful Christian home. Both of my parents had powerful Evangelical conversion

Editor's note: the author adapted her essay from a piece that first appeared in the Coming Home Newsletter.

experiences in high school, my Dad coming from a Christian Science background and my Mom from a nominally Catholic background. I cannot remember a time when Scripture study was not a part of our family life. We sang the Greek alphabet as kids, had family Bible studies, and attended church regularly. My Dad had a voracious love of the Scriptures. He studied Jewish history, mapped out the Gospel accounts in chronological order, and even translated the New Testament from Greek—for fun. Our family was always involved in ministries at our Baptist church in Southern California. I had a gift for memorization that won an awkward kid a fair amount of attention in AWANA (a Bible verse memorization program for kids). By the time I was in sixth grade, I had memorized hundreds of Bible verses.

During my high school years, I went on a mission trip through nine countries in Europe. I was devoted yet naive and had no real concept that the whole point of the trip was to "save" Catholics. Our mission leaders talked about all of the people in Europe who go to church every week, but have no personal relationship with Jesus. I knew plenty of people in my own Baptist congregation who fit that description so I thought nothing of it. We toured Europe sharing our Four Spiritual Laws, often in front of cathedrals we would later tour.

The following year our family moved to Washington State and I began work at a Christian Camp nearby. (I had a love for the ministry because my Dad had come to Christ at a Christian camp.) We worked with a number of Christian denominations and saw many lives ignited by the Gospel message. We had daily prayer with the staff and in my time off I worked with the high school staff and taught Sunday school for kindergarteners. I was constantly involved in ministry activities.

In the beginning of 1999, I began dating Stan, who had attended Christian college with my sister. Half a year later we were planning our wedding. We were to be married just after he returned from his upcoming six-month deployment with the US Navy. However, six weeks before he deployed, at a doctor's appointment for an unrelated issue, I found out I was pregnant. I was shocked, embarrassed, and humiliated. How could I let this happen? What would people think? I had let down my parents and so many others who looked to me as a witness to the faith. In that moment the temptation flashed into my mind, "You could have an abortion, and no one would even know." It was a startling thought for someone who was adamantly pro-life, but it was a dizzying temptation in my moment of humiliation. I knew I had to tell someone to "make it real" and to dissolve the temptation in the light of the truth. Stan was at work for another six hours, and there was no way of contacting him. I went to my sister's house (her husband was also on staff at our Baptist church) and asked if we could talk. Immediately after confessing to my sister, the power of the temptation was gone. A few hours later, Stan and I talked, and in the following days he told my parents and our pastor, and I wrote a letter to the staff at the camp repenting of our sin and asking for their forgiveness. It was an extraordinary experience of the power of confessing your sins to someone with some authority to retain forgiveness—of exposing and repenting of our shortcomings out loud and thus receiving God's grace and freedom through that confession. Two weeks later we were married. Two weeks after that Stan deployed. He returned after a six-month deployment and two weeks later our first beautiful daughter was born.

As the years passed we remained very involved in our Baptist congregation. I headed up women's ministry, Stan was a deacon, and we had a weekly Bible study in our home. One week in our adult Sunday school class, in which we were discussing the Parable of the Sower (Matthew 13:3-23), Stan asked about the seed that fell on rocky ground. He mentioned that it sounded like it refers to someone who had been saved, "received the word with joy," but then "falls away" or loses their salvation. Now, if you'd like to see a room full of "once saved, always saved" Baptists turn on you, this is a good way to do it. On our way home that afternoon, we mused about the hostile reaction to what seemed to be a fairly clear Biblical account. But then we were not really willing to bet our eternal salvation on a hunch, so the incident fell like a seed on our rocky path.

In our home Bible study we were going through the Book of Acts. Each week, Stan and I would read a chapter, research all of the best commentators we could find, and then discuss it with our Bible study group. It became more unnerving the more commentators we read. They each had a different take on the passages, and not just personal reflections, but often opposing theological views. How could we be sure that we were reading the right interpretations? We had, of course, been choosing which to agree with based on our understanding of the Scriptures, but these commentators had years of study under their belts yet still had dozens of different views on how the passages should be interpreted. How could faithful believers, who were not disposed to spend several hours each day studying, know which interpretation was correct? Then came Acts 15 and the Council of Jerusalem.

Acts is a picture of the early Church in action, and as Protestants we were always trying to get back to an authentic early Church experience. But in studying the early Church in the Book of Acts, it didn't look much like my Baptist experience. They met in council and spoke with authority to all the other churches about issues of faith. Where was that in my denomination? We had no councils, nor did we have the ability to define with authority matters of faith and morals. Again, these unsettling notions remained as seeds on our path as we navigated a busy life with faith, kids, and a bunch of deployments.

In 2003, my Dad announced, much to the horror of my Mom and surprise of our Baptist friends, that after several years of studying he was going to enter the Catholic Church. This tore my Mom up, devastated our pastor who had been very close to my Dad, and shocked the congregations whom my Dad had taught often through the years. For me, it didn't seem like the huge tragedy others thought it to be. My Dad studied more than anyone I had ever known. He asked questions that stumped pastors and seminary professors in his quest to know Christ. Since he had been meeting with a couple of priests for a few years, they had directed him to more resources and answers than he could dig through in a lifetime. He'd grown deeply in prayer with the help of these Carmelite priests. The Catholic Church seemed like a great fit for someone like my Dad, who studied so much. I viewed it as more of a personal preference, that we were all Christian—the people who loved the Bible were Baptist, the ones who were drawn to ritual and study were Catholic, the ones who were charismatic were Pentecostal, etc. Out of respect for my Mom's struggle with his conversion, my Dad shared very little about his conversion with us unless we asked directly. It must have been a terribly isolating time for him.

Several years later, after hearing a news story regarding Pope Benedict XVI and contraception, and knowing better than to take the news media's word about any denomination's teaching at face value, I asked my Dad about the Catholic Church's deal with contraception. I knew very little about it, only that they taught something against using contraception. It seemed like such an odd place to draw a line in the sand. My Dad's brief explanation of the Church's reasoning was shockingly reasonable. But what struck me most was that every single

Protestant denomination had held the same teaching as the Catholic Church on contraception until 1930 after which each denomination in turn changed its teaching with the times. I had never even heard anything about this in our denominational history. It was a non-issue; it was simply a given that people had always used whatever form of contraception they wished without being in opposition to any teaching of the faith. It was another seed on our path.

In early 2010, part way through our seventh Navy deployment, I was chaperoning a field trip for my daughter's class. I was paired up with Janet, another mom who I hadn't met before. Throughout the field trip Janet and I talked about religion, the spiritual state of the nation, and all of the subjects generally frowned upon in polite conversation. We got along famously and talked for several hours after the field trip was over. I ran into Janet and her family again a few weeks later at the hardware store and she mentioned that she thought my Dad went to their church. I asked, "Oh, you go to St. Cecilia's?" It was their parish also, and they asked me what I thought of my Dad being Catholic. I said I thought it was a good fit for him, and that I was happy for him. She then asked what my Mom thought about it. I said, "Well… not so much. It's been really hard for her." (My Dad had now been Catholic for about seven years.) She recommended a book by a former Protestant minister who had converted to Catholicism. Because the book addressed how the former minister's wife struggled with his conversion, Janet thought it might be a help to my Mom. I thanked her and finished my errands.

A month or so later Stan returned from overseas, and we were prepared to spend some much needed family time on a road trip to several national parks. While driving through our town a few days before our trip, I decided to stop by the Catholic parish to ask them where I might find this book Janet had recommended. I had never seen a Catholic bookstore (or a priest or nun for that matter). When I arrived the doors were locked, but I noticed someone moving boxes around the side of the building. I walked around to ask her if she knew where I could find the book. She said that she didn't have a copy of the book, but had a conversion CD by the same author if I was interested. (I had planned to read the book before deciding if I should give it to my Mom. I knew what kind of firestorm might follow if I gave her a Catholic book, especially if she thought it actually had come from my Dad.) The lady at the parish was cleaning out her office and asked if I would be interested in any other CDs. I told her I would, and she loaded me up with more than 30 CDs and a Seeker's Catechism. I thanked her and headed home.

A few days later we left for our road trip. On our first drive through the night, after the kids were asleep, we popped in the conversion CD. We were dumbfounded. How could we have missed all of this? At every rest stop we were scouring our Bibles to confirm that all of these verses were really there. We read passages such as Matthew 16:13-20, John 6, Isaiah 22:22-23, John 20:23, 1 Timothy 3:15. Of course they were there, some I had memorized back in my AWANA days, but now they all came together and had a place. They were like tumblers in a lock, nothing was being pressed to fit; it fitted the lock and opened the door. It was like being handed the answers to every question about the faith I'd never thought to ask and yet felt I should have thought to ask them years ago.

The most profound revelation for me was that, according to the Scriptures, Christ clearly founded a Church and it had His authority and protection (Matthew 16:13-20). Jesus granted Peter the power to bind and loose on earth and in heaven. Since we know that nothing impure can enter heaven, we know that whatever this Church, founded on Peter, binds on earth would not and could not be counter to Christ. Then when Jesus says the gates of hell will not prevail against this Church, He gives His word that this Church would be specially protected. If this was true, then it meant that Christ had founded a Church and it was still present today, not in a simply mystical way, but in a real and visible way. It was very clear through my own experience that denominations struggle with unity because they lack authority. Someone who disagrees with the biblical interpretations of the pastor can simply break off and start another church, and they often do. But here the Catholic Church stands with authority given by Christ, as it has for two thousand years, led and protected by the Holy Spirit. If this claim is true, I had to come in line with the Church and not the other way round. The scriptural evidence especially on the issues of the authority of the Church, Christ's Real Presence in the Eucharist (John 6), and the necessity of faith and works rather than faith alone (James 2:14-24) was staggering. By the end of our road trip we had listened to more than 30 hours of Catholic teaching and spent countless hours poring over the scriptures.

When we arrived home, we got ahold of as many Catholic books as we could, including several on the early Church Fathers of whom we had never heard, and began reading. We studied the Bible with new eyes, having removed the Baptist lenses we didn't know we had. We continued to study for months with a growing conviction that the Catholic Church was really what she claimed to be — one, holy, catholic, and apostolic—but we had yet to attend Mass. After some discussion we settled on a date to attend our first Mass, with the intention that we would keep going to our Baptist church. Then we could slowly attend Mass more over the coming months to lessen the blow to the Baptist community I had been a part of for nearly 18 years.

I then told my Mom that we were considering becoming Catholic. We had always been close and generally talked every day. She went to all of my prenatal appointments when Stan was on deployment and we even went grocery shopping together. But when I told her what we were considering, she was speechless, which shortly turned to hysteria. Following this, she could no longer talk to me without tears often accompanied by shouting. She even went to counseling to try to get a handle on what to her felt like utter betrayal.

On August 1, 2010 we attended our first Mass. Stan, knowing what a hardship conversion would mean for our family, prayed for divine direction. At Mass we listened to the prayers, responses, and readings which all poured out from the Scriptures. The Responsorial Psalm rang out as if speaking right to me: "If today you hear his voice, harden not your heart." In his homily the priest spoke about Cortez and his men landing in the Americas. They encountered so many hardships that the men wanted to return home to safety and comfort. However, Cortez burned the ships and the men had to move forward to complete the mission they had been chosen to do. I leaned over to Stan and said, "I think our ships are on fire." Then came the consecration and we watched as people from every age, race, and social status received Christ. The room literally filled up with Christ. I turned to Stan again and this time there were tears streaming down his face. This Navy Chief could not speak about it for several weeks without being moved to tears. It was the reality of all we had been studying. We never went back to the Baptist church. Within days, the life and friendships we had before fell suddenly silent. In the loneliness of those days we dove deep into the Scriptures and Catholic teaching. I was introduced to Catholic writers like Fulton Sheen, Karl Keating, Frank Sheed, Pope John Paul II... and especially G.K.

Chesterton, who would become one of my jovial and genius guides on the path of conversion.

Chesterton began to convert my conversion from merely an intellectual ascent to a whirling adventure thundering toward the historic Church. His clear brilliance coupled with extraordinary humility and contagious mirth began to open a vision of a path to holiness that was possible even for the likes of me. Chesterton presented the common sense of the faith with a great love for the ordinary man that brought clarity to the muddle of modern thought that had crept into my thought process over the years. I began to devour his books beginning with *Orthodoxy*, then diving into *The Everlasting Man*, followed by every book I could find in print. The *Illustrated London News Essays* from the *Collected Works,* spanning more than thirty years and every topic under the sun provided a means of combating the barrage of half-truths hurled mindlessly about with a clear vision of the true, the beautiful and the good. The Church was right where I was wrong, and there had never been so much joy in being wrong.

A couple days after our first Mass, a member of the parish told us about a Catholic conference in a nearby town the following weekend. That Friday afternoon we arrived early to the conference and ended up having dinner with Tim Staples from Catholic Answers, who was one of the speakers. We tripled the number of Masses we had attended to date, prayed our first Rosary (very awkwardly), and were connected to a number of resources for our journey. We also ran into an old friend, who after recovering from his shock at seeing us at a Catholic conference, offered to bring us more CDs and books. The following week he dropped off dozens of CD sets as well as the three-volume set of the writings of the early Fathers and much more.

The main theological issues I struggled with were: did Christ really found a visible Church with His authority and, if so, was it still in existence today? Being a Baptist, the Bible verses I had never seemed to notice especially struck me, particularly Matthew 16:13-20 and 1 Timothy 3:15. In my study of the Scriptures over the years I had focused much of my study on Paul's epistles rather than the Gospels. I think this was because they occurred after the Resurrection; therefore they were more relevant to the living of the Christian life. In studying the Catholic Faith, I was starting to see how little I had regarded the words of Jesus in relation to the structure of my faith as a Baptist. I had always believed that the Church was an invisible, Mystical Body of all believers who had a personal relationship with Christ, not an actual visible Church with a hierarchy. Reading Matthew 16, it seemed clear that Christ gave particular authority to Peter and the Church he would lead. If Jesus said, "whatever you bind on earth will be bound in heaven" then whatever Peter bound in this Church would have to be infallible or it would make Christ a liar.

Then I began reading some of the early Fathers of whom I had never heard before beginning my study of the Church, and began to study how the Church believed, thought, and taught in the first centuries. I had no idea that writings from the disciples of the Apostles existed. It was equally shocking to read what they had to say about the authority and structure of the Church. St. Ignatius of Antioch, a disciple of the Apostle John, said in A.D. 107, "You all should follow the bishop as Jesus Christ does the Father. Follow too the presbytery as the apostles, and honor the deacons as the command of God. Let no one do anything that is proper for the church without the bishop. Let that Eucharist be considered valid that is under the bishop or performed by one to whom he entrusts it. Wherever the bishop appears, let there be the fullness [of the church] as wherever Christ Jesus appears, there is the catholic church." I became convinced that the Bible and the earliest accounts of Christianity in the world were profoundly Catholic, not Baptist, in their structure.

Janet, whom I had met on the field trip, and her husband became our sponsors through the RCIA process. It was wonderful to be united in faith with my Dad in the Catholic Church. It is difficult to put to words the thrilling and terrifying adventure of conversion. Chesterton describes it thus: "It is impossible to be just to the Catholic Church. The moment men cease to pull against it they feel a tug towards it. The moment they cease to shout it down they begin to listen to it with pleasure. The moment they try to be fair to it they begin to be fond of it. But when that affection has passed a certain point it begins to take on the tragic and menacing grandeur of a great love affair." Our family entered the Catholic Church together at the Easter Vigil Mass in April 2011. Both our girls received the Sacrament of Baptism, and the entire family was confirmed and received our first Eucharist together that night.

The years that have followed have been a great and growing love affair with Christ and His Church. They have included the most heartbreaking and joyful moments of my life. Just eight months after we were received into the Church, my Dad fell seriously ill and would need a transplant to survive. Ten days after that, my Mom was driving and her hand fell off the steering wheel. A few weeks later she underwent brain surgery for a terminal brain tumor. Both my parents moved into our home where we cared for them. The Lord provided a powerful time of healing and reconciliation with my Mom during those months. Once after one of our long talks my Mom said, "I know you are experiencing Christ in the Catholic Church… I just don't know why God would do that!" It was a long way for my Mom to come, and we both got a hearty laugh from her closing line. In September 2012, I lost both of my parents just three weeks apart. As I watched my parents receive last rites as they died, I saw the Church's sacraments pour out God's grace on them. My Mom had been baptized and confirmed Catholic, but she had been attending Baptist churches since she was 18. The day before she died, a parish priest came and anointed her. There were no words to express the weight in my heart as the Church militant and the Church triumphant prayed together with us. It was a moment when the veil between earth and heaven is so thin you can nearly see through it. The following year, my 84-year-old Grandpa was baptized and entered the Catholic Church.

The Christmas following my parents' deaths we attended Midnight Mass, followed by the Feast of St. Stephen the Martyr on December 26th. It struck me again, that even the calendar of the Church encompasses the human experience of faith. We experience the peak of joy at the birth of Christ immediately followed by the depths of the sorrow at the death of the first martyr. Our lives are a compilation of feasts and fasts, yet neither are in vain. They both hold vigil in our lives. God works in both according to the good for those who are in Christ Jesus. He directs our paths through both joy and sorrow with His word and His very self in the sacraments to sustain us. In His great mercy, Christ directed our path to Rome.

To doctor one last line from Chesterton to summarize my experience to date, "I know that Catholicism is too large for me, and I have not yet explored its beautiful and terrible truths. But I know that [Protestantism] is too small for me; and I could not creep back into that dull safety, who have looked on the dizzy vision of liberty."

THE ORACLE OF THE DOG

By Br. Neil B. Conlisk, O.Carm.

I WAS BAPTIZED AND CONFIRMED in the Catholic Church but didn't think much of it. I stopped attending Mass as soon as I could. The environment I grew up in wasn't religious, but rather the opposite. My father was an anarchist, and my mother a dead-head. I identified as a Socialist, and made sure people knew that. Eventually, during my undergraduate years, as I neared the end of my rope, I would, as Chesterton said of Gabriel Syme, "rebel against rebellion."

Many factors contributed to my reversion but the one relevant to the task at hand was reading G.K. Chesterton's *Orthodoxy* in a political philosophy course at Marquette University. I did not consider myself a Christian before reading *Orthodoxy*, but after reading it, I did. "That tremendous figure which fills the Gospels…towers above all thinkers who ever thought themselves tall." There is a chapel dedicated to St. Joan of Arc on Marquette's campus, and Joan plays a pivotal role in the argumentation of *Orthodoxy*, thus Joan and Gilbert became my first two patron saints.

I have heard people say that they have tried reading Chesterton but were put off. That was not my case. As soon as I read Chesterton I knew that I had found a friend. I devoured his works: *The Everlasting Man*, *St. Francis of Assisi*, *St. Thomas Aquinas*, *The Thing*, the *Autobiography*, *The Catholic Church and Conversion*, and countless essays and murder mysteries. Everything. Chesterton accompanied and guided me along my journey back into the Catholic Church. I was like that English yachtsman rediscovering England under the impression that it was an island in the South Seas.

Following my abrupt conversion I began to feel a calling from God. To say that I was considering a religious vocation would be too generous; I was running away from a religious vocation like Jonah. I bounced around jobs: I taught music with the Jesuit Volunteer Corps and the Boys and Girls Club, I worked two stints as a clerk at law firms, eventually I ended up working for a dog boarding facility called "Pooch Hotel", driving a van through downtown Chicago picking up and dropping off dogs. It was miserable, and I likened it to how the Prodigal Son must have felt at the pig farm.

I inquired with a Trappist Monastery about joining. I visited during the Advent season. The monks usually did not welcome retreatants or inquires during those weeks, as they were preparing for the Solemnity of the Nativity. They made an exception for me because I was interested in joining, sooner rather than later. I helped an elderly brother named Placid bind firewood and move out Christmas trees throughout the monastery. The Vigils at 3 in the morning made me feel weak and lazy. I ate with the monks in their refectory, silently, listening to a reading. During those weeks the lector was reading through a biography of Dorothy Day.

As I talked with the monks, it became clearer, to myself and themselves, that I did not belong. God was not calling me to be a monk at their monastery. I was impetuous and lost; I would have joined the military if I were younger. One afternoon, after supper, the Abbot motioned for me to join him in his office. I was nervous and ashamed. He spoke in a taciturn manner, letting me know that he did not wish to psycho-analyze me but advising me that we all have a God-sized hole in our hearts, but he saw me with a father-shaped hole in my heart as well. He recommended that I read the book *Iron John* by Robert Bly.

At a later meal time I sat downcast, feeling uncomfortable and out of place. I had ruined years of my life foolishly wandering down a dead-end road. I resigned myself to returning to Chicago and continuing to pick up dogs in a van. The lector finished the biography of Dorothy Day, and began reading a book titled *Silence: A Christian History* by Diarmaid MacCulloch. The first paragraph of the introduction spoke of G.K. Chesterton's Father Brown story, "The Oracle of the Dog". The oracle in question was an anguished howl of a dog that had swum out to sea to retrieve a walking stick that it presupposed would float, only to be cheated by it being a sword stick that had sunk.

Whether or not this was a message from Gilbert in heaven is debatable, but the effect of hearing Chesterton's name, and the oracle of the dog, was certain. It was a grace that can be best described as an "elevation of the spirit." I went from a tragedy, ending up in a desert of desolation, to a comedy, a joke with my friend Gilbert in heaven. I could have laughed out loud in the silent refectory. I know Chesterton is in heaven. I know it. Whatever else may have been a delusion, I knew that my connection with Chesterton was real. Wherever I belonged, I knew that I was meant to be there at that time to hear Chesterton and the dog mentioned.

Now, a few years after that episode, I am a brother with the Order of Carmelites, teaching High School in Chicago. Chesterton still informs my understanding of the Catholic Church more than most. I quote him constantly. I probably think about him every day. I regularly attend meetings with the local Chesterton Society and enjoy our conversations very much. A new member arrived recently, and as we were discussing an essay of Chesterton's on Shakespeare's sonnets he joined in sharing what he knew about the Earl of Southhampton. I told him, "I'm glad you found us." I contemplated the amazing variety of people in the room. How does Chesterton bring these people together?

St. Joan and St. Therese, please join us in praying for the canonization of our friend Gilbert. He has touched so many, and brought so many to the Faith. He is so funny. "We are perhaps permitted tragedy as a sort of merciful comedy: because the frantic energy of divine things would knock us down like a drunken farce. We can take our own tears more lightly than we could take the tremendous levities of the angels. So we sit perhaps in a starry chamber of silence, while the laughter of the heavens is too loud for us to hear."

The Everlasting Quest

By B. Frederick Juul

WHEN I FINISHED HIGH SCHOOL, I went to work as a deckhand on merchant ships that sailed from West Coast ports to Asia for a few years, which included one trip to France on a coal ship out of Newport News. I had been tired of school and decided to educate myself from available books. But as this project turned into a fool's errand, I realized that I needed help. Perhaps help from what everyone else thought was obvious—a local college. Thus, in my early twenties, I finally went back to school. I was hungry for knowledge and had a growing need for what seemed like truth, or perhaps wisdom—which was fast eluding me in my self-serving lifestyle going nowhere fast.

Prior to my adolescent apostasy and deep skepticism for all things religious, my former religion came from my mother's faith in Christian Science. She was a deeply religious and prayerful personality. She had become committed to this faith-healing sect following a psychic and physical healing experience in her 35th year. I was close to my mother and tried to follow her intensely spiritualist faith and ideas when I was younger. However, it became increasingly difficult to comprehend the contradictory, matter-denying theology of the founding thinker of Christian Science, Mary Baker Eddy. Much later, I came to understand that many of her teachings in late 19th century Boston were a kind of reappearance of a couple of ancient heresies in the gnostic vein—teachings stunning in boldness and apparently appealing to some people, perhaps in their radicalness.

Both the liturgies and official prayer methods of this church were in the stark or puritanical style, with much scripture reading and meditation. There was a well-organized daily prayer routine based on assigned readings, from both the Old and New Testaments, in the great King James Bible. In some ways a peaceful, almost contemplative, lifestyle was encouraged, with prayerful reading room stations scattered around the cities. Yet it was fraught at some level with the intense, hopeful, painful, and at times tragic, spirit of emotional faith-healing ideals and practice, including professional "Practitioners" who would pray and strive for a medicine both mystical and practical.

Later, as I struggled through the years with all this, I often thought of the apparently painful dimension of my mother's faith, as well as that of others in this sect. Faith in an ontologically ambivalent divinity, to whom you pray to heal and to be healed in (what seemed to me) a dis-unified, conflict-ridden cosmos did not make complete sense to me.

There was also a kind of strong, prayerful spirit and hope in the positive side of this divinity and in the Holy Scriptures (weirdly interpreted, but still…). This, along with my mother's deep faith, did give me a solid impression, though laced with ambiguity and sadness, of God's possible existence. In my memory I give her that with gratitude, her strong faith and quiet joys. Especially in her last cancer, I dearly hoped for her what Christ offers us all: His redemptive suffering.

From what I knew of the coastal lands in my travels, it was not difficult to choose an appropriate and beautiful area offering both an entry-level college and university: the Santa Barbara area. I hoped the beauty of the old town, headed by the Mission Church, cascading down part of the fertile coastal plain at the foot of the great sandstone mountains to the sea, could be both nurturing and healing for me. I enrolled in a local college, set in the wooden enclave on the hillside above the town. My expenses were paid for by the G.I. bill and temporary manual work. My needs for study, for place, and for steady human relations were to be met as time worked its way.

I decided this peaceful area would be the base and home in my new adventures. Living at first in town in a small shack near the beach, before moving up to the mountains, I enjoyed the interesting and lovely order of Santa Barbara. Most of the public (and many of the private) buildings were unified by a kind of adapted Spanish Colonial architecture and lush landscaping, with trees and flowers everywhere in the spring sunlight and, in summer, the air would be stirred by orange-blossom-scented winds that brought warmth and hope. I would stroll along the handsome, palm-lined, twilit beaches stretching south along the great bight in the Pacific shore, with stars slowly appearing in the vast vault above and lights in the nearby hills. It was a fine way to conclude a long day of studies and work.

Along with learning and appreciating the area, I continued to be periodically plagued with attacks of depression and intense anxiety, akin to vertigo, which had begun during my recent months at sea. These attacks would strike unpredictably in a classroom, or a meeting, or while walking in the woods or beach; a black perception of death, emptiness, and meaning-lessness would pervade my mind and my feeling. At times, aside from fear, the lack of feeling was the worst feeling of all: the pain of nothingness. It could endure for hours, though sometimes it would be over quickly. Once it struck me on a pleasant, quiet af-ternoon, while I was walking into the library on the old, hillside campus. In sheer desperation to do *something*, pointless as it all seemed, I sat down in the warm sunshine of a wood-paneled alcove with a literary journal. I opened it to a short lyric poem by H.D. Reading it, I was calmed by a rich sense of peace, order, and beauty—and everything was together in a unity that felt like meaning. It seemed like the power of art could put things in harmony, at least for a time.

I read widely, in history, philosophy, fiction, and poetry (both assigned and otherwise). I enjoyed lectures and lively discussions with other students. I was trying to fathom it all. *Was everything a vast confusion or what?* I delighted in reading translations of Lao-Tzu, Confucius, Chuang-Tzu, Hui-Neng, the work of Suzuki, and the folk Buddhist ghost stories of Lafcadio Hearn. Often these readings served as a calm way to end a long day.

The quest continued with studies in comparative religion. I read sacred texts from both East and West. I attended, spo-radically, a variety of faith meetings and services: mainline Protestant, Vedanta, Mormon, Sufi, Buddhist, and even the Catholic Mass in Latin (which seemed to be the most authen-tic and profound). I was praying and meditating in different traditions, feeling drawn at some level (more or less subtly, but relentlessly) towards the religious and spiritual. The endless questions I had had seemed to devolve into just one or two: *How do things flow? How is the obscure, hoped-for unity found?*

At this time, I would have a recurring memory: an image of the sunny afternoon, with a view through the cargo gear on the foredeck toward the distant old waterfront of the city of Rouen as we approached up the Seine River, and the sight of an enormous building with towers looming in the distance. I was amazed by its size and the intricacies of its design and surface décor. It was unlike anything I had ever seen before. My main question at the time had been: *What is this distant building of such unearthly beauty, seemingly infused with some kind of energy or force that makes it, to me, vividly vibrate in the blue air?*

It turned out to be the Gothic Cathedral of the ancient town, a type of work of supreme social and cultural and religious art that I, in near-perfect Californian ignorance, had not even heard of! It served as well to be the first Catholic item to catch my attention as an adult.

Gradually, I was inspired by the vast philosophical, hierarchical, historical, and mystical order of the Christian vision. Increased prayer and meditation became part of my struggle in life to find order and meaning. But for a long while I remained hesitant and non-committal in this spiritual search. I was plagued by periodic doubt and confusion and anxiety over all the options, as well as a secret stiffness, or fear of "bending the proud neck." But always, though usually elusively, in one way or another, through thickets and around obstacles, the sense of truth was drawing me on.

I was plagued at times by such ambivalence of thought that would twist from anger and doubt to affirmation and hope. But this could be calmed by work or by positive readings from essays or Scripture.

I befriended a bookstore owner, Kristina: a hard-working, charming, and sweet older woman with a deep love for Christ such as I had never witnessed before. She led me gradually toward the Catholic Church. Two other friends helped: an old Russian museum curator, Andrei, and an L.A. poet, Jerry.

At the time, I was becoming acquainted with a variety of arts: Fra Angelico, the great Medieval and Renaissance paintings, and both secular and sacred classical music. It all tended to validate or affirm the Christian search. I experienced this same affirmation in readings of scholastic theology and of Étienne Gilson and the metaphysics of realism. I took a seminar on Aquinas that was especially helpful. Add to that Shakespeare, Kierkegaard, Newman, Belloc, Peguy, Mariac, Hopkins, and Eliot—they all pointed the way. But above all was the glory of Catholic (and perhaps world) poetry: The Divine Comedy of Dante.

In the coolness of parks or under trees near the beach, during long quiet afternoons, I read with deep appreciation the meditations and poetry of Thomas Merton. And then, finally feeling ready, I began studying G.K. Chesterton's two seminal works: *Orthodoxy* and *The Everlasting Man*. I found these works very inspiring during my Christian studies and throughout my life.

Orthodoxy helped me to focus my thinking on the meaning and power of Christ as the Incarnation. Chesterton validated the concrete and physical and human sense of place and reality. It was the common sense of Aristotle. Another of Chesterton's books that I worked through at this time, *What's Wrong with the World*, explored various aspects and challenges of human relationships and the morality of commitment, especially in marital love.

> For Western religion has always felt keenly the idea "that it is not well for man to be alone." The social instinct asserts itself everywhere as when the Eastern idea of hermits was practically expelled by the Western idea of monks.

Together, my friends and I attended different churches where I could observe the Mass, hear sermons, and practice certain common prayers with the people. Eventually I heard a priest whose calm and masculine definiteness and intelligence I especially liked. Kristina urged me to contact this priest, Father Martin, if I wanted to pursue any questions or interest in the Church. I very tentatively did so, and he agreed to meet me—thus beginning focused discussions and, later, systematic teachings in the Catholic Faith.

What followed was a procession of divine forces: the spiritual lilt of Gregorian chant in the Franciscan Convent, the social compassion of the religious sisters in schools and hospitals, the excitement of learning about the worker priest movement in France where they were apparently attempting to counter the workers' attraction to Marxism, the colorful interiors of Catholic churches, rich with stained glass and flickering candles, tapestries, paintings, statuary, faint residues in the air of wax and incense...the vital Corpus Christi procession of hundreds of chanting people led by vested priests with golden monstrance and boys carrying a tall crucifix and colorful banners and incense streaming in the wind, and the poetics of Scripture and the Mass, and the mystery of the Eucharist. All these combined to direct my whole being: mind and body and heart.

Watching Andrei—my lean, old, Russian friend—I was struck with the thought that his sensitive face reflected both the suffering of his motherland and the intensity of his intellectual strivings. He was a widower who had converted from Eastern Orthodoxy through love and respect for his deceased wife, whose memory he continued to adore. He was an art historian, a scholar of Robinson Jeffers, and a quiet and intense student of mysticism. Once I was watching him supervise the hanging of paintings for a new realist show at the gallery where he was a curator. We were discussing one image by a late 19th century Russian Master of a stripped-to-the-waist, lean, pale, suffering Christ with burning deep eyes staring at a casual, stocky Pontius Pilate with the title, "What is Truth?"

"Great picture."

"Yes, technically, the way the light focuses on Christ both from above and, to a degree, from within, and in terms of the title, a wonderful pictorial presentation of the answering silence."

I met with Andrei periodically at his cottage to discuss literature, Church traditions, and his great devotion to St. Teresa of Avila. At times his close, young friend Jerry, from L.A., would join us, and we all took turns reading from our own poetry, followed by good talks with wine at the evening meal. Jerry would then regale us with tales from the artistic underground in L.A. and from the artistic and academic worlds as he knew them from his job teaching English at a Catholic college.

I went through long months of thought, prayer, ambivalence, and of studying catechetical truth with Father Martin at Catholic Social Services. After close to two years, finally (at Kristina's urging), we all agreed that I would be baptized, with Andrei as my sponsor, at the small church in a nearby coastal town. At the end, I remember Father Martin saying, "Welcome to the joy of the Faith, and find peace—but remember, it won't solve all your problems!"

Later that day, I walked alone on the trail by the stream in Cold Creek Canyon, feeling what seemed like an electric charge in the marrow of my bones!

I was confirmed half a year later at Our Lady of Guadalupe, an old wooden church in the Mexican neighborhood on the east side of Santa Barbara. It was a church full of families and grade school children, with many colorful decorations and images, including a violent one of a life-size crucifix at the right of the sanctuary, the corpus covered with whip marks and bloody wounds — from red drops running down beneath the crown of thorns to pathetic-looking raw scrapes on the knees, to the poor feet smashed with a great nail. Beauty and pain. Redemptive suffering. It is the answer to Christian Science.

One Sunday, the bishop was there and, leaning kindly toward a youngster, asked, "What are the four marks of the Church?"

"One, Holy, Catholic, and…and…Apostolic!"

He then turned to another, older child and asked, "What would you say was the spiritual seedbed for growth in the early Church?"

"The blood of the martyrs."

While attending a Franciscan ordination of two young men at the Old Mission, amidst the pomp and panoply and color and the golden light of the lovely old church, I felt suddenly a kind of ravishment at the beauty and meaning and the love of God in the sacraments, grace, and all the divine contact with earth and man. I was overwhelmed, feeling low and nearly infinitesimal in the awesomeness and joy of the divine order of love, justice, and communion. Later, after relaying this experience to Father Martin, he told me, "Men have spent their entire lives in the religious life after an experience such as you've had."

My periodic times of unprovoked dread or depression did not disappear completely. They still occasionally hit me, perhaps in memory of my former days of pointless wandering or in imagining vast, bleak seascapes surging endlessly, like they did in my time as a deckhand. But while they would still come, after my conversion I noticed a certain lessening of the frequency of these events and their intensity over time. As I went through the years of studies, counseling, relationships, and conversion to Catholicism, I think my perceptions, feelings, and reasoning settled in ways that helped me. I found an increased awareness of purpose and meaning in my life. Though these mini-events continued for years in varying degrees, dependent at times on social and economic stressors, at times, they seemed to be a prod or a reminder to "wake up" to things I had been neglecting, and even serve as a sudden *memento mori*.

In my studies, from the time of the great cathedral in Rouen to the time of the local bishop asking questions of his lively confirmation group, I found that Chesterton stayed with me. As Chesterton moved through the Middle Ages with Thomas Aquinas, St. Francis, and Chaucer, he developed his ideas of "thingness," place, reality, actuality, and being, all to a fine pitch. He described the good poets, like Chaucer, as master artists and celebrators or being and existence. As Chesterton proclaimed, better than any of the rest of us could:

> There is at the back of all our lives an abyss of light, more blinding and unfathomable than any abyss of darkness; and it is the abyss of actuality, of existence, of the fact that things truly are, and that we ourselves are incredibly and sometimes almost incredulously real. It is the fundamental fact of being, as against not being; it is unthinkable, yet we cannot unthink it, though we may sometimes be unthinking about it; unthinking and especially unthanking. For he who has realized this reality of light knows that it does outweigh, literally to infinity, all lesser regrets or arguments for negation, and that under all our grumblings there is a subconscious substance of gratitude. That light of the positive is the business of the poets, because they see all things in the light of it more than do other men. Chaucer was a child of light and not merely of twilight, the mere red twilight of one passing dawn of revolution, or the gray twilight of one dying day of social decline. He was the immediate heir of something like what Catholics call the Primitive Revelation; that glimpse that was given of the world when God saw that it was good; and so long as the artist gives us glimpses of that,

it matters nothing that they are fragmentary or even trivial; whether it be in the mere fact that a medieval Court poet could appreciate a daisy or that he could write, in a sort of flash of blinding moonshine, of the lover who "slept no more than does the nightingale." These things belong to the same world of wonder as the primary wonder at the very existence of the world; higher than any common pros and cons, or likes and dislikes, however legitimate. Creation was the greatest of all Revolutions. It was for that, as the ancient poet said, that the morning stars sang together, and the most modern poets, like the medieval poets, may descend very far from that height of realization and stray and stumble and seem distraught; but we shall know them for the Sons of God, when they are still shouting for joy. This is something much more mystical and absolute than any modern thing that is called optimism; for it is only rarely that we realize like a vision of the heavens filled with a chorus of giants, the primeval duty of Praise.

THE DIVINE DOCENT
INSIDE THE DOOR

By Laurie Robinson

SOME MONTHS AFTER I ENTERED the Roman Catholic Church on Easter Vigil 2009, a nasty bronchitis sent me to bed with a flagon of hot toddies and G.K.'s *The Everlasting Man*. I am still not entirely sure whether the rum-laced toddies or my desperate need for reassurance inflamed his writing with the healing remedy I needed at the time. But those three days down with the book and the man set my soul on its feet again—at least for the next crucial miles before the next juncture of growth emerged.

After being born, bred and baptized Mennonite, in my late 30s I began to make what would become a 15-year journey into Mother Church. During that long sojourn, I heard of G.K. through friends who attended the American Chesterton Society summer conferences. Here and there I read snippets of articles in *Gilbert Magazine* and managed to navigate *Orthodoxy*—but that was about it. I respected the passion my friends had for him, but I had not yet met the man face to face.

In hindsight, I understand that the gigantic girth—in mind, soul and body—of G.K. didn't show up in full force until I really needed him. And I really needed him that weekend. I had begun to question my decision to step across the door of the Church, and fitfully stirred after the first infant days of resting in the Mother's arms. Emotional challenges had emerged in my largely-Protestant family that evoked feelings of rejection. And some social challenges within the Church piqued a depth of loneliness and invisibility I had not expected. As a well-known writer within the Mennonite fold that had bred generations of Mennonites in my ancestry, I had been a public figure with a loyal Anabaptism threaded into my DNA. As a newbie convert, I was forced to start all over in a mid-life vertigo after breaking ties and loyalties with the old before finding a way to bond significantly with the new.

As the box of Kleenexes emptied and the flagon was refilled, I read *The Everlasting Man* with the intensity of a drowning woman who tossed about in the Barque of Peter on a stormy sea of doubts. Christ and His Mother—with all the Saints —were there, yes—but also asleep. Or so I thought. Until G.K. became a divine "docent" (guide) leading me into the inner rooms of the Roman Catholic Church. It's where Her heart beat calm and steady and unruffled by fluctuating feelings.

Just what was it that G.K. said and did in that book that turned the tide for me from insecurity to increased certitude— at least at the early stage of my conversion? (He since has done similar acts of restorative invigoration when new layers of doubts have ground me down). In this book, at that moment, there were three things.

Leaving the myopic for the mystery: From the get go, Chesterton in *The Everlasting Man* lays the ground rules for exploring the history of the world as informed by the Incarnation. In the very first paragraphs of the Introduction, he states, "There are two ways of getting home; and one of them is to stay there. The other is to walk round the whole world till we come back to the same place... in other words, the next best thing to being really inside Christendom is to be really outside it. And a particular point of it is that the popular critics of Christianity are not really outside it."

Indeed, in this work, Chesterton helped me to grasp the riches inside the Church by journeying far outside the boundaries of Her treasures. By presenting an overview of world history from the perspective of my being a pagan citizen rather than a Mennonite or a Catholic, he helped me to detach from my myopic fears. He helped me gain a breathtaking and roomy aerial view that allowed me to better see the full Truth among the half truths.

In the chapter, "The God in the Cave," he reminded me that the Catholic Church would always be larger than the smaller pieces of Her which broke away during the Reformation—including the Mennonites. He helped me connect with the fact that the main driving force behind my journey Home was this: I began to cramp up in the brand of my childhood tradition of smallness—though it brought me to a solid faith for which I am forever grateful. Yet I longed for the grandeur of the greater vista that shimmered on the other side of the Tiber. That meant crossing the wet and wild river of separation. I finally did so. But after the initial honeymoon elation, I was not a little weary, worn and chilled.

Chesterton's words warmed and renewed me:

"But it is to whatever philosophy or heresy or modern movement we may turn. How would Francis the Troubadour have
fared among the Calvinists, or for that matter among the
Utilitarians of the Manchester School? Yet men like Bosuet
and Pascal could be as stern and logical as any Calvinist or
Utilitarian. How would St. Joan of Arc, a woman waving on
men to war with the sword, have fared among the Quakers or
the Doukhabors or the Tolstoyan sect of pacifists. Yet any number of Catholic saints have spent their lives in preaching peace
and preventing wars. It is the same with all modern attempts
at Syncretism. They are never able to make something larger
than the Creed without leaving something out..."

This excerpt sparked for me another metaphor I had read
and heard many times before: Mother Church is an entire
stained-glass window. All the other denominations that splin-
tered off her during the Reformation and later contain only one
or two, or at the most, several colors of the vast array of hues in
the Church Christ founded. In my conversion, I sought the full
spectrum and was not betrayed. My current fears were a col-
or-blindness that allowed me to see only grayish green where
there was royal blue, glittering gold, blood red. G.K. helped to
heal my blindness so I could again apprehend the good, the
true and the beautiful as handed down by the Apostles through
the ages to us.

Unlocking the right door with the right key: As a convert,
one of the most powerful G.K. quotes for me is from the chapter
"The Witness of the Heretics":

> The Early Christian was very precisely a person carrying about
> a key, or what he said was a key. The whole Christian movement
> consisted in claiming to possess that key. It was not merely a
> vague forward movement, which might be better represent-
> ed by a battering-ram. It was not something that swept along
> with it similar or dissimilar things, as does a modern social

movement. As we shall see in a moment, it rather definitely refused to do so. It definitely asserted that there was a key and that it possessed that key and that no other key was like it; in that sense it was as narrow as you please. Only it happened to be the key that could unlock the prison of the whole world; and let in the white daylight of liberty.

During that weekend of coughing fits and fits of doubts, Chesterton helped me to face the reality of why conversion was the only way to apprehend the fullness of the faith. Breakaways from Mother Church strove to change the locks on the only Door that led into the One True Church. That meant that each group forged a new key that did not have the whole shape of the key of the kingdom given to Peter. There was something about my experience as a young adult that began to feel as if no amount of locksmith magic would allow me entrance into the fullness for which I hungered. Only when I was willing to throw away the partial-shaped key of my childhood heritage could I cross the threshold into an everlasting hope for holiness with no perimeters. That weekend, Chesterton beckoned me inside the mansion with his good-humored common sense that articulated clearly: the only way to open the right door is to use the right key.

Giving up the temporary that fades to grasp the everlasting that shines ever-new, I found other pivotal passages on which my spiritual health turned for the better; the squishy became more solid. The doubts gave way to the blustery gusts of dogmas that still the shifting winds of time. In the conclusion of the book Chesterton writes:

> In the Catholic Church, which is the cohort of the message, there are still those headlong acts of holiness that speak of something rapid and recent: a self-sacrifice that startles the world like a suicide. But it is not suicide; it is not pessimistic,

it is still as optimistic as St. Francis of the flowers and birds. It is newer in spirit than the newest schools of thought; and it is almost certainly on the eve of new triumphs. For these men serve a mother who seems to grow more beautiful as new generations rise up and call her blessed. We might sometimes fancy that the Church grows younger as the world grows old... For this is the last proof of the miracle; that something so supernatural should have become so natural. I mean that anything so unique when seen from the outside should only seem universal when seen from the inside.

On that fateful weekend, when I met Chesterton face to face, he guided me on a tour that solidified my conversion. The journey took me around the world and all its ages, only to bring me back again to the inside of the timeless Home. To the only dining room in which bread and wine become the body, blood, soul and divinity of our Lord. To the only true food and the true drink that I could imbibe as a child-like convert by returning to the only Mother who can mature me fully into an everlasting woman.

THE TRYSTING PLACE

By David W. Fagerberg

I KNOW THE MONTH AND THE YEAR when I met Chesterton for the first time. Like some people keep a guestbook in their home for visitors to sign so they can remember who has visited, I keep a register of authors whom I have read, treating them like visitors to my mind. Some only make a short call; some leave a faint impression; but some make themselves at home, and take up residence. In September, 1990, I carried a sum of birthday cash into a bookstore and spent the afternoon calculating how to spread it across my interests. If I bought these books in liturgy and metaphysics, would I have to skip these books in Scripture and history? If I put back this hardcover, could I buy two softcover books? After a series of compromises and much internal bargaining, I started for the cash register with only five dollars unaccounted for. Standing in line, I saw on the shelf a $4.50 Doubleday Image Book publication of *Orthodoxy*, by G.K. Chesterton. I recognized the name, but did not know who he was. I tossed it on the pile. It took one chapter to get used to his odd writing style; it took two more chapters to get a sense of what he was complaining about; but in the fourth chapter, "The Ethics of Elfland," I started to grin, and have not stopped since. Eleven months later, and another dozen Chesterton books, my family and I were received into the Catholic Church.

Chesterton was not the only influence on me during this time, and among the numerous nudges by God's providence, I should mention three. First, I sometimes say that I wrote myself into Catholicism in chapter five of my dissertation. A thesis does not ordinarily have such an existential effect on its author, but in my case I was studying liturgy as an ordained Lutheran pastor intending to raid the Catholic pantry for some liturgical geegaws to bring home, and in chapter five I saw a difference between liturgy and *leitourgia*. The former is ritual, temple etiquette, pomp, and ceremony. The latter, I was being told by Alexander Schmemann and Aidan Kavanagh, is the cult of the new Adam left in the hands of his mystical Body to exercise for the glorification of God and the sanctification of man. In other words, *leitourgia* proved to be the interior form of an ecclesiology. I might hammer this round liturgical peg into my square ecclesiastical hole, but it would be forced and there would be gaps. I was writing a dissertation on liturgical theology, and then I blinked and saw a Catholic ecclesiology. (Does the reader remember the optical illusion of black on white looking like a vase, but white on black looking like two faces staring at each other?) Second, there were the works of Fr. Louis Bouyer, himself a Lutheran pastor who converted and became an Oratorian. His writings explained to my satisfaction theological issues like sacrifice and saints, spiritual issues like mystery and sacrament, and ecclesiastical issues like hierarchy and magisterium. Third, we began attending a Catholic parish, and their sincere liturgies and cordial spirit gave me a peaceful place in which to come to terms with the decision. We went to Mass one Sunday morning, and didn't ever not go back; that community drew us in.

That is a quick description of my pathway, but of more interest to the reader is what Chesterton was whispering to me as he accompanied me on it. When I began reading him, I had no more design on becoming a Catholic than a cannibal (his description of himself in the *Autobiography*), but a series of quotations placed steppingstones across the Tiber at just the intervals I needed if I was to stride across.

In his essay "Why I Am a Catholic," Chesterton describes the Catholic Church as "the trysting-place of all the truths in the world." This is parallel to an illustration he remembers from a display venue in London. We are wrong to consider Catholicism as one among the displays of churches and sects and religions inside the Crystal Palace when the Catholic Church is the Crystal Palace itself. She can contain all the truth, beauty, and goodness that the world can bring, which she receives, and plants in a domestic garden where they can grow more healthy than they could in the wilderness, isolated. For me, conversion was not so much a move from false to true, or wrong to right, it was a move from small to large. This was behind my operating metaphor of referring to the "*size* of Chesterton's Catholicism" in my book title. He was an irenic apologist to me. He said, "I was converted by the positive attractions of the things I had not yet got, and not by negative disparagements of such things as I had managed to get already," and so was I. Inklings of truth I had managed to get so far were given a more spacious home and powerful impact by Catholicism. Neither Chesterton nor I regretted our past, but we were both glad for now having room for things to run wild that our earlier tradition could not accommodate.

This idea was made even more pointedly for me in Chesterton's biography of St. Francis. At the end he discusses how the order came eventually under papal administration. Chesterton is speaking about Francis and Franciscans, but I read it about Luther and Lutherans, to wit:

> The Pope was right when he insisted that the world was not made only for [Lutherans]. For that was what was behind the quarrel... [Luther] was so great and original a man that he had something in him of what makes the founder of a religion. Many of his followers were more or less ready in their hearts to treat him as the founder of a religion. They were willing to let the [Lutheran] spirit escape from Christendom as the Christian spirit had escaped from Israel. That was the point the Pope had to settle; whether Christendom should absorb [Luther] or [Luther] Christendom. And he decided rightly... For the Church could include all that was good in the [Lutherans] and the [Lutherans] could not include all that was good in the Church.

Lutheranism was not large enough to hold all that is in Catholicism, but Catholicism is large enough to hold all the positive things Lutheranism had given me. It is a capacious Church, which is the opposite of heresy. The Greek word *airesis* meant a choice or disposition to something; then it meant a chosen mode of thought; and finally it meant a party or sect. It is one-sidedness, or only looking at one side. So Chesterton says "Every heresy has been an effort to narrow the Church," and sets the mood against the mind. "The mood was indeed originally the good and glorious mood of the great [Luther], but it was not the whole mind of God or even of man."

The convert has more liberty, not less. Here are three quotes that spoke to me about greater, not lesser, liberty of thought.

From *The Catholic Church and Conversion*: "To become a Catholic is not to leave off thinking, but to learn how to think. It is so in exactly the same sense in which to recover from palsy is not to leave off moving but to learn how to move."

From "Why I Am a Catholic": "There is no other case of one continuous intelligent institution that has been thinking about thinking for two thousand years."

From *The Well and the Shallows*: "A Catholic has fifty times more feeling of being free [because a Catholic] has the range of two thousand years of twelve-hundred thousand controversies, thrashed out by thinker against thinker ..."

Tradition does not stifle, it is the democracy of the dead; complexity does not smother, it is the key that fits an intricate reality; dogma does not strangle, it puts up warning fences so we don't plunge to our death. This is the most adequate way to account for the impression that Catholicism is always at odds with the world. To the charge that Catholicism is unrealistic we can give the same reply that Chesterton gave to his contemporaries when they accused the Victorians of being prudish. "What disgusted [the Victorian], and very justly, was not the presence of a clear realism, but the absence of a clear idealism. Strong and genuine religious sentiment has never had any objection to realism; on the contrary, religion was the realistic thing, the brutal thing, the thing that called names." Entering the Catholic Church did not mean abandoning realism.

Chesterton delights in pointing out that the Church continues in continuity while the heresies rage in contradiction around her. At the present moment, Catholicism is protecting liturgy against a secular rationality that has no use for ritual, but when the pendulum swings we may find the Church protecting the rationality of the faith against over-emphasized ritual superstition. At the present moment, Catholicism is protecting the soul in the face of materialism, but one day she may have to protect the body in the face of spiritualism. She has in the past. This is an example of the famous conclusion he came to, recorded in *Orthodoxy,* that if Christianity was wrong, it was very wrong indeed. How could it be attacked from all different angles? "Quakerish and bloodthirsty, too gorgeous and too threadbare, austere, yet pandering preposterously to the lust of the eye, the enemy of women and their foolish refuge, a solemn pessimist and a silly optimist." Then the thunderbolt hit him: perhaps the Church is the normal thing, and all its critics are mad, in various ways.

This capaciousness of the Catholic Church derives from the fact that she is still living, which means she is responsive, which means she can remain our teacher.

> The Church in its practical relation to my soul is a living teacher, not a dead one. It not only taught me yesterday, but will almost certainly teach me tomorrow. Once I saw suddenly the meaning of the shape of the cross; some day I may see suddenly the meaning of the shape of the mitre. … This, then, is, in conclusion, my reason for accepting the religion and not merely the scattered and secular truths out of the religion. I do it because the thing has not merely told this truth or that truth, but has revealed itself as a truth-telling thing.

Chesterton felt as if he was being asked why he could not take the truths, but leave the dogmas and magisterium. The answer was clear: "Henry VIII was a Catholic in everything except that he was not a Catholic." If the Church was going to be my living teacher, she must be my teacher tomorrow about things I do not yet know, and not just confirm things I had already concluded. While I was studying with the Benedictines, I had become quite fond of the Rule of Benedict, but I imagined

Chesterton saying to me: "So you like the Rule of Benedict? You should try Benedict's Church. It has lots more rules, and some of them you will not like as much!" He had managed to see the meaning of the shape of the cross, though not the mitre. I substituted a number of other things for that mitre: I did not yet see the meaning of Mariology, the papacy, five additional sacraments, hierarchy, merit, the communion of saints, etc., but I might be taught their meaning any day, if I could remain patient and docile.

The reason I could not simply remain a Catholic-sympathizing Lutheran was the same reason Chesterton could not simply remain a high Church Anglican: "I believe one of my strongest motives was mixed up with the idea of honor." He gives an example of a young prig who refuses to live at home because wine is drunk in the house or there are Greek statues in the hallway. When that Puritan snob develops broader ideas, he should come back to his father and say, "You are right and I was wrong, and we will drink wine together." He should not set up his own house mimicking the house he had so hastily abandoned in the sixteenth century. The day I drank my first glass of Catholic wine and saw a liturgical theology of the Mass (including its sacrificial dimensions), and the synergistic relationship between grace and works, and divine love as the key to liturgical asceticism, and the relationship between ordained priesthood and baptismal priesthood, and the importance of ritual, and the purpose of monasticism, and the Queen of Heaven, and the name of a hundred other flowers in the garden—on that day it seemed that I should stop work on my separate abode, and set sail for home on Chesterton's yacht.

THE LATEST VERSION OF MY CONVERSION

By Emma Fox Wilson

MR. AHLQUIST SAID, "Write something about how you were converted to Catholicism by Chesterton." And I said "Okay."

Except I wasn't converted and it wasn't Chesterton and I can't write about it. I can't write about it because that would set it in stone—and every time I finish writing this, I look at it the next morning and disagree with everything I wrote the night before.

Still, if a thing is worth doing, it's worth doing badly. Let's get cracking.

My mother was vaguely, uncertainly Christian; my father firmly atheist. We kept Christmas and Easter in a gentle, C. of E. [By these initials, Emma means to indicate "Church of England," and, being an Englishwoman, she just assumes Americans are familiar with this usage. – Editor (who is starting to have second thoughts about having asked Emma to contribute a chapter to this book.)] sort of a way, usually without going to church. My mother's extraordinary mother and aunts—the Goldsmith girls (who deserve a book of their own)—came from the generation just after Chesterton's. They were warm, vigorous, English figures, living in Norfolk and Sussex—all crisp linen, warm wool and practical hands for teaching, baking and caring. They were steeped in Christianity, which washed over my brother and me without our really noticing. They also had vigour in spades—that kind of beautifully-enunciated, Margaret Rutherfordish oomph that you just don't see much nowadays. They knitted and cycled, and swam naked in the Norfolk Broads in the 1920s—and they laughed a lot.

I grew up in London—like Chesterton—and, so I'm told, I used to plaster myself to the car window, every time we drove past a big convent that was on our route to the local swimming pool. God lurked around the place, mentioned in school assemblies and present in Mother's assumptions about the world, and in her gentle attempts at bedtime prayers with us when we were small—but there wasn't really a formal introduction. There are stirrings (or are they memories?) of God for all small children, I think: staring hypnotized at the brief, rounded perfection of the bubbles created by each individual raindrop as it falls into the puddle beside your small wellington-booted foot; nearly understanding what the branches of the trees against the evening sky are trying to say, as mother tucks you into bed.

My parents had stuffed the house with books, and Father bought more books like other people buy food. Mother read to me from before I can remember until I was well into my teens: Austen and Dickens and Wilkie Collins and George Eliot. Some of these writers were more obviously Christian than others—but it didn't matter. They, and the world they described, were steeped in it: mercy and forgiveness; sin and redemption; God and Man and the baby who was born in Bethlehem.

These were the days of vinyl records and no headphones, so if my parents listened to a lot of Mozart and Bach and Beatles, my brother and I had to, too. And some of that—although this thought never reached the surface of one's mind—sounded a bit like what it might sound like if you could hear God making bits of the Universe. Mother made sure that we infested the National Gallery from an early age, so I also grew up with Giotto and Raphael and all the crowded glories of religious art from the Middle Ages and Renaissance—pictures packed with scenes, events and huge ideas that you didn't even know you were gulping down. Father took us to the Science Museum and the Natural History Museum. I was awed by the blue whale, suspended above our heads in a vast hall, all to itself. Father had a microscope and a telescope, too—and we peered at all the little lives thrashing about in a single drop of pond-water or wrestled with the unimaginable distances that were so casually described as "light years."

All this was dangerous: the study of anything properly, will lead to awe—and is hence filled with paths that might point you at something that might be God. I read a lot of science and science-fiction from Father's bookshelves and learned extreme scepticism and the rudiments of logical thought from Asimov and Houdini and Randi and Sagan and Sladek (Don't miss Sladek's *New Apocrypha*—a joyous debunking of a slew of pseudo-sciences from astrology to ESP. And any biography of Houdini will give you a very jaundiced view of psychic seers and spiritualists). More danger: logical thought, the sceptical pursuit of truth, attempts to see behind mysteries—all this can land you back on those same damned paths to God again, shucking out the chaff and being left with what looks suspiciously like it might be wheat.

And I'm leaving out *Star Trek* and the Muppets and the funny lady with the bandaged legs at number 57 and the Beach Boys playing on a tape in Father's car and things about Churchill and P.L. Travers' *Mary Poppins* books and the great chunks of the Christian story that were snuck into Captain Scarlet and the smell of dust and stone and holiness inside my great-aunt Le's parish church and the calmly questioning typeface of the ads in the paper that said 'Once a Catholic…?'—you see, once you start to look, you see that everything had something to do with God in your life, because everything made you who you are, and who you are is someone who has God washing about inside them, because that's what God does.

Or at least, that's what God does…if He's there at all. Which I sometimes don't know. Conversion stories make it sound like a one-off, once-in-a-lifetime thing. But it's not. Sure, St. Paul was knocked flat—but he struggled and wrestled after that. St. Teresa of Avila, St. Therese of Lisieux, Mother Teresa (this list suggests that if you want a life of calm spiritual certainty for your child, you should maybe avoid calling her "Teresa")—all had decades of an almost complete absence of God. Sometimes, it's all just a bloody great mystery: if Cardinal Basil Hume can say that (and he did, very wisely and very sadly, only without the swearing, when someone asked him to comment on God during an IRA atrocity) —then I can too. It's a mystery and one that I don't seem to be getting any better at.

Everything that I was reading and experiencing churned around inside me and at different times, different bits reached the surface—but by the time I left school, I was firmly if unreflectingly atheist, with that rather smug certainty that some atheists have.

Then I bumped into some good Evangelical Christians, with some crummy Evangelical ideas—but who nevertheless managed to give me a better idea of Biblical and salvation basics. At least I now knew what I was disagreeing with more clearly. Then I met some of their friends, but these people were Catholics—and I got to know them better. We talked about God and books and films and music and I asked questions and they explained stuff and one of them said, of becoming a Christian: 'It's not something you do. You are done by it'. I came across Lewis on Miracles and Pain and he grappled my obvious questions with enough fearless and forensic logic to raise doubts in my mind as to whether this atheism lark was quite as foolproof as I had assumed. You want to do Logic? Do Lewis. Fearsome.

We all went to University during all this, and one of my two best female friends there turned out to be a rather recently lapsed Catholic. (Another Catholic: they were everywhere: it was at about this time that I found out that my granny Goldsmith had flirted with Catholicism as a girl, and my father discovered—to his absolute horror—that he had been christened in a Catholic church.) In my girlfriend, even that lapsed touch of Catholicism had still left her with more decency, goodness and wisdom in her supposedly atheistic little finger than most of the people around her. Of course, I wasn't fool enough to think that Catholicism was any assurance of goodness: dear God, even the most recent history of the Church spells that out in letters of flame.

I was studying English Language and Literature and so I read Herbert and Vaughan and Hopkins and Shakespeare and both Eliots and Wolf and Golding and Anglo Saxon poetry, and everyone you can think of in between. I found that D.H. Lawrence was utter tosh and that *The Dream of the Rood* wasn't. Authors who wrote about the grim side of life—the realists, the

atheists, the early T.S. Eliot of the evening like a patient ether-
ized on a table—they were clearly telling the truth, and talking
about things that I could see right in front of me. But I started
to find that the authors who looked even more unflinchingly
at all of that—at the mundane, the real, the sordid and mean-
ingless—but who also saw the something more that was lying
right next to (or within, between, behind) all of that—these
authors seemed to describe far better, far more fully, the actual
world in which we were all stumbling about. I found that the
writers who portrayed the fullest and clearest pictures of what
it was like to be here, seemed repeatedly to be the writers who
also saw God. Worrying.

I decided to peer a bit more closely. I survived the sweat-making embarrassment of Christian Union meetings run by
Evangelicals, for about a term. But they often seemed to confuse
how willing you were to experience artificially whipped-up
states of emotion—and to wave your arms in the air to indicate
it—with real evidence of holiness or an encounter with God.

I gradually also found that I really couldn't see the point
in a service that faffed around with bread and wine and all
that kneeling and standing, and men in dresses—only in order
to remember what Jesus had done. Why bother with all that
guff, if "This is My Body, this is My Blood" didn't mean exactly
what it said? God. Right there. On the altar and in your hand.
Transubstantiation. The real deal.

And so—just to have a look, of course—I started to go to
Mass. And Mass was even more sweat-making. I'd like to say,
with Chesterton, that my fear was of the great Mystery at the altar ("I am afraid of that tremendous reality," he said), but it was
mostly the far more mundane fear of all these mysterious people who knew when to stand up and sit down and cross themselves, people who would certainly detect an incomer and—oh

horror—might even try to welcome me. Why churches have greeters, I will never understand: any normally constituted human being will shrivel up like a mollusk, when confronted with a phalanx of eerily smiling strangers, all trying to push damp missals and a parish bulletin into your hand.

The Masses I attended during term-time were at Blackfriars in Oxford. There I found monastic psalmody (which you could join in) used as an ordinary tool to probe the meaning of things, and I found preaching of the highest scholarship and theology. All of this was dished out by a bunch of men who sometimes wore Reebok kickers under their mediaeval habits and who would often nip quietly to the back of the church to prop up the meths-addled tramps (or eminent and holy professors of theology: the two were quite indistinguishable)— who had come in to hear the Word and get warm.

I had to force myself to go each time. But I stuck with it. God knows why—I certainly don't. In the later stages of the fight against believing there might be something in any of this, it was sometimes as if God was no longer whispering, he was SHOUTING INTO MY FACE. Everywhere I turned, it seemed that God was chasing me down. The film (and then the play) of *Amadeus*, Anthony Sher in *Richard III*, Mozart's music (again); the trees against an evening sky; the shapes of the fences outside the Bodleian, with the final little arabesques that turned from palings into carved wild leaves—all of it was talking about God and saying "Come in."

Sometimes I would come out of Mass and walk back to college (past The Eagle and Child, where Lewis and Tolkien had once sat drinking pints with their friends and reading out chunks of *The Lord Of The Rings* and *Narnia*, to see how they sounded) and I was filled with a sense of good things found. At other times, I wondered if the whole secret of the Catholic faith was simply that they were putting something dodgy in the incense—I felt so inexplicably happy. But mostly, I was merely horrified.

My two closest male friends throughout this time were still the Catholic chaps I'd met just as we were all leaving our school. (They're now both extremely eminent doctors, which suggests that the opposition between science and religion isn't as straightforward people like to say.) They were rowdy and wild and threw beer about and got into trouble and made fart jokes—but they were also brimming with something that seemed to be God, and specifically God mostly as described by Catholicism.

As I was leaving Oxford University, one of them also found just the right priest for me, back in Birmingham (where he was studying and where my family and I now lived). My friend explained that this was a priest who would be just as terrified by my knocking on his door and asking to receive instruction, as I was, to be knocking and asking. And so it was that one day—after lots of false starts and a desperate and sweaty last reading of *The Catholic Faith* by Msgr. Ronald Strange, just to see if I could find anything that I definitely disagreed with—I quaveringly walked down the road and knocked on the office door of Father Nicholas Latham. May God bless and save him.

Fr. Nicholas and I worked slowly through everything—over about six months: all my questions and all the things I thought were nuts; and all his questions and all the (different) things he thought were nuts-but-true—and then all the usual canards about the Pope and Mary and the Saints. You didn't have to despise homosexuals. You didn't have to approve of Vatican wealth. You didn't have to think that sex was a sin (indeed, it would be a sin to think so). You didn't have to have blind obedience to the Pope.

Most important for me, you didn't have to abandon your intelligence (Aquinas and Lewis and Chesterton—and my friends from university and millions of others, all witnessed to that)—and you didn't have to abandon your conscience.

And now imagine a Laurence Sterne-ish blank page, to indicate a pause in which I am failing to write what (or Who) exactly it was that convinced me, and how, and why. I would need to sit with you and read out bits of books and show you corpses and babies and universes and birds—and wave my arms—and you would need to ask questions and I would get confused, and then you would get confused, and then we would both come back the next day and understand a bit more... but I'm not Lewis or Chesterton and so I can't put it all in here. Hence the pause instead.

I was received—in a long, rather tatty sports-hallish sort of a room that was the chapel downstairs from Fr. Nicholas's office. And I have never regretted stepping in through that door of faith, for even a millionth of a second. I have not had a straightforward life (who does?) I have known huge failures and sins and disasters of all sorts. But I have never regretted coming to Catholicism—and when I did come to it, it felt (as everyone always says) like coming home, and knowing it for the first time.

But of course, that's not the end because I wasn't converted. And where's Chesterton?

Conversion? Sure—when I was received into the Church, that was a moment as solid and final as a birth or a death. But—it's like a marriage or anything important: you have to be reconverted every day. Every moment. You doubt, you worry. You get slack. Worst of all, you go back to who you were before you converted—but with a sickly "Catholic" icing on top. Over there, we have the converted racist who simply replaces her tribal-hatred of the Other who-are-black, with a nice, new

"Catholic" hatred of the Other-who-are-homosexuals. Or here, the converted politician, who simply replaces his blind loyalty to his party, with a nice, new "Catholic" loyalty to the further reaches of the Pro-Life movement—and thus justifies his continuing to vote for his beloved party, no matter how low it sinks, because after all, a good, Catholic hatred of abortion justifies any crime. Or—before some of you start to choke—have a look at the converted me: always snobby and superior about people in general, and now with an added "Catholic" veneer of being snobby and superior and judgemental about people if they commit the unforgivable sin of not doing Catholicism as I think it should be done. So—sure: I was converted. But I wasn't. I'm still in there, pitching. And hoping that God understands. And He does. If He's there. Which He is. I think.

And Chesterton? Well, you can see that Chesterton didn't convert me, because so many other things did. But he was certainly inextricably mixed up with all of it.

How could anyone stumble onto this, as I did at the age of about 12, and not be knocked sideways:

> "Did you catch this man?" asked the colonel, frowning. Father Brown looked him full in his frowning face. "Yes," he said, "I caught him, with an unseen hook and an invisible line which is long enough to let him wander to the ends of the world, and still to bring him back with a twitch upon the thread."

Or this:

> [The man coming from the confessional] believes that in that dim corner, and in that brief ritual, God has really re-made him in His own image. He is now a new experiment of the Creator. He is as much a new experiment as he was when he was really only five years old. He stands, as I said, in the white light at the worthy beginning of the life of a man. He may be gray and gouty; but he is only five minutes old.

Or even just this:

> The winter afternoon was reddening towards evening, and already a ruby light was rolled over the bloomless beds, filling them, as it were, with the ghosts of the dead roses.

Or this:

> And through thick woods one finds a stream astray
> So secret that the very sky seems small.

You start to think there might be something in this Catholicism lark, if someone who could see that clearly, and write that beautifully, was grabbed by it.

And what about the millions of little girls who are born to starve, or be raped, or drown in mud, or be killed by parasites that destroy a child's eyeball from the inside out? Religion is just a comforting fairy-tale for people who can't face the hard truths of the real, scientific world, isn't it? But then you read a bit more Chesterton—and he doesn't seem to be full of fairy-tale. You wouldn't write "A Ballade of Suicide," if you hadn't plunged pretty deeply into the mud and the blood and the sights that might lead you to suicide in the first place. This was a man, who'd said with Wilde, "Atys with the bloodstained knife were better than the thing I am". He had seen stuff that was worse than anything the hard-truth guys were coming up with:

> While dull atheists came and explained to me that there was nothing but matter, I listened with a sort of calm horror of detachment, suspecting that there was nothing but mind. I have always felt that there was something thin and third-rate about materialists and materialism ever since. The atheist told me so pompously that he did not believe there was any God; and there were moments when I did not even believe there was any atheist.

And yet, still—he emerged into Catholicism.

And when you slide towards using your faith as a reason to hate, you find Chesterton's there with a slap-in-the face reminder, straight from Jesus:

> Christianity …came in startlingly with a sword, and clove one thing from another. It divided the crime from the criminal… We must be much more angry with theft than before, and yet much kinder to thieves than before. There was room for wrath and love to run wild.

And all the time, you're also falling in love with Chesterton just because he makes you laugh. You read "On Running After One's Hat" or the episode of the Vicar and the Oswego biscuit in the *Autobiography*—and you reflect that such a rowdy sense of humour is unlikely to accompany a sheep-like tendency to be brainwashed.

And I haven't even started to tell you about Chesterton's "Hammer of God" and "The Queer Feet" and the (genuinely disturbing) "Secret of A Train" and the true story about the student and the bonfire and the devil on the steps of the Slade School of Art. And then there's his biography of Aquinas (and the time Aquinas forgot he was sitting with a King), or his biography of St Francis, or his rotten but occasionally brilliant novel, *The Man Who Was Thursday*. And his poetry: good heavens, "Glencoe" is only 20 lines long, but it's a walk with giants. And *The Ballad of the White Horse*. And anything he ever wrote on Christmas—and you should jump out of your chair and read all of these straight away.

But let's throw all of that out of the window. Here's the shocker—that makes you begin to grasp the reach of Chesterton. You see, even if I had never read a single word written by Chesterton, his fingerprints would still have been all over this story. So, you might say that Lewis was the writer who most directly brought me in. But Lewis was there to bring me in, because he'd read Chesterton. You might say that my Catholic friend brought me in. But he was there to bring me in, because at the same time he was talking to me, he was struggling with a crisis in his own faith, and he survived it by re-reading Tolkien's *Lord of The Rings*. But Tolkien was only there for him, because Lewis had been there for Tolkien (Lewis was the first person to tell Tolkien his book was worth finishing) and Lewis was there for Tolkien, because he'd read Chesterton. Even the Goldsmith girls, right at the beginning of my tale? They'd all read Chesterton, of course—everyone had, in those days. And even if they hadn't, they might not have been around to beam so kindly and so fruitfully upon me at the start of my journey, if they hadn't survived both the First and the Second World Wars. And English soldiers in the First War famously shouted bits of Chesterton as they launched themselves over the top. And in the Second War, it is arguable that one of the things that gave England the strength to fight on (and to fight in the right direction) was Lewis's hugely popular "Broadcast Talks." And he wouldn't have written them if he hadn't been Christian, and he wouldn't have been Christian if he hadn't read Chesterton.

And so it goes. You keep bumping into Chesterton like he keeps bumping into God. So, yes, what I said at the beginning is true: I wasn't converted and it wasn't Chesterton. But also, I was and it was.

And here we are in the present. At the end of a day this week, which had started with no God and a woman in the car in front of me who was hitting her child, I lay in bed and the window was open. I smelled approaching summer and heard the sounds of English birds singing in a May evening, and the voices and footfalls of children who were laughing and running up and down the pavement, for the sheer joy of it—and

I thought for the millionth time that you can't look at all the children who are born into horrors, without also looking at all the children who aren't. And that you can't be furious about one, without being grateful for the other—even "by one thin thread of thanks." And yes, Jesus died a bloody and horrible death. But it does look very much as if He then got up again. And—He is there, as the Curé d'Ars used to say, pointing at the host in the tabernacle. And when God was asked His name, He replied—impossibly—"I Am." And what can you do with that, except lay beside it the story of Elijah waiting to see God, and hiding in the cave, and God not being in the earthquake, or the fire, or the great wind, but in the still small voice?

Now it's time for me to go, and for you to read some better things.

And may all of us—the Evangelicals and the atheists and the racists and all the little girls born to die of starvation in the mud and all the happy children on the pavement and even Mr. Ahlquist—and of course, you as you hold this book in your hands—may we all (to steal a beautiful thing that St. Thomas More came up with at a particularly bad moment, because God had filled him, too)— may we all meet merrily in Heaven hereafter.

God bless us all. Amen. Oh—and thanks, Tim.

A CONVERTED IMAGINATION

By Matt Swaim

I N MY EARLIEST DAYS AS A CATHOLIC, having been received
into the Church in the mid-2000s, I was asked about the
decision so commonly that I came up with a short stock
answer for those who were only inquiring as a matter of small
talk. I had read my way into the Church, I would say, and then
go on to list a few examples of the authors who'd influenced
me. If I was listing essayists, I would cite Chesterton, Belloc
and Knox. If theologians, Chesterton, Newman, and probably
Augustine. If modern apologists, Chesterton, Frank Sheed, and
toward the end of my decision making process, Scott Hahn. If
novelists, I would usually bring up Flannery O'Connor, J.R.R.
Tolkien, and of course, G.K. Chesterton.

In those first few years after the Easter Vigil of 2005, I had
the internal sense that because I had "read my way into the
Church," my journey to Rome was the result of an intellectual
conversion. After more than a decade of reflection, I've come

to understand that's not quite so; it would be more accurate to say that what I had undergone was a conversion of the imagination. And my tutor, muse and traveling companion for all of that was G.K. Chesterton, dead for more than half a century and yet more lively and relevant than most of the contemporary thinkers I had been browsing in my spiritual search.

I was of course originally primed to understand Chesterton in my childhood, because anyone who's read him knows that Chesterton only makes sense to people who have been children at some point in their lives. I discovered G.K. in college, but I was prepared for him by Aesop and Grimm, by Narnia and *A Wrinkle in Time*, and even by Spider-Man and Luke Skywalker. I was always a big reader growing up, from classics to comics, and even in my own mind, I often saw my immersion in those worlds as a way to escape from reality. As a sheltered and socially awkward kid who had a fairly rough time running the gauntlet every day at public school, I looked at books as a way to shut out the world I was in and escape to a world that I could only inhabit through imagination: a world of adventure, romance, magic, and the cosmic triumph of good over evil.

Throughout my childhood I had been conditioned, whether intentionally or not, to understand that the worlds I read about in books were full of awe and mystery, and the world I walked around in was, well, a complicated mess. According to the churches and youth groups I attended, the world was a dangerous and scary place that should be converted, condemned, or avoided, while according to the public school system, that same world was progressing, always progressing, and we were all amazing fantastic unicorns in it who could be anything we wanted to be as long as we believed in ourselves. The Evangelical culture presented a world that was fearful. The secular humanist culture presented a world that was fake. The former was dissatisfying because it seemed to posit that the main purpose in life was salvation, and everything else was a waste of time or energy. The latter was dissatisfying because it seemed that every message encouraging positivity and self-esteem was a thin veneer for selling some product that I didn't have.

Suffice to say that by the time I was ready to enter college, I had become a complicated jumble of thoughts and ideas, an anti-composite of the worldviews I'd been soaked in for nearly two decades (the 80s and 90s). Because of my immersion in the Evangelical world, I had remained a committed Christian, but because of my dissatisfaction with late 20th century Evangelicalism, I was extremely cynical toward mainstream Christianity and the shallowness of both its conservative and liberal manifestations. Working part-time for a Christian bookstore chain didn't help this. Because of my being bombarded with a chaotic stream of postmodern noise from the consumer culture, I felt a rebellion towards that as well. I started playing in Christian alternative, punk and metal bands, which may not make much sense to the reader but made perfect sense to me at the time, and still makes a fair amount of sense to me now.

It was in these raw and philosophically discontented college years that I encountered G.K. Chesterton. I'm not sure exactly how I first came across him; I think I might have read one of his safer quotes in another person's book, something true, but not overly challenging, like "A dead thing can go with the stream, but only a living thing can go against it." I think at one point I even picked up a volume containing both *Heretics* and *Orthodoxy* using my Christian bookstore employee discount, but I didn't read it immediately. I read *The Man Who Was Thursday* over a summer, but didn't really understand it because I hadn't read *Orthodoxy* and still had no sense of where Chesterton was coming from.

I was attending Asbury College in the early 2000s when the revolution came. Several things happened around the same time. Of course, there were the September 11 attacks, which caused everyone to rethink everything. My disillusionment with even the Christian punk rock counterculture was starting to manifest, and I was beginning to think that if the communications degree I was earning would land me working for the same media I'd grown to loathe and mistrust, then I would never figure out what to do with my life.

It was around that time that I was scheduling classes for an upcoming semester, and noticed that a Chesterton seminar was being offered by a recently appointed English professor. I had taken two classes on C.S. Lewis already, one through the English department and the other as a Philosophy elective, and I figured I might as well study this man who was said to have had an impact on Lewis. Since I didn't know what someone like myself was going to do with a college degree anyway, I saw it as a healthy diversion. I had no idea what was about to hit me.

I've read a lot of people who say true things. I've also read a lot of people who say things in interesting ways. But G.K. Chesterton set my brain on fire.

I finally cracked open *Orthodoxy*, highlighting half of it and copying the other half into my personal journals. His biography of St. Francis of Assisi was required for class, but I ordered his St. Thomas Aquinas biography shortly thereafter (from a secular bookstore, oddly enough; it wasn't carried by the Christian bookstore chain). I read the essays and chapters that were assigned, and then I scoured the internet (it wasn't as big then as it is now) for everything else I could find from Chesterton. Everything I read was giving voice to the unspoken angst I felt both against megachurch Christianity and secular consumerism. However, Chesterton did more than that for me, because the more I read him, the more I realized he wasn't so much speaking *against* things (as I seemed to do with every bad song lyric I penned), but rather speaking *for* something. He was championing Christian truth, in all of its adventure, paradox, mystery and beauty, whereas I had merely been complaining about hypocrisy and mocking what I saw as the shallowness of the zeitgeist.

There is much to say about the various ways his thought began to impact my own: his prophetic take on eugenics, his musings on Distributism, his scathing critiques of postmodernism. But two significant chapters in *Orthodoxy* were probably the main steerers of my theological and philosophical trajectory: "The Ethics of Elfland" and "The Paradoxes of Christianity."

Firstly, in "The Ethics of Elfland," Chesterton's understanding of the importance of fairy tales to understanding the "real world" was formative for me. St. Therese of Lisieux's gift to the world of the Little Way helps us understand how we can view the most ordinary of activities as an opportunity for holiness; Chesterton's "Ethics of Elfland" helps us understand how we can view the most ordinary of activities as an opportunity for adventure. I had been under the impression that my exploration of science fiction and fantasy was a way to escape from reality; Chesterton helped me understand that they could be a way to see reality itself with new eyes. Previously I had understood my Christian faith as adversarial toward the world and a way to bide my time in the present age until I could slog my way to Heaven and escape the madness of it all. Now, I was beginning to understand that everything I experienced, from the creative work of God to the handiwork of humans, whether trial or triumph, was a clue to help me understand the broad and beautiful mystery of the genius of God, who endowed us with the gift of free will that makes both sin and love possible.

Before absorbing this concept from Chesterton, I had
something of an essentialist view of Christianity, the kind of
Christianity that has as its most basic expression the question,
"What must I do to be saved?" and sees anything beyond that as
unimportant, and even a potential obstacle on the path to salvation. Now, I was seeing art, architecture, history, poetry and
creation itself the way that a rock climber views outcroppings
on a sheer face: as aids to get one closer to the summit. It's impossible to overstate how much this re-oriented my relationship
with God, which had previously been cliquish and cynical, and
was now becoming magnanimous and joyful.

Secondly, Chesterton's thoughts on paradox upended my
philosophical assumptions. In the theological debates I'd been
engaged in through high school and college, I had tended to
find myself on one side or another of what was usually some
kind of false dichotomy. Did salvation depend upon grace,
or free will? Was God ultimately just, or ultimately merciful?
Should Scripture be interpreted literally, or metaphorically?
Almost in a single fell swoop, Chesterton helped me replace
my "either/or" mentality with a "both/and" paradigm. And as I
began to gravitate more and more toward the Catholic Church,
I found that "both/and" was a handy way to answer a lot of
questions, such as "Should a follower of Jesus feast or fast?"
"Should the Church have beautiful worship spaces, or should
it help the poor?" and "Should Christians be celibate, or have
lots of babies?"

Of course, as Chesterton points out, the idea of paradox is
at the very heart of Christianity, whose Savior descended from
the Godhead to become an infant in a manger, told us that the
first would be last, and died on a cross—a scaffold on which
the vertical beam points upward and downward, the horizontal
beam points to the left and right, and there, at the meeting of

all of it, is our crucified Lord who calls us to follow Him into the mystery.

I would go on to graduate from college in 2002, and it would be another three years before I would come to the full acknowledgement that the adventure, paradox and wonder I was seeking could ultimately be found in the Catholic Church. Those last couple of years before entering the Church, especially that last year, were wrapped up in a lot of apologetics and catechism and the like. But those were more like working out the itinerary after booking a trip. Once my imagination had been converted, all the rest of the "Catholic stuff" was just a matter of connecting dots. And there in the background of it all, encouraging me to embrace the path with joy, humor and vigor, was G.K. Chesterton, always leaping off the printed page to invite me into the great adventure of being Christian.

THE MANIAC
Chesterton's story of my conversion in Chapter 2 of Orthodoxy

By Fr. Simon Heans

YOU HAVE TO HEAR THE BAD NEWS before you can be told the good news."

That is excellent advice when presenting the Christian gospel, and it is one that Chesterton himself heeds in *Orthodoxy*. For the preacher—which I am every Sunday and frequently on weekdays too—the bad news is about sin. In this the preacher is following his Master. Chesterton observes: "The ancient masters of religion... began with the fact of sin." For Chesterton that is "a fact as practical as potatoes." But that is not where Chesterton begins his argument for orthodoxy. The reason he gives is that even Christian thinkers now deny the reality of sin. Quoting some disciples of the Rev. R. J. Campbell as his witness, Chesterton maintains that for society at the beginning of the 20th century, sin has ceased to be the uncontroversial, self-evident premise from which to construct a case for Christianity. And so unable to found his apologetics on the presence of moral disorder, he proposes to base it instead on the fact of mental disorder. As he puts it: "though moderns deny the existence of sin, I do not think they have denied the existence of the lunatic asylum."

Over a hundred years later, sin is even less popular as an explanation for human behaviour than it was in Chesterton's day, but there has been an explosion of mental ill-health even if the buildings which once housed the sufferers—like Chesterton's Hanwell—have been replaced by psychiatric drugs. I have never taken any of those, but I want to own up to having been mentally ill. I am encouraged to make the admission by the example of Chesterton himself. In Chapter 4 of the *Autobiography*, "How to be a Lunatic," he recounts his own experience of madness. He ends that chapter by expressing the hope that "in this, my period of lunacy, I may have been of little help to other lunatics." Chesterton is writing about the composition of *The Man Who Was Thursday* while he was still in his lunatic phase so the comparison with my own experience of madness is far from apt. However, I offer this brief narrative of my mental disorder in the same spirit of charity. I want to show "other lunatics" that Chesterton is a doctor of the modern soul and that his diagnosis of the maladies of the modern mind are as relevant now as when he first proposed them. They certainly struck me as true when I reread them in the second chapter of *Orthodoxy*. I realized that I was the Maniac of the title.

I was brought up as a Jehovah's Witness. Members of the sect do not identify themselves as such to each other. "Jehovah's Witness" is an outsider's label. Anyone on the inside is said by their co-religionists to be "in the truth." By the age of fifteen I had decided there was no truth to be found in that organization—the term "church" is never used by JW's. Leaving the sect was difficult emotionally because my family remained staunch, but it was even more difficult intellectually because in a sense, I never left. Truth remained what I wanted from life, and I believed that I could satisfy that desire for myself. Chesterton begins Chapter 2 by defining the Maniac as "the man who believes in himself." That was the frame of mind in which I entered Cambridge to study History. Of course, I was not alone—I encountered lots of conceit and arrogance among my student contemporaries who set out again to win the "glittering prizes" of the university in order to launch what they hoped would be their brilliant careers. However, the prize I sought, and the career I wanted, was knowledge of the truth. Again, the aspiration to find life's meaning is a common theme of adolescence, so in that sense I was no different from many of my peers. But where to look for it? Chesterton writes criticizing "a notion adrift everywhere that imagination, especially mystical imagination," is dangerous to man's mental health, adding that "when a poet really was morbid it was commonly because he had some weak spot of rationality on his brain." I had tried to be a poet at school in a very silly and juvenile way as one might expect, but I lacked "a mystical imagination." I had rationality on the brain for that is how I had been brought up. My father was a rationalist in that sense and, in his nineties, even now makes the occasional attempt to argue me back to his religious opinions. He certainly did when I saw him during the long university holidays, but by that time, I had, so I fondly believed, left behind such nonsense. I had become a Marxist.

Marxism appears in Chapter 2 of *Orthodoxy* as "materialism." Chesterton clearly has Marxism in mind when he writes, "The materialist is sure that history has been simply and solely a chain of causation." Marx proposed a materialist theory of history in which it is fundamentally a succession of modes of production each having its origin in the previous one. Chesterton describes this materialism as "having a sort of insane simplicity" concluding that "it has just the quality of the madman's argument, we have the sense of it covering everything and yet leaving everything out." I certainly recognize the truth of that verdict for I studied European medieval history for a term at Cambridge when I was firmly under the sway of the "insane simplicity" of Marxist theory and I then taught the same subject for many years in the sixth form. The comprehensiveness of Marxist history is indisputable, but as I taught medieval history, I soon came to realize that, paradoxically, it also leaves things out. This list is not exhaustive: monks, popes, kings, bishops and crusaders. They don't figure unless they are economic actors. As Chesterton says: "There is such a thing as a narrow universality; there is such a thing as a small and cramped eternity; you may see it in many modern religions." That was obviously true of the Biblical Fundamentalism of my childhood, but now I had found for myself another "narrow universality." And it began to drive me mad. Chesterton makes a memorable distinction in Chapter 2 between the poet and the logician, the first of whom wants "to get his head into the heavens," while the second "seeks to get the heavens into his head. And it is his head that splits." Cracks were definitely appearing in my head as I followed the "perfect and narrow circle" (Chesterton's description of the Maniac's thought process) of Marxist logic, believing that there was nothing in the heavens or on the earth that could not be explained in materialist terms.

The Marxism that I professed was what is often called "structuralist." The feature of this kind of Marxism which is relevant here is its anti-humanism. "Man is but the ensemble of his social relations," wrote Marx, and the structuralist Marxists, most prominent among them being the French philosopher Louis Althusser, took him at his word. But structuralists were not just reinterpreting Marx. There were other French thinkers who were reworking the thought of Freud and Nietzsche in the same anti-humanist way. Taking his cue from Freud, Jacques Lacan was eliminating the human subject from psychology, and Michel Foucault was drawing inspiration from Nietzsche to do the same in social and intellectual history. What will seem strange to anyone reading this—it does to me as I write—is the pleasure, the sheer exhilaration, I felt at the blows landed by these thinkers on traditional approaches which continued to take the idea of the integrity of the human person seriously. I rejoiced at the iconoclasm of these and other thinkers as they destroyed the image of man as a free and rational being. This was the exaltation of the Maniac. Chesterton did not write about anti-humanism in Orthodoxy for his opponents, Shaw, Blatchford, McCabe et al, were all humanists and could not have anticipated the use to which these French thinkers put the nineteenth century philosophers who influenced them. However, Chesterton was more prescient than they were about the "main deductions of the materialist," pointing out that "they gradually destroy his humanity." Looking back on my own life at the time, that is the effect that they had on me. Chesterton elaborates on the destructiveness of materialism: "I do not mean only kindness, I mean hope, courage, poetry, initiative, all that is human." The truth of that observation was painfully brought home to me by a debate about socialism and the society of the future in which I was one of the main speakers for the socialist side. My argument, as I recall, amounted to asserting that socialism was the future whether they liked it or not and they had better get used to it. The inevitability of socialism was the doctrine of the "scientific socialist." To think otherwise was to be one of that despised breed (at least by me), a "utopian socialist." But it was the latter whose doctrine had a place for "kindness, hope, courage, poetry, initiative, all that is human." That is why Chesterton could debate with Shaw and Wells. It was the common ground on which they met. But it was not the ground on which I stood. I was "in the truth," a "scientific socialist," but at the cost of a good deal of my humanity.

It diminished further as I embarked on a period of postgraduate study which was hardly supervised at all. Chesterton writes of "the two boxes" in which modern thinkers imprison themselves. By the time I left Cambridge with a degree that was good enough to get me a postgraduate grant and to give me a renewed sense of that self-belief Chesterton identifies with madness, I was well-ensconced as I have described, in the materialist's box. However, I was about to leave it to enter the second of Chesterton's boxes where the skeptic dwells. Although they are different they are both places where the Maniac is found:

> The man who cannot believe his senses, and the man who cannot believe anything else, are both insane, but their insanity is proved not by any error in their argument, but by the manifest mistake of their whole lives. They both have locked themselves up in two boxes, painted inside with the sun and stars; they are both unable to get out, the one into the health and happiness of heaven, the other even into the health and happiness of the Earth.

The equivalent to the skepticism Chesterton condemns here and which I embraced is post-structuralism or post-modernism. Its basic premise is that there is no reality accessible to the senses, no reality "out there," because it arrives "always already" (a favored phrase) constituted by language. "For the sake of simplicity," writes Chesterton describing this state of mind, "it is easier to state the notion that a man can believe he is always in a dream." He can indeed—and I did. Freud took over from Marx, but not Freud the scientist. Under the influence of Jacques Derrida and Paul de Man, I wrote a paper for a seminar run by my Marxist structuralist comrades in which I argued that the patient in one of Freud's most famous cases (the "Wolf Man") knew more than Dr. Freud himself. This proposed role reversal was a step too far even for these avant-garde intellectuals. My talk was greeted with a hostile silence and I left the room alone. To this day, I continue to think that my argument was water tight, but then (as Chesterton says above) that is not the point. The "Wolf Man" was also thinking logically. Chesterton's verdict on the two types of mania he identifies, materialism/structural-ism and the skepticism/post-modernism ("equally complete in theory and equally crippling in practice") applies *a fortiori* to the "Wolf Man" and to me as his interpreter: "Their insanity is proved not by any error in their argument, but by the manifold mistake of their whole lives." Yet this is not a practical error; it is intellectual, the consequence of false philosophy. Chesterton traces these mental illnesses to "reason without root, reason in the void." The madmen are mad because they lack true "first principles" and begin "to think at the wrong end." The Maniac cannot be cured by therapies or chemicals. The only hope for him is conversion to orthodoxy. He must come out from among the heretics and adopt orthodoxy.

It would be a satisfying conclusion to this autobiographical study of Mania if I could write that Chesterton saved my sanity. But I cannot: I had not heard of *Heretics* or *Orthodoxy,* and I don't think I would have made much of them if I had tried to read them at that point. But I like to think that these works were ultimately responsible if we accept providential as well as proximate causality. The evidence for that statement is that my recovery from my mental disorders can be expressed in terms Chesterton uses in Chapter 2 of *Orthodoxy*. He describes exactly what happened to me.

We have now left the "two boxes"—my two boxes—of the Maniac behind and arrived at the point in the chapter where Chesterton gives what he calls "a general answer touching what in actual human history keeps men sane." His answer is mysticism. "The ordinary man," he insists, "has always been a mystic... He has permitted the twilight... He always has left himself free to doubt his gods, but (unlike the agnostics of today) free to believe in them." That quality of doubting the gods but being free to believe in them I found in the commentaries of Heidegger on pre-Socratic Greek philosophy and Holderlin, Rilke, Trakl and other German poets. Having discovered Heidegger through writing a critique of the use of his work by Jacques Derrida, I took him up and avowed myself his disciple. His Question of Being became mine too. I had, to the extent that this question is for Heidegger a mystical one, adopted mysticism.

However, I do not think the study of Heidegger could have been sufficient to guarantee my sanity. As Chesterton puts it, "It is not enough that the unhappy man should desire truth; he must desire health." My desire for truth had been the cause of my mania and I knew it could be again as I became preoccupied with Heidegger's pre-Socratic notion of truth, *aletheia* or un-concealedness. As Chesterton explains, when the Maniac's "mere reason moves, it will move in the old circular rut... just as a man on the Inner Circle will go round and round the Inner Circle unless he performs the voluntary, vigorous and mystical act of getting out at Gower Street." Earlier in the chapter Chesterton has told us that there are two ways in which the desire for health on the part of the Maniac manifests itself: through "the will and faith." The act of will in my case was getting a job—and keeping it—in a school teaching History. And it was at Lancing College, an Anglo-Catholic foundation, that I discovered faith, not of course the heterodoxy of my dear mother and father, but the orthodoxy of Chesterton which, of course at the time he was writing *Orthodoxy*, he also found in Anglo-Catholicism. However, like him, I have made a further discovery, viz., the Catholic Church. After Anglican ordination in 1994, in 2011 I was received into the Church with a small group from my parish and was ordained a Catholic priest of the Personal Ordinariate of Our Lady of Walsingham.

There ends the story of my conversion—at least as told by Chesterton in Chapter 2 of *Orthodoxy*. I am no longer The Maniac. I could go on, but I fear that I might contract a bout of mania if I did. In other words, I might be tempted to start believing in myself again. So, I'll stop here at the point where I can say unequivocally that this has been Chesterton's story of my conversion.

CHESTERTON HIS AND HERS

By Yasha and Denise Renner

YASHA

THE FIRST TIME I HEARD the name of G.K. Chesterton was on the lips of the Evangelical Christian apologist Ravi Zacharias, a figure well known to Protestants. Anyone familiar with Ravi's style of rhetoric knows that he is something of a compilation author; that is, the backbone of his preaching consisted of borrowed prose, and some poetry, from various Christian intellectuals as well as a handful of notorious anti-Christs. Of all his aides, Chesterton stood out as a truly inspired and original thinker, a fact which was later confirmed as I began to read his writing for myself.

With ease did Chesterton see the profuse irony of a world turned upside down by the original sin, a world drowning in fads and still groaning for more, as well as the only solution in the One he named the Everlasting Man.

Of our Lord, Chesterton wrote in the final chapter of *Orthodoxy*:

> Joy, which was the small publicity of the pagan, is the gigantic secret of the Christian. And as I close this chaotic volume I open again the strange small book from which all Christianity came; and I am again haunted by a kind of confirmation. The tremendous figure which fills the Gospels towers in this respect, as in every other, above all the thinkers who ever thought themselves tall. His pathos was natural, almost casual. The Stoics, ancient and modern, were proud of concealing their tears. He never concealed His tears; He showed them plainly on His open face at any daily sight, such as the far sight of His native city. Yet He concealed something. Solemn supermen and imperial diplomatists are proud of restraining their anger. He never restrained His anger. He flung furniture down the front steps of the Temple, and asked men how they expected to escape the damnation of Hell. Yet He restrained something. I say it with reverence; there was in that shattering personality a thread that must be called shyness. There was something that He hid from all men when He went up a mountain to pray. There was something that He covered constantly by abrupt silence or impetuous isolation. There was some one thing that was too great for God to show us when He walked upon our earth; and I have sometimes fancied that it was His mirth.

It was these very words which, in the early days of my religious formation, first sparked my interest in their author as they were being broadcast like poetry from Ravi's pulpit. For in them I heard the eloquence of a true genius, the aptly named Apostle of Common Sense whose mastery of letters, and paradox, made him the most fitting critic of modern man.

And so it happened that through Chesterton's merits, and those of many others besides whom Ravi had compiled into his stimulating exposition of the Christian faith, that I began to appreciate the intellectual weight of a religion I implicitly trusted, or perhaps never found reason to doubt.

I was not raised in any particular religion, though I believed in God, and even the God of the Bible, from an early age. In fact it was my mother, who was raised a secular Muslim in Iran but then practiced a kind of gnostic spirituality, who first introduced me to Ravi Zacharias when she gave me his book *Deliver Us From Evil*. Ironically, her purpose in doing so was not to evangelize me, for she herself was happily indifferent (but always respectful) toward the great prophet of the Christian religion. Probably it was out of a mother's frustration, as my misguided teen years gave way to early adulthood and it became apparent that my life had stalled. I was unmotivated, still living at home while finishing my undergraduate degree, and spending all my free time playing computer games.

My introduction to Christian doctrine helped to reawaken in me an interest for reading and learning, which I had long stifled. As for the faith itself, I am pleased to say it was not entirely erroneous, but that did not matter: my assimilation of the truth as such amounted to nothing more than an intellectual pursuit that lulled me into a false sense of security, even as I continued on a steady diet of Protestant radio, sermons, and books by various self-appointed pastors of one stripe or another. One might say I was a faithful member of the Christian Opinion. Of sanctifying grace and the sacraments I knew nothing. My politics were steadfastly libertarian, which seemed quite compatible with American Protestantism, and my philosophy of morals was implicitly Pelagian.

Clearly I had been deceived, and not only by the traditions of men. My own pride had caused me (and every heretic before me) to create a religion of my own making. Indeed, it is precisely this capital vice that imperceptibly leads to the rejection of all authority, resulting in a punishing ignorance of the truth which sets us free.

On this vital point I think again of Chesterton, who reminds all who would glory in the name of Christ of our indispensable need of true humility as a precondition for the gift of faith. In *The Catholic Church and Conversion*, he writes, "We do not really need a religion that is right where we are right. What we need is a religion that is right where we are wrong." Can there be anything more obvious and still missed by countless followers of Jesus? These are words I heard not once in Ravi's repertoire (it is no accident) but read for the first time several years later, in the little book that would eventually be thrown across the room by my future wife.

For the time being, however, I continued in my arrogance. Small wonder, therefore, that my newfound "religion" was powerless to effect the awesome change promised by our Savior. On the contrary, I persisted for some time in a deeply flawed understanding of the spiritual life and of prayer, which were based on superstitious beliefs that, as I look back now, were the real cause of so much personal anguish; indeed, that vice drove me to the abyss.

By the time I finished my undergraduate degree at Portland State University and began my first professional job as a graphic designer at a well-known craft brewery, I had lost all interest in religion, and things very quickly got worse from there as I sunk into intemperance, vulgarity, and other vices too shameful to mention.

This trajectory may have gone on indefinitely had it not been for the woman who is now my wife, whom I met at the height of my arrogance and moral depravity but the depths of loneliness. In more ways than one, our relationship quickly exposed my hypocrisy as a self-identifying Christian who still enjoyed, if only tacitly, the moral safety of fiducial faith. It was during this formidable time that Almighty God began to prepare us in a special way for the miracle that He would accomplish seven years later, when she and I were both received into full communion with the Catholic Church.

It would not be long before the grace of God revived in us an interest in the Christian religion, which helped to order our relationship toward the good. And just as I had done in those unfruitful years before we met, the two of us immersed ourselves in the world of Protestant Christianity, mostly through radio sermons and books by popular authors. This positive momentum culminated, for the time being, in my baptism by our Lutheran pastor three months before he witnessed our marriage. And it was this singular and irrevocable moral act (viz., matrimony) that reawakened what till then had become indifference toward the Catholic Church.

The awful events that led to my initial conversion to Christianity is, for the present purpose, a story too long to tell. Suffice it to say, it was the grace of attrition (i.e., an abiding fear of hell) and the conviction that neither the passage of time, nor faith alone, could free me from my moral anguish and the eternal punishment that surely awaited me. Into such a soul as this did Christ begin to speak His graces, granting me a relentless desire to live according to the truth, a desire which drove my quest to be reconciled with God through his Son and the Church he founded. I am in good company then, as far as sinners go, with our man Chesterton, who when asked why he converted from Anglicanism simply stated, "To get rid of my sins."

My wife Denise was raised Lutheran (Missouri Synod), but she too had lapsed many years earlier as a teenager. Yet she had a fiercely Catholic spirit, even though she did not know it at the time. She loved to travel and experience different cultures. By the time we met, she had already been to 20 countries. In fact she had just returned from a two-year stint in Ethiopia, where she wanted to live out the rest of her days. Unlike me, she was well read and literary, an arts and letters major. And she valued everything small, unique, and full of character, as well as the "most important things in life," a frequent topic of discussion as we were getting to know each other. Whereas for me, I had never travelled of my own free will and thought the desire to do so was absurd and bordering on the irrational. My favorite stomping ground was Fry's Electronics and Costco of all places, where I would (as Pope Francis says in *Gaudete et Exsultate*) "spend with abandon and live only for the latest consumer goods."

It was Chesterton who finally helped me see the truth of Denise's intuition, namely, that small is not just beautiful but objectively better; and that the desire for more things, or more for the mere sake of novelty, is a vain and worldly attitude unbecoming a Christian—or as my wife would say, the equivalent of chasing after your own tail. "I think the big shop is a bad shop," writes Chesterton in *The Outline of Sanity*. "I think it bad not only in a moral but a mercantile sense; that is, I think shopping there is not only vulgar and insolent, but incompetent and uncomfortable."

But I was not so far gone into the cold labyrinths of individualism and hedonism that I could not relate to what is still for me a frequent reminder, which she first posed in the form of a question: Will any of this stuff matter on your death bed? In this gentle admonition my would-be Catholic wife was preaching on the first of the Four Last Things, becoming, as it were, an ancient echo of our sacred tradition: "Remember, man, that thou art dust, and unto dust thou shalt return." Just as these words mark the beginning of Lent each year with the imposition of ashes, so too I would begin my own pre-Lenten *Quadrigesima* to mortify in my own flesh all those impulses that incline fallen man to seek his last end in created things.

During this time my wife and I were living in Virginia, where I was studying law at a well-known Evangelical university. Law school came easy for me, and during my free time I read the Church Fathers, Papal Encyclicals, and the Catholic Encyclopedia, all of which beautifully supplemented my legal education. In contrast, my experience among such a religiously diverse student body and faculty only amplified my Catholic convictions, which finally saw the light of day in my second semester when I handed Denise a copy of Chesterton's *The Catholic Church and Conversion.* Till then I had not shared my doubts with her about the Protestant religion, or my research about the Catholic Church. Still, I hoped that her genuine appreciation for the author would have at least prepared her for the obvious meaning of my gesture. It did not, and she reacted by throwing the book across the room. She refused to read the book, and insisted that we remain Lutheran.

To navigate our differences and accent our shared beliefs, I enlisted Chesterton in the role of mediator. I knew she would appreciate his literary genius, but also identify with many of his (unpopular) views, especially regarding marriage and family life. My goal, humanly speaking, was to concede ground on issues which Denise held dear (and about which I had already begun to come around), and at the same time acclimate her to Catholicism, which Chesterton could not help but politely indicate in his writings. Together we read all his major works, and after she would finish a book, we would discuss the pages she had marked. I immensely enjoyed that activity because it brought us together intellectually; but it was quite practical too, as I could then gauge her tolerance for discussing the Catholic faith and discover in what ways she was already Catholic, as well as any misconceptions or hot-button issues.

But reading Chesterton during this period began to have a subtle effect on me, too, as I already mentioned. He helped to widen my vision and enculturate me with all things authentically Christian. In short, he communicated the *sensus fidei* and the surprising beauty of revealed religion.

Hence the whole affair played itself out as a divine comedy, something which clearly would have amused Chesterton who saw the hidden paradox in everything. That is, as I was grooming my wife to accept Chesterton the Roman Catholic, Chesterton the Apostle of Common Sense was grooming me to accept my wife's instinctive catholicity. All the while my wife was secretly delighting in my developing worldview.

But most of all, it was Chesterton's arguments in defense of marriage and the family, and everything traditionally associated with them, that provided the most fertile ground for friendly discussion, as the two of us not once diverged on these matters. Indeed, before we had ever heard of the "domestic church" or the concept of vocation, we knew that we wanted to raise a family, a traditional division of labor, and to homeschool our children, all of which Chesterton promoted often and with great veneration as the objects of the greatest common sense.

In our day these institutions are under fearful attack, and common sense is on the wane. Such a pity, then, that our prophet is so underappreciated and little known, in spite of his notoriety and monumental influence on countless souls, including such notable converts as C.S. Lewis. Maybe it is better this way, that is, to leave the discovery of such a gifted soul to them who seek for buried treasure, or in my case, to them who sought his intercession.

And so it was with the man I discovered, the man whose imagination and charming wit would profoundly influence so many of us as we crossed the Tiber.

DENISE

As a teenager I rejected what I would have called "organized religion," and had maintained my distance for a decade. When I met my future husband, Yasha, I was of the opinion that God's church existed in an invisible web of believers known only to Him. The Lutheran church was my default denomination, the one I had been raised in and appreciated for its reverence and solemnity, its familiar hymns and Bach. But it wasn't until he handed me G.K. Chesterton's book on conversion that I realized how much I wanted to remain Lutheran, and how much I hated the Catholic Church.

When he first broached the subject of conversion, we were still newlyweds, having been married in Oregon a few months before moving cross-country so he could attend law school at an Evangelical university in Virginia. He wanted to learn the foundations of law from a Christian viewpoint, and I wanted to escape the dreary rain and liberalism of Oregon. The curriculum was appealing, the foothills of Virginia looked beautiful, and so we embarked on our first adventure as a married couple.

We arrived in Virginia and found what my mother called a "church home," a tiny Lutheran church with only two other young couples. This formal religious life was relatively new for us. Yasha had been baptized and confirmed in the Lutheran church just prior to our marriage, and he received communion for the first time the morning of our wedding, in the church basement with its folding tables and chairs and large chalkboard with a portion of our wedding verse written on it: "a cord of three strands is not easily broken." I was back to my roots, with a liturgy I still knew by heart. I had a new job to keep me busy while he was studying around the clock. We had a less-than-wonderful apartment we had rented sight unseen from Oregon, but were settling into Virginia (which boasted the promising motto, *Virginia is for lovers*), and our new roles at work and school.

There were many changes during that time, but the Lutheran faith was untouchable, or so I thought. I was totally unprepared to be ambushed one Saturday morning by the Whore of Babylon—as presented by G.K. Chesterton.

I heard the words, "I think we should become Catholic," and then my husband handed me a book with the ulcer-inducing title *The Catholic Church and Conversion*. I remember spouting off something about Martin Luther and the Bible being chained up in a Catholic Church, and the sound of the book slapping against the wall after I threw it across the room. It's possible I noticed the author's name, but in my panicked state maybe it didn't register. At that time, I had read snippets of Chesterton's work and enjoyed them, but still knew him to be a card-carrying member of the superstitious, sacrilegious Roman Catholic Church.

I had no intention of reading the book. I remember saying, "I would never have married you if I'd known you wanted to be Catholic. *I'm Lutheran.*" In other words, when people said the Pope was the Antichrist, I would think, "Well, if the shoe fits." We didn't formally agree to disagree, with the exception of celebrating Reformation Sunday, when I would ask for a reprieve from any and all discussion of the Catholic Church, which meant no snide comments about Luther, please.

I'm not sure how Chesterton made his way back into the house after that, but eventually we were both reading *Orthodoxy* and *Outline of Sanity* and enjoying them. Chesterton appealed to the rebel in me. He said what people might think privately, but out loud and in print. The Apostle of Common Sense had a little something of the original apostles in that his words were audacious, roundly rejected by a large segment of the population, and spot on.

He was a tolerable sliver of the Faith; and I also had Saint Augustine poking holes in my Catholic prejudice, as I had previously read some of the saint's writing and readily accepted everything he said on the subject of contraception and family. After all, Luther was an Augustinian monk, so the bishop of Hippo couldn't be all bad. And I knew from my work in adoption that new life wasn't something to be taken for granted.

So while I was willing to accept the truths of faith as proffered by Saint Augustine, as well as Chesterton's witticisms, I never looked closely at the writings of Martin Luther—works I should have held dear, given that I had become the great defender of the Lutheran tradition. But there was plenty that was amiss, if not downright abhorrent, in his work; nonetheless, I neatly disconnected the man Luther from the faith and church that are pleased to share his name—something many Lutherans do to some extent, cherry-picking his teachings and conveniently ignoring others, like his devotion to the Blessed Virgin Mary and her perpetual virginity.

The war of words continued on all fronts. No topic was safe. If we discussed history, Europe, contraception, women's rights— it always led back in some way to Rome, the Reformation, and Protestantism. And that led to an argument. For my part, it was easy to take pot shots at the Catholic Church, a huge institution made up of humans and now existing for over two millennia. What was interesting, however, was Yasha's responses to these charges of corruption, superstition, and manipulation: he was able to defend his position with *so much information.*

Wanting to go toe-to-toe with my loving husband, I searched out information from the Lutheran Church Missouri Synod. I found a booklet and the date of its founding: 1847. I was shocked to realize there was nothing to bolster the faithful or refute the Catholic apologist. I would raise some issue—play the indulgences card, for example—and receive a three-page email smoldering with everything from writings of the Church Fathers to the *Summa* of St. Thomas Aquinas to modern apologists. There would be links to books, articles, and podcasts, and I would respond with . . . my opinion, in all its glory.

At one point, he wanted to buy a Catholic book and I said, "Shouldn't we buy *Lutheran* books, since we are, in fact, *Lutheran?*" Expecting some push back, I was surprised when he responded, "Sure. Do you know of any?" I did not. I googled. And I came up with Albert Schweitzer.

In addition to the conflict at home, I was struggling to defend my faith while working at a Baptist university. My interview had felt more like an inquisition, and my "faith trajectory" had been called into question because I did not have a "conversion story" a la Chuck Colson. I had no Nixon, no Watergate, no Jesus moment. I had "just" been baptized as an infant and raised Lutheran. Even having strayed and returned, making the leap from West Coast to Bible Belt, from open rebellion to a Sunday churchgoer, I still failed miserably as an extroverted cheerleader for Jesus. And of course I saw Southern Baptists as a newfangled, regional religion, totally different from my Lutheran Church Missouri Synod with its deep sixteenth-century, European roots.

One perk of the job was the opportunity to go back to school, so I dove into my Masters in Theology—at a Baptist school. As a Lutheran. For fun. The crowning moment in this muddled period was probably when I chose to write a paper on the Eucharist. In support of this "Lutheran" teaching, I used a few Catholic sources, believing these early Christians were trustworthy souls before the Catholic Church went south and the Reformation became necessary. I presented the Lutheran understanding of communion and received an "A" with the advice that I should read the Bible more: this was Catholic doctrine. I was failing (and flailing) spiritually as I struggled to be Lutheran by birth and opinion, an enthusiastic evangelical by day and defender of Protestantism (not in whole, but in part) against the full weight of 2,000 years of Catholic Tradition by night.

It's no wonder Chesterton was such a welcome respite. I liked that he was converting Yasha from his materialistic mentality, and Yasha liked that he was bringing me closer to the Faith of our Fathers. Chesterton spoke from a place that was not laden with emotionalism, and was not overtly antagonistic. He managed to be deeply religious but also concerned with the day to day, with man and his journey on earth, and also with newspapers and big business and homemaking. He spoke frankly and honestly in a way that appealed to my Midwestern sensibilities, and he pushed and pulled at the barriers I had erected around "my" religion through his own story:

> I did strain my voice with a painfully juvenile exaggeration in uttering my truths. And I was punished in the fittest and funniest way, for I have kept my truths: but I have discovered, not that they were not truths, but simply that they were not mine. When I fancied that I stood alone I was really in the ridiculous position of being backed up by all Christendom. It may be, Heaven forgive me, that I did try to be original; but I

only succeeded in inventing all by myself an inferior copy of the existing traditions of civilized religion.

It was the giving up of my Lutheran traditions that stung the most—and right at the time when I was about to become a mother, too, and would be passing them on. As a child of divorce, the Lutheran tradition represented continuity for me. My father had been raised Catholic, but left the Church to marry my mother, who had generations of Lutherans in her family. I grew up making blankets for the Aid Association for Lutherans to send overseas and singing "Stille Nacht" in the choir during the children's program at our Lutheran elementary school. (Incidentally, that piece was written by a German priest and sung for the first time at midnight Mass.) The Lutheran faith was what was left to pass on to a future generation in the absence of personal family traditions that were dissolved upon divorce and then decimated with remarriage.

But, as Chesterton wrote, "Tradition means giving votes to the most obscure of all classes, our ancestors. It is the democracy of the dead. Tradition refuses to submit to the small and arrogant oligarchy of those who merely happen to be walking about." Tradition wasn't as small as my first eighteen years of life, or as small as my once intact family. Tradition was a big thing, much bigger than a family or a geographical region. There was a wealth of "tradition" that was mine for the taking, beyond anything I could have imagined—far more than a song removed from the midnight Mass and tucked into a children's program two weeks before Christmas.

And as for divorce, a reality with which I was all too familiar, Chesterton spoke eloquently and convincingly on that subject as well:

When the reformers propose, for instance, that divorce should be obtainable after an absence of three years (the absence actually taken for granted in the first military arrangements of the late European War) their readers and supporters could seldom give any sort of logical reason for the period being three years, and not three months or three minutes. They are like people who should say "Give me three feet of dog"; and not care where the cut came. Such persons fail to see a dog as an organic entity; in other words, they cannot make head or tail of it.

You are charmed, I am sure. So was I.

As a teenager, Christianity had struck me as painfully unthinking and dull. But Chesterton was a thinker, and he had a way about him. After reading his words, you weren't quite so sure of your position anymore. In a perfectly pleasant way—so pleasant, in fact, you didn't want it to end—he could dash your wrong-thinking to bits and build it back up so that it looked an awful lot like Saint Peter's at sunrise on a feast day: glorious, beautiful, holy.

Even at the threshold of conversion, my beliefs were radically incoherent: I still believed the teachings of the Catholic Church to be deeply flawed but thought G.K. Chesterton, despite his profession of faith, was an absolute peach. It was surprising that I was reading a book written by a Catholic, and astounding just how enjoyable it felt. For the traveler and reader in me, Chesterton was a delightful companion. As he himself described the second stage of conversion: "It is like discovering a new continent full of strange flowers and fantastic animals, which is at once wild and hospitable."

But then came the third stage: the "truest and most terrible. It is that in which the man is trying not to be converted. He has come too near to the truth, and has forgotten that truth is a magnet, with the powers of attraction and repulsion." This prophecy was fulfilled on my birthday, two weeks before our first child was due. We were watching a movie when the DVD player started acting up. Yasha got his laptop so we could finish the movie and that's when I saw it: the familiar figure dressed in blue—it was the link to some podcast about the Virgin Mary. And it bugged me. I was tired of the tension between us, and she symbolized two years of talks and tears and stalemates. As we stood in the kitchen cutting slices of birthday cake, I asked, "Are you really okay with raising our children Lutheran?" And he said, "Sure." But then he asked me if I would trust him.

He wanted to give me some books of his choosing. If, after reading them, I still didn't want to become Catholic, then he would let the thing go. I just had to promise to read with an open mind; and we know what Chesterton said about an open mind: "The object of opening the mind, as of opening the mouth, is to shut it again on something solid."

Well, I could have chipped a tooth on the stack of books Yasha gave me. Ludwig Ott's *Fundamentals of Catholic Dogma* was among them. There was no Chesterton, because I had read most of his nonfiction by then, although a Father Brown mystery would have been nice. I dove into Catholic apologetics: *The Faith of Our Fathers* by Cardinal Gibbons and *The World's First Love: Mary, Mother of God* by Fulton Sheen. I had fallen hard for Chesterton's worldview and now embarked on a study of Catholic doctrine. He inspired me to not reject *all* things Catholic, for he himself was Catholic, and his words were dreadful only in their catholicity and perfect in every other sense. Since all roads lead to Rome, as Chesterton observed, it is only fitting that he was the first author to accompany me as I read my way into the Church; it was my loving husband who introduced him to me.

"What is the good of words if they aren't important enough to quarrel over? Why do we choose one word more than another if there isn't any difference between them? If you called a woman a chimpanzee instead of an angel, wouldn't there be a quarrel about a word? If you're not going to argue about words, what are you going to argue about? Are you going to convey your meaning to me by moving your ears? The Church and the heresies always used to fight about words, because they are the only thing worth fighting about."

A COMPANION ON THE JOURNEY

By Thomas Storck

MY CONVERSION TO THE CATHOLIC FAITH began over fifty years ago, in the summer of 1967, and proceeded in several distinct stages. I clearly recall the main points and the main influences at each stage, while I recognize, of course, that the chief cause was God's action, behind the scenes, and at first not even suspected by me. My conversion that summer to theism from a doubtless immature and unformed atheism was externally the work of a rather improbable source, a book by the Methodist missionary, E. Stanley Jones, entitled *Abundant Living*. A few months later I haltingly came to accept the fundamental truths of the Christian revelation, and it was primarily Ronald Knox's book, *The Belief of Catholics*, which taught me that revelation had been entrusted to a definite society, a Church, not written down in a book meant to be interpreted by any and every one according to his own lights and preferences. Then finally, about ten years later, it was by reading St. Irenaeus, the early Church Father, that I saw that the Church about which Knox and others spoke, and of which I had wanted to see the Anglican Communion as a branch, was made up of Christians in ecclesiastical communion with the See of Rome and that therefore there was no choice but to become a Catholic. Shortly afterwards I was received into the Catholic Church on February 12, 1978.

How was Chesterton a part of this process? In fact, Chesterton, along with C.S. Lewis, were my companions in this journey, and even if neither of them was ever the determinative factor at any particular turning point, they still played a very important role.

In the fall of 1969, as a very immature Christian believer, I entered Kenyon College, a college nominally affiliated with the Episcopal Church, but in which very little Anglican Christianity—or Christianity of any kind—was practiced by either students or faculty. I suppose that most of the faculty was atheist or agnostic, skeptics of some kind, at any rate. Yet there was little direct attack on Christian faith. Mostly it was just ignored. I do not know whether this was because of indifference, perhaps born of contempt, or from fear of attacking religion at an officially Episcopal institution or what, but in its own way, to ignore Christianity can be more destructive of religious faith than outright attacks or hostility. If the faculty had been composed of rabid atheists, students at least would have seen the religious question as important, would have been forced to confront real arguments, and possibly some would have found the arguments for atheism wanting. But if atheism is simply assumed, if religious faith is treated as so obviously false or irrelevant as to require no refutation, an intellectual and spiritual atmosphere results which is very dangerous to religious belief. In addition, it relieves the opponent of Christianity of the task of coming up with actual arguments. How much easier just to ignore religion and trust that the pressure of opinion will operate in an atmosphere of moral promiscuity to keep students from any serious consideration of the claims of Christian faith. And this lack of any need to make arguments means that students, most of them away from their parents for the first time and in a heady atmosphere of freedom from rules, can likewise ignore the religion in which they were raised—and even more so if they were only nominally raised in that faith. This is convenient for all—on the one side, no need to make arguments, on the other, no need to grapple with them, no need for a real intellectual or spiritual search or struggle.

In an intellectual atmosphere such as this it is easy for a new Christian, a lowly freshman thrust among teachers and professors of presumed vast learning, to lose his faith. Even if, as in my case, one had come to Christian faith by an intellectual process, that intellectual process can be undermined. For example, as a student of philosophy, I was told that God's existence could not be proven by reason. But it was precisely by reasoned argument that I had come to accept the existence of God. Given the fact that the arguments I had read back in high school for God's existence, as presented by E. Stanley Jones, were not exactly specimens of philosophical rigor, and that I had not yet encountered a genuine philosophical demonstration of God's existence, who was I to argue with such a host of learned men? Why was I not overwhelmed by the indifference of the cultured despisers of religion, as Schleiermacher called them?

Here it was Chesterton and Lewis who were my friends and safeguards. Neither of them was the least bit intimidated by the anti-Christian intellectual atmosphere of their times, and anyone who absorbs their writings will be able to see through most of the glib dismissals of Christianity of his own time.

Thus I never had any serious intellectual difficulties about religion either in college or later in graduate school. The few overt attacks on Christianity that I encountered did not trouble me, nor did the general indifference to the truth claims of faith. Chesterton and Lewis were important chiefly for giving me confidence, a sense that the skeptics didn't have the best arguments, and that most of their pretensions were pretenses. I had read Chesterton's *Heretics* in high school, sometime during this period I read *The Everlasting Man*, and I read *Orthodoxy* during one of my college summer vacations. I did not fully appreciate the latter work till I reread it years later, and realized that under its surface of paradox and brilliant turns of phrase there is actually a tight and compelling argument. But even on an initial and doubtless superficial reading, these books, together with C.S. Lewis, especially his *Screwtape Letters*, fueled in me a confidence that the claims of Christian faith could stand against skeptical attacks and against the even more intellectually and spiritually corrosive indifference that I found all around me.

In his autobiography, *The Church and I*, Frank Sheed spoke about his youth in a Catholic ghetto in Australia, where many Catholics had accepted the valuation which the non-Catholic world put upon the Church and her members.

> In the second half of the nineteenth century the outside world had grown into a kind of automatic contempt for the Catholic intellect.... It was part of the siege mentality that too many Catholics believed this themselves. They were proud of being Catholics, but there was an unstated feeling that while we had the Faith, the others had the arguments!

For Sheed himself all this changed during his last year of high school. One of his teachers handed him two volumes, one of Chesterton's, the other of Belloc's, "with the remark, `These will suit you.' They did indeed." In fact, those two books "turned my mental world upside down." Chesterton and Belloc, along with other writers of the Catholic intellectual revival, helped Frank Sheed and many other Catholics of that generation throw off their feelings of intellectual inferiority. "For lots of us, Belloc and Chesterton meant an end of the three-century old siege mentality."

Even at the removal of a hundred years one can get some feeling for that exuberant and contagious confidence that Chesterton embodied and communicated so well. It is present in *Orthodoxy*, a relatively early work, written while he was still an Anglican, and even more palpably in two works published after his reception into the Catholic Church, *Where All Roads Lead* (1922), and *The Catholic Church and Conversion* (1927). These are both triumphalist books (I use this term without any pejorative meaning whatsoever), joyous affirmations and celebrations of the excitement of the Catholic faith. *Where All Roads Lead* begins, "Until about the end of the nineteenth century, a man was expected to give his reasons for joining the Catholic Church. Today a man is really expected to give his reasons for not joining it." The Church was now on the world's mental map. "The world has become conscious that it is not Catholic. Only lately it would have been about as likely to brood on the fact that it was not Confucian."

In the second book, what we might call this jaunty assurance is even more in evidence, and even more delightful. He speaks of Catholicism as appearing like one of the new religions, like one of the "enthusiasms that carry young people off their feet and leave older people bewildered or annoyed."

> The worthy merchant of the middle class, the worthy farmer of the Middle West, when he sends his son to college, does now feel a faint alarm lest the boy should fall among thieves, in the

sense of Communists; but he has the same sort of fear lest he should fall among Catholics.

Now he has no fear lest he should fall among Calvinists.... He is not likely to await with terror the telegram that will inform him that his son has become a Fifth-Monarchy man, any more than that he has joined the Albigensians. He does not exactly lie awake at night wondering whether Tom at Oxford has become a Lutheran any more than a Lollard. All these religions he dimly recognizes as dead religions; or at any rate as old religions. And he is only frightened of new religions. He is only frightened of those fresh, provocative, paradoxical new notions that fly to the young people's heads. But amongst these dangerous juvenile attractions he does in practice class the freshness and novelty of Rome.

Even in our utterly changed cultural and ecclesial environment Chesterton's enthusiasm for the Faith retains its contagious vitality; indeed, in the dreary present state of things I find my own faith and enthusiasm nourished and revived whenever I reread these words. This is, note, apart from any particular arguments that he makes. In fact, in neither book does one find a carefully laid out apologetic, as in Knox's *The Belief of Catholics* or even in Chesterton's own volume, *The Everlasting Man*. I cannot remember when I first encountered *The Catholic Church and Conversion*, whether before or slightly after my own reception into the Church, and, as far as I can recall, there was no particular argument of Chesterton's that was a mainspring in propelling me from atheism to theism, then to an acceptance of the Christian revelation, finally into the one Church of Christ. But without the confidence that I did not need to be ashamed of my faith, which Chesterton and C.S. Lewis helped instill and maintain in me, in the atmosphere of indifference in which I found myself, I might have abandoned or lost sight of the particular individual arguments which had carried me through the major turning points of my religious trajectory.

There was one other way I should mention in which Chesterton was a helper. This was in the mere example of his conversion from Anglican Christianity to Catholicism. I was well aware that Chesterton, and several of the other writers I was reading during this time, Ronald Knox, Cardinal Newman (whose *Apologia* I had read during high school) were converts. Thus, unlike many American Episcopalians for whom the Episcopal Church appeals as merely a respectable and dignified kind of Protestantism and for whom the Catholic Church is something fundamentally alien, the thought of going from Anglicanism to Catholicism was never far from my thoughts. In fact, for many reasons the Catholic Church exercised a strong emotional pull over me, so that even after I had gotten a reasonable grounding in High Church Anglican theology and was a convinced adherent of the Anglican branch theory of the Church, I was tempted more than once simply to go over to Rome forthwith and forget my intellectual disagreements about Papal authority. Fortunately I did not do so, for it would have meant entering the Church while not really convinced of all that she teaches. But still Chesterton and those other convert witnesses never let me rest in the comfortable insular Christianity that Anglicanism can be for so many.

Conversion is not a process that ends with our reception into the Church, but rather not until we enter that final "sabbath rest for the people of God" (Hebrews 4:9). Thus reading and rereading Chesterton can be part of our effort, in cooperation with grace, to bring our minds "into captivity to the obedience of Christ" (2 Corinthians 10:5), surely a continual project for most of us. In particular, Chesterton's vibrant confidence can be a singular help in these days when Catholics are divided and often discouraged, it can refresh us not only with a reminder of a happier time in the history of the Church, but give us a hope that something like that happier time might return someday.

In his Foreword to Chesterton's *The Catholic Church and Conversion*, Hilaire Belloc wrote of converts: "Men and women enter by every conceivable gate, after every conceivable process of slow intellectual examination, of shock, of vision, of moral trial and even of merely intellectual process." In every one of these ways of entering the Church, Gilbert Keith Chesterton's varied writings can be our faithful friends and companions. Thus to one still outside the Church, I will counsel: Read Chesterton. And to new or old converts, the same: Read Chesterton. To born Catholics: Read Chesterton. There are few authors who will repay us our time better.

Fundamentalism, Fairyland and Father Brown

By Fr. Dwight Longenecker

IN MY HAPPY EVANGELICAL HOME in Pennsylvania we were nurtured on the King James Version of the Bible and frightened by the apocalyptic fantasies of dispensationalist preachers. There was a great computer in Belgium named "The Beast" that had the names and addresses of all the Christians. The Jesuits were the Pope's storm troopers who had made a blood curdling vow to obey the Pope under all conditions, and they were awaiting his order to march out and round up the Bible-believers. The rapture was about to occur at any time. The Lord was about to return in glory and "in a moment in the twinkling of an eye" all the saved would fly up to heaven while all the damned would be left behind to suffer seven years of tribulation enslaved by the anti-Christ.

Really.

The fantastic prognostications of the dispensationalists were combined with Calvinism—or at least enough Calvinism to convince you that everybody who wasn't Fundamentalist was worldly and wicked, and indeed you yourself were "dead in your trespasses and sins," there was "none righteous no, not one" and "your righteousness was as filthy rags." So between the dispensationalist fantasies and the Calvinist doctrine of total depravity, was it any wonder that I, and so many others, grew up to view ourselves and the world with a kind of panicked personal pessimism?

Added to this heady brew of religion, I was sent off to Bob Jones University after high school. In South Carolina the temperature of both the climate and the religion was considerably hotter. Whoo, boy and was it hot! Billy Graham was a liberal compromiser, the president's wife Betty Ford was a "slut," and Jimmy Carter was "one of Joe Kennedy's boys." We weren't particularly anti-Catholic at home, but Dr. Bob was. I was there when Pope Paul VI died and Dr. Bob Jr. said from the pulpit something along the lines of, "Paul the sixth, that old imposter has gone to his place next to Judas his brother."

But God is always doing secret things, and it was at Bob Jones that I joined a little Episcopalian breakaway church deliciously named "The Holy Trinity Anglican Orthodox Church." On Sunday nights I trooped off with some other hoity-toity friends to the little stone church in the bad part of town to light candles, chant psalms and kneel down to say beautiful prayers out of musty prayer books. I was an English and Speech major, so I was delighted when I discovered that this odd church called "Anglican" was the church of T.S. Eliot, George Herbert, C.S. Lewis and John Donne.

I very quickly fell ill with an incurable disease called Anglophilia and decided that I wanted to be a country parson like George Herbert. By this time I had visited England a couple of times and had my heart set on taking up residence in a rambling vicarage in a country village in England.

I would sip tea and munch biscuits while writing poems, then step through the garden gate to wander through the churchyard to a church of mellow stone as old as Methuselah to ring the bell and say evening prayer. That evening I might stroll down to the Goose and Garter for a pint of ale—puffing my pipe as I played drafts with one of the locals. You get the idea.

So, after Bob Jones, when I was accepted to study theology at Oxford, you can imagine that I was quite a happy young man. Like Bilbo Baggins, I set off on my great adventure, and I will never forget my first approach to Oxford. It was early September as I stepped from the train still groggy from the flight. I loaded my big trunk into the back of a taxi and we headed for the Banbury Road.

The hilarious fact was that I arrived on the day of the St. Giles' fair. In the middle of Oxford is a wide avenue called St. Giles' after the church that stands at the head of this open space. Every week during late summer this street is closed for the St. Giles' fair which sounds delightfully medieval you think—jousting and jesters, the odd ox roast, archery competitions, the dupping of the swan and so forth.

It's not. Instead, for the St. Giles' fair, all the traveling carnival people turn up and the place is turned into a sprawling, overcrowded, amusement park. There are whirligigs and spook houses, carnival games with big pink teddy bears for prizes, kiddy cars, shooting galleries and ferris wheels. You can buy hot greasy sandwiches and bad beef burgers, cotton candy, pints of beer, fish and chips and sausage rolls. Loud music is blasting away, the neon lights are flashing and the girls on rides named "Terminator" or "Spill Your Guts" are screaming.

C.S. Lewis described his first arrival in Oxford, and how he was disappointed because he turned the wrong way out of the station and ended up in the working-class part of the city with factories, grubby pubs, and unsatisfying row homes. He thought, "Can these mean streets be Oxford?" My disappointment was far more dramatic. I was looking for the city of dreaming spires and inspired dreamers. Could it be true that in the middle of this venerable university there was a crass amusement park? How could one study with a fun fair going full tilt? I had heard of the rowdy pastimes of the students, but thought it was the odd boat race, a particularly hardy scrum on the rugby pitch or leaping into the Cherwell from Magdalen bridge on May Day. Did the students really spend their free time eating pork sandwiches, swilling cider, then riding Long John Silver's Swinging Pirate Ship? Tell me it wasn't true.

It wasn't.

The St. Giles' fair was only there for a few days before disappearing into the mist like Brigadoon. It wasn't long before I was cycling through the same square going to spirituality lectures at Blackfriars, dozing in the Bodleian library, having a pint at the Bird and Baby or Mass at Pusey House. The serious study of theology had begun, and it was there in my attic room in the Victorian pile of Wycliffe Hall that I discovered G.K. Chesterton. C.S. Lewis had mentioned the portly prophet in his biography *Surprised by Joy*, along with the warning that a young atheist can't be too careful in his reading, else his mind and imagination will be captivated by that enchanting seductress called Truth. He might have warned an eager young Evangelical likewise.

I was first enchanted by Chesterton's rambunctious review of fairy tales in *Orthodoxy*. The whole passage is Chesterton at his best as he glorifies the fairy tale for being Truer than true. "Here I am only trying to describe the enormous emotions which cannot be described. And the strongest emotion was that life was as precious as it was puzzling. It was an ecstasy because it was an adventure; it was an adventure because it was an opportunity. The goodness of the fairy tale was not affected by the fact that there might be more dragons than princesses; it was good to be in a fairy tale."

While Chesterton's understanding of true fairy tales was enchanting, he should have warned his readers more about the difference between fairy tale and fantasy. It is very important to distinguish the proper delight in fairy tales from fantasy. A fairy tale is a fantastic story that is true. A fantasy is a fantastic version of reality that is deeply untrue. A fantasy is a fiction that pretends to be true. A fairy tale is a fiction that we know to be true.

You will say I am being paradoxical in a Chestertonian way. I admit it. One of my weaknesses is, if not to be a Chestertonian mannequin, then to be a Chesterton manqué. Forgive my weakness and allow me to explain: a fairy tale is a magical myth that we know is a fabrication. It is a story that mysteriously incarnates and communicates the truth. A fantasy, on the other hand, is a fabrication about real life that we wish were true, and that we actually attempt to make come true. We try, if you like, to become the fairy godmothers in our own self authored fairy tales.

My own example was my fantasy of bucolic Anglicanism. I held in my mind a romanticized version of a George Herbert Anglicanism. It was my own fantasyland Anglican world, and what a lovely fantasy it was! Furthermore, in the 1980s it was actually possible to become an Anglican country parson. Ten years after going to England I became the vicar of two ancient churches on the Isle of Wight. Each night I meandered over to the church, rang the bell and said Evening Prayer. I drank beer in the pub, lunched with the Lord of the Manor and even wrote a few poems.

The fantasy was all the more seductive because it had every appearance of reality. It was not a pipe dream. As time went on I added another layer of fantasy to my Anglican idyll: I became Anglo-Catholic. I spent time in monasteries and went to Walsingham. I went to India and met Mother Teresa. I liked the people to call me "Father." I even prayed the rosary and liked the Pope much better than the Archbishop of Canterbury. I told people I was "Catholic, but just not Roman Catholic." I was adding fantasy to fantasy as an aging ingénue might lay on yet another layer of makeup.

In *The Catholic Church and Conversion* Chesterton lays out three stages of conversion: Correcting the Falsehoods, Discovering the Truth, and Resisting Conversion. As I became first Anglican, then Anglo-Catholic, I tripped happily through the first two stages, but then the fantasy, like a beautiful bubble radiating a rainbow of colors…burst.

I was in conversation with the Abbot of Quarr Abbey, and without embarrassment explained that I was a Catholic in the Anglican Church. He smiled, "Yes, but we Catholics define Catholicism rather differently than you do. You see, to be a Catholic one needs to follow all the teachings of the Pope."

"But I do!" I protested. "I believe everything in the Catechism. I love Pope John Paul. He's my Pope, too. I do all I can to follow the teachings of the Pope!"

"But one of the teachings of the Pope is that to follow the teachings of the Pope you need to be in full communion with the Pope."

I gulped. If Peter was the Rock, I was between a rock and a hard place.

I resisted. To become a Catholic meant giving up my dream. It meant giving up my country vicarage and my two lovely old churches, my ministry, my people and my vocation. I was newly married by this time with two young children. I hadn't trained for any other career. What would George Herbert do? He'd stay put in his country vicarage and hunker down. Right? What would John Henry Newman do? I knew the answer to that question and looked the other way.

As I read further, I realized that I had not only entered my own personal Anglican fantasy, but that Anglicanism itself was a kind of fantasyland—a form of Christianity that imagined itself to be a branch of the ancient Church when it was, at best, a branch that was cut off from the vine, and we know what happens to such branches. They are thrown on the fire.

As my quest continued, Chesterton's writings hit home again and again. It was not only his wit that captivated and disarmed me, but also his common sense and genial hopefulness. He poked fun at Protestant sects, but he never mocked them. He was humorous about heretics, but he didn't heckle them. He loved fairy tales, but had no time for frivolous fantasy.

I suspect that most converts who have been influenced by Chesterton point to his apologetics, his essays and the brilliance of *The Everlasting Man* and *Orthodoxy*. They generally don't point to Father Brown. But for me, it was the famous priest-detective who helped to push me past stage three of the conversion process—to move from resisting the faith to submitting joyfully to the call to Catholicism.

Father Brown sneaked up on me. I was reading the stories as light entertainment. They were fun. Father Brown was engaging, smart, humble and most of all, real. He was real in the way a stiff walk on a May morning or a swim in a cold lake is real. There was not a whiff of humbug in Father Brown, not a trace of vanity, silliness or the Anglican fantasyland.

I had come to perceive my own Anglican fantasyland with increasingly realistic vision, and was dismayed but not surprised to discover that I was not the only Anglican fantasist. In fact, all the other clergy were fantasists too, but we all had different fantasies. The evangelical charismatic vicar was wrapped up in his fantasy of a church that was full of happy, clappy Christians speaking in tongues and melting over "signs and wonders." The feminist Anglican was in a fantasy campaign for women's ordination and saw the church as a fellowship of female peace and justice warriors. The Anglo-Catholic priest was ensconced in his own fantasy of chasubles, china teacups and choirboys. The left wing vicar in his sandals and rumpled jumper saw the church as the religious face of socialism. The promotion of fair trade coffee and tea was his fantasy of faux Franciscanism. Meanwhile the ambitious clerical social climber was following his fantasy of becoming the dean of a cathedral or a bishop or even becoming the Queen's High Almoner or a Chaplain to the Chapel Royale.

In the midst of all this fantasy, Father Brown in his soutane, saturno and rotund figure was a representative of reality. Although he was a fiction, there was nothing fantastical about him. He was salt of the earth and down to earth. He was common sense incarnate. Chesterton may have created the most wildly unreal figures in *The Napoleon of Notting Hill* and *The Man Who Was Thursday* but Father Brown was real, and it was his crisp and curt reality that helped to burst the bubble of my own, admittedly rather eccentric Anglican fantasy.

Father Brown is not a fairy tale character, but he functions like one. Like Merlin, Gandalf or Dumbledore, Father Brown wields an almost magical power as part and parcel of his patriarchy. He is the old man, the mentor, the source of wit and wisdom and the one who sees through the lies with clarity and charity. He is the one who asks the right questions so that we can discover the right answers. In every case Father Brown punctures pomposity, unveils vanity and sees through the fantasies, fabrications and fictions that always accompany crime.

It was therefore the true fairy tales of the Father Brown stories that helped to bring me out of the fantasyland of the Church of England into the reality of Catholicism.

In a sense, that first arrival in Oxford was symbolic of my foray into the world of Anglicanism. At the heart of Oxford was the St. Giles' fair—which was a kind of Vanity Fair. Somehow it came to symbolize for me the fantasy at the heart of Anglicanism. On becoming a Catholic that fantasy, like St. Giles' fair, vanished overnight.

Cardinal Newman experienced the same thing. In *Difficulties of Anglicans* he described how Anglicans created a fantasy that their church was the ancient and original church. He says they are "as men who have fallen in love with pictures of knights in romance who do battle for high dames whom they have never seen." They are entranced by their fantasy "but at length, either the force of circumstances or some unexpected accident dissipates it; and, as in fairy tales, the magic castle vanishes, the spell is broken, and nothing is seen but the wild heath, the barren rock, and the forlorn sheep-walk…So it is with us as regards the Church of England, when we look in amazement on that we thought so unearthly, and find so common-place or worthless."

But Newman would agree that the fantasy was not all wasted. It was a beautiful dream that set us on the quest. It was not wrong to look for the fantasy castle, for when the magic castle vanished we saw not only the wild heath and the barren rock, but also the rock on which the Church was built, and that Church was not a magic castle, but a sure stronghold and fortress, for is not the Vatican is a little walled city with the Castle of the Archangel on the edge of its ramparts?

That reality stands in Rome even today as a sign of that castle that draws and enchants us like every other magic castle, except that it really exists, and is not only our fortress and defense but also our everlasting home.

THE MYSTERIOUS WAY

By Arthur Livingston

A

S WAS THE CASE WITH CHESTERTON, a rumor perpet-
uated by some legal documents and verbal testimony
suggests that I was born in a Norwegian hospital in
Chicago, and Norwegians in some sense haunted much of
my childhood, as you will learn anon. According to the paper
trail, I entered the world seven years and several weeks after
Chesterton shuffled off his mortal coil. Also, my parents told
me so, and I can lick any man in the house who denies it; or, I
could at one time. Fighting for truth gets into the blood. Were
the non-metaphorical war fought in my youth a just one, I
would probably have been, like every male in my father's family
for three generations, a military man—a high percentage career military personnel; but even as a child, I cringed at a film
like *Thirty Seconds Over Tokyo*, in which people were to rejoice
at bombing civilians. Yet I have never doubted the wisdom
of a strong militia defense. Most of the women in my family

married military officers as well. The role of protector is apparently highly developed in my family.

My earliest memories began at age three while living in the genuinely Southern part of Florida, the Gulf panhandle, near the Alabama border. From the beginning, then, my life shaped itself into paradoxes. My strongest memory apart from my family started with feeling a deep, numinous desire as I wandered about an enormous manicured lawn full of pinecones. Somewhere nearby must have been pine trees, but I do not remember them. Many years later I learned that I was walking on the grounds of a Catholic seminary in the space adjacent to our home. Although it had nothing to do with my later conversion, the providential nature of a small boy desiring he knew not what in that setting surely means something. Mysterious ways, indeed.

After my father's discharge from naval service, he, my mother, and I became part of what has increasingly been called the Southern diaspora. Because of continuing poverty in the South, droves of Southerners reluctantly moved north to work, but many did not leave their culture behind them. My maternal grandparents were part of the first wave in the 1920s. They scrimped so that my mother could attend a Lutheran grammar school and thus exempt her from the compulsory state indoctrination of the public institutions, i.e. public school. To my chagrin, I found myself semi-imprisoned in these places from 1949 to 1961. I have regretted every day of the experience.

My religious education was as pragmatic as something out of Dewey. I would have been a Methodist like my father, but that would have required a little boy crossing an arterial street without a stoplight. On the other hand, I could amble to the local Lutheran church, with only a couple of allies on the way. That it was an evangelical Lutheran church that believed in its own interpretation of scripture more than in the faith of the Apostles did not seem to bother anyone. We were all happy; we were all one big Protestant family after all. When I eventually put two and two together I left, but the irony was that my parents turned a little Southern boy (as I then was) over to Norwegians from Minnesota to foster his religious education. Head-scratching stuff.

Luckily, under those circumstances, they still taught basics of the faith unless they went out of their way to attack Catholicism, which was more of a ritual than real vituperation. On the good side, they made me memorize much of Luther's *Smaller Catechism*. Most certainly, because the odder features of Luther's thought never arose, the doctrines taught us were mostly sound, although the faith was severely truncated, I was to learn in retrospect. Pastor Munson was a fine Christian gentleman of the separated brethren. After I had become completely engrossed in the first chapter of the Gospel according to St. Luke at age twelve, I asked Dr. Munson what Luther thought about the Virgin Mary. When he told me the truth, that Luther venerated her, I became internally upset that we were never taught that. Also, it seemed that whenever I went to the Scriptures after somebody tried to present a proof text, I discovered that far too often in context these private opinions were entirely wrong. This was the train of thought that followed from discovering that church's internal contradictions, and they made me throw in the towel on Protestantism when I was fourteen.

I had tasted what C.S. Lewis called joy on that seminary lawn at three; I had taken a putty knife and stabbed it repeatedly into a concrete wall when I was eight crying and saying "I want it, I want it." And then at fourteen, unbeknownst to anybody, I fell in love with Mary, even though by that time I was not sure I believed in God.

In my family's home, we presented one face to the world and another to ourselves. Usually that kind of behavior masks something ominous, but not in our enclave. We were consciously, even self-consciously, Southern, wanting to hang on to every fragment of a life we could only retain with effort. I imagine, but do not know, that this was happening to hundreds of thousands of other folks of the southern diaspora. In my home, when we shut our door and were together, all that happened there smacked far more of Savannah, Georgia, than of anything north of the Mason-Dixon line. I met many such people in my youth, but few have maintained Southern ways into later life. One of my goals still is to remain rooted culturally. As Hank Williams, Jr. put it, "We say sir, and we say ma'am/And if you don't like it, we don't give a damn."

At every opportunity, the world that met me outside tried to undermine faithfulness to anything that smacks of traditional ways; in the case of those with a Southern background, this takes the form of trying to maintain that my people had been slave drivers and quite inconsistently that they were also ignorant fools. Any stick I have discovered is good enough to try to beat a Southerner or a Catholic; protecting myself was good training. Every aspect of my people's ways was considered an object of ridicule. Fortunately for me, not until I was over forty years old did I even consider the motives of the ridiculers as anything but being envious, and that happened because I really knew what they thought, if that is the correct word, was untrue.

Something antithetical, and also paradoxical, was to enter my life eleven days after I first slogged my way to high school. In the review section of the Sunday supplements in our newspaper, I learned of a new book published that week and then spent the following Saturday hurrying to Marshall Field's to purchase a copy. The very next day, that same supplement published a second review of the volume, this time scathing. The party line had apparently changed within the week. The object of what amounts to a retraction was Jack Kerouac's *On the Road*, which is doubtless the most misunderstood novel in American letters. In truth, it is a cautionary tale about a road not to take. Dean is, as our narrator finally learns, "a rat." Beware of false prophets. If one reads the corpus of Kerouac's writings, he has created one vast cycle that begins and ends in the Catholic Church. Just as much as *Brideshead Revisited*, America's Sebastian Flyte writes the Dulouz legend. Not Evelyn Waugh. Sebastian. What if Sebastian had written about his experience? That is the real essence of what Kerouac is about, and hardly anyone has still noticed, it seems. In short order, I became a cautious bohemian from my Kerouac experience, and an even more self-conscious Southern aesthete from reading Thomas Wolfe. The ridiculous reaction against Wolfe, the one that proves repeatedly that these people are empty, is most likely the product of emasculated critics who learned everything they know about literature in school, and thus have no real opinions or they would never come to one that attempts to discredit a literary giant (no pun intended) like Wolfe.

Nothing shook my agnostic aestheticism for several years until I became involved with a subset of older bohemians, with whom I had pounded the table in argumentative delight for several years already. Several of us formed for a few years what I referred to in later years as the Confederate Beatniks. We all had southern backgrounds; we all wrote imaginative literature; all but me had Catholic formation. This connection became the catalyst that led me to the Church. Also, an occasional guest at our little soirees was the rector of the most sky-high Anglican Church in Chicago, the buckle of the so-called biretta belt. Many, if not most, of our discussions would turn to religion.

Many of the people peripheral to our gang were Catholics from nearby DePaul University and, as a group, they convinced me that I would get an honest shake if I switched to DePaul from the somewhat Marxist joint I had been attending. DePaul was then still openly Catholic, and I arrived just in time to still be required to take five courses in Thomistic philosophy, four of them from Dominicans—one of the best times in my life. Not once, however, did I hear the name Chesterton mentioned by any of the faculty; but the bohemian Catholics close to me mentioned the name. Almost on a daily basis, or so it seems.

Many times one of my pals would say something like, "Livingston, have you read any Chesterton yet?" "Hey, what's stopping you from reading *Orthodoxy*?" "Get that 'art for art's sake' nonsense out of your life and read some Chesterton." Finally, one cold day after a final exam, I trundled off to the DePaul library and took out *Alarms and Discursions* for the sole reason that it was the first volume alphabetically in the card catalog.

That impulsive move took place in December 1964. By the vernal equinox, I had downed twenty titles and was asking the rector for instruction. The clincher, as it is for many, was *The Everlasting Man*. Here is where Chesterton provides compelling answers to that most basic question, "What think you of Christ?" One of the older men in our group recapitulated GKC's argument one night, stripping GKC's argument to the bone. Before we got into it, though, I had joked about Plato by saying that although I loved reading and studying Plato, I do get tired of others saying, "Yes, Socrates; you are right." After he re-presented Chesterton's argument in a succinct manner I said, "Yes, Chesterton; you are right."

All early history looks forward to Christ; all subsequent history looks back to Him. All sanity is a matter that maintains a rational balance, perhaps a balancing act, between two sides of a paradox: Start with any idea or any object. All truth is relative—relative, that is, to one central truth. This man called God. The logic is quite different than Aristotle's. It does not contradict it, but is, to use the square of opposition, its contrary. That in itself is paradox. Finally, a thought once thought cannot be unthought. Christ remains the center of history because the argument Chesterton offers cannot be refuted.

Like Chesterton, under influence of Fr. Hildebrand (that really was the rector's name), I became an Anglo-Catholic, even what is sometimes called an Anglo-Papalist, for decades. (Consult the architecture of Ralph Adams Cram.) The lure of Donne, George Herbert, Thomas Traherne Swift, Dr. Johnson, the young John Henry Newman, C.S. Lewis, and I would add the first two-thirds of Chesterton's career—these had too strong ahold of me to bring me yet all the way to Rome. Like all Anglo-Catholics, I was convinced of my Catholicism until it was proven otherwise. Only after finally being hit as with a two-by-four that, because of the nature of its modernist politicking, the Episcopal Church was not catholic, and that Canterbury had been the one who strayed from Christ, not Rome, did I finally enter the Catholic Church at the age of 57. And my wife, then in the thirty-first year of our marriage, thank God, decided to enter with me.

I am aware, as is common, that when looking back at our lives we can readily see that the hand of Providence had guided all along, drawing straight with crooked lines, as that other bastion of Orthodoxy, St. Athanasius, has truly said. I pray that this old sinner meets with some approval at his particular judgment, although I know damned (oops, I don't mean that) well that I will need at least a few swift kicks in the pants before all is over. At least that is the best I can hope for. Sure beats the alternative.

But there it is: Without Luther I would not have had childhood spiritual training; without the South I would not have had her true culture; without bohemia I would not have had an artistic and intellectual training ground; and without the synthesis of all of them in our little Confederate bohemia, I would not have been led to Catholicism; and also without all of them, I would never have even heard of Gilbert Chesterton for a good many years. And it was Chesterton who led me finally to say that I was a Catholic in a conversion that was akin to that of a C.S. Lewis or T.S. Eliot—or even akin to GKC until 1922.

Oh, by the way, rereading *The Thing*, one of his few overtly Roman Catholic books, was the last ingredient that took me all the way to Rome. Thank God for Gilbert Keith Chesterton.

GOD AND CHESTERTON AT YALE

By Leah Libresco

I SPENT THREE YEARS WAITING TO READ the second chapter of G.K. Chesterton's *The Man Who Was Thursday*.

The trouble was, I'd managed to read the first chapter without knowing the source. A classmate at my high school submitted the first chapter of the book to our school literary journal, and his plagiarism wasn't caught. Neither the student editors, nor our faculty advisor, nor (as far as I know) any reader of the magazine recognized Chesterton's dueling poets.

I loved what I thought was a short story, and I asked the boy who submitted it to tell me if he ever wrote any more of it. (I also told him that it felt more like it was set in England than America—he had changed the place names to cover his tracks). From then till graduation, I asked him every couple of months if he had written any more, even as a draft, that I could read. So I guess God set me on as his guilty conscience. Still, he never 'fessed up.

I was hooked on the story when I fell in love with Syme, Chesterton's "poet of order." I was an atheist, a rationalist, a person who read works on higher dimensional topology for fun, someone who liked to know the hidden causes of everything and bring them to light. But the one thing I wasn't was a reductionist.

In the opening debate of *The Man Who Was Thursday*, Syme rejects the idea that knowing and ordering the world is a matter of reducing it to something tame and mastered. He sees us as navigating the world, not commanding it.

I had a similar sense of the marvelous givenness of the world, even if I had no sense of the Giver. Mathematics was something I understood as received—it was a series of truths that we discovered, but could not create and recreate as it suited us. Morality was the same way. The reason to uncover these laws was to become conformed to them, not to overturn them.

It wasn't until I was in college, attending one of my debating circle's weekly gatherings, that I heard Chesterton's words again, as one of my classmates quoted Syme's riposte to the anarchist's claim that order was unpoetical, that trains running on tracks are unromantic:

> "The rare, strange thing is to hit the mark; the gross, obvious thing is to miss it. We feel it is epical when man with one wild arrow strikes a distant bird. Is it not also epical when man with one wild engine strikes a distant station? Chaos is dull; because in chaos the train might indeed go anywhere, to Baker Street or to Bagdad. But man is a magician, and his whole magic is in this, that he does say Victoria, and lo! it is Victoria."

I thrilled to hear it, and then, a little later, I smelled a rat. I didn't believe that my college classmate had happened to run across that high schooler's short story. I tracked down the citation from my debating friend and headed straight to the library.

I read the whole gripping story, from the election of the new Thursday to lead the anarchists to Scotland Yard's clandestine recruitment of secret policemen to stymie the forces of chaos. The end, with its pageant of creation, was harder for me to make sense of, but I liked the whole thing too much to quibble with it.

The debate group that had led me back to the book had a habit of recruiting members in a Chestertonian way. In addition to our actual organization, we had a number of front groups, all designed to recruit people who would be excellent members of our debating circle, but might not realize that they ought to seek it out. We had the Yale Transhumanist Society, the Yale Shakespeare Project (which ensnared my eventual husband), and, most outrageously, the Objectivist Study Group at Yale.

It wasn't Randians we were interested in so much as ex-Randians. So the Objectivist Study Group existed as a sort of carnivorous pitcher plant. We promised discussion of Ayn Rand's thought and works, but the upperclassmen running the group really intended to talk attendees out of her philosophy.

As for what we intended to talk them into… that was a matter of debate. And debate was an every Thursday night affair.

It was at those debates that I started to hear Christian ideas articulated deeply for the first time. I had been used to encountering Christians primarily on TV or in the news: the people who wanted to require prayer in schools, who opposed teaching evolution, who hated questions and curiosity.

The people I met on the floor of my debate group were curious in both senses of the word. Like many undergraduates, they were trying on personae, many of them a little outrageous, a little full of Chestertonian brio.

I wasn't any different. While one classmate gave a 20-minute stemwinder on the virtues of Mary (at a debate decidedly not on that topic), I exhorted the body to be Kantian-Stoics like me, acting out of pure duty, uncorrupted by a desire to be treated well or liked by others.

We cross-examined each other at debates lasting till 2am, during walks around campus, sometimes even in some poor professor's seminar if two of our group ended up registered for the same class. By the time I graduated, I didn't believe Catholicism was true, but I had begun to find it lovely and coherent. And I was much better read than I'd been when I started school.

Mere Christianity by C.S. Lewis made Christianity seem reasonable to me. *Orthodoxy* by Chesterton made it seem dangerous. Lewis proposed the Lunatic, Liar, Lord trilemma to those who consider Christ simply a good teacher. Chesterton suggests that perhaps the first and final horns of the trilemma aren't so far apart—at least not from our starting, not-as-sane-as-we-think perspective.

For someone who had spent freshman year staring at the ceiling of my dorm room, puzzling out my advanced fractal geometry proofs by figuring out what a fractional dimension looked like, it was wasn't so strange to see sense in Chesterton's praise of paradox in Orthodoxy:

> Christianity is centrifugal: it breaks out. For the circle is perfect and infinite in its nature; but it is fixed for ever in its size; it can never be larger or smaller. But the cross, though it has at its heart a collision and a contradiction, can extend its four arms for ever without altering its shape. Because it has a paradox in its centre it can grow without changing. The circle returns upon itself and is bound. The cross opens its arms to the four winds; it is a signpost for free travellers.

One year after graduating, on Palm Sunday, back at Yale for an alumni debate, God granted me a collision, an apocalypse (in the full Greek meaning of unveiling), and invited me to do what I'd always wanted: to become fully conformed to reality, docile to morality, reshaped by beauty.

My conversion was least remarkable to the members of my debate group. Every other debater in my year who had stuck with our group till graduation had already converted to either Catholicism or Eastern Orthodoxy. I was bringing up the rear. We had a reputation on campus as "the Catholic factory." Something about seeking truth in friendship tended to do that.

My husband, Alexi, wised up faster than me, and was received into the Church from Anglicanism in the Eastertide of his sophomore year. In the spring of his senior year, I was in town to see Arcadia, and was genially press-ganged by him to help him load in sets and furniture for his stage adaptation of *The Man Who Was Thursday*.

He gave me a backstage tour of his props (paper rolled up for dynamite, a cruciform lamp) and his stage tricks (how to have Sunday escape in a hot air balloon onstage?). That fall, we had our first date. One year after that, we were married, embarking on what Chesterton's Michael Moon calls in Manalive, "a duel to the death, which no man of honour should decline."

THE ESCAPE FROM PAGANISM

By Stuart McCullough

I HAD JUST FINISHED A GAME OF SNOOKER with friends in the centre of Cardiff and was walking back to the bus stop to go home, I heard a shout of, "He's one of them! Get him!" I started to run for the bus as fast as I could with four or five black chaps in hot pursuit. I jumped on the bus, as it pulled off, I looked through the window to see my pursuers being left behind and noticed a "National Front" sticker on the window (The National Front were at this time a right wing political party that wanted the UK for white people only). I peeled the sticker off the window and took it home with me.

I wasn't from a particularly nationalistic or racist family, but a month or so before I had been to a birthday party where a fight took place between a couple of my friends who happened to be white, with a couple of black gate-crashers. When the party ended the gate-crashers had returned with 20 or 30 of their friends and a small riot ensued. The only person arrested was one of my friends who was of mixed race. Most of my friends who were followers of Cardiff City Football Club lived on the opposite side of the city from me and so we would meet up in the town centre. When I say followers, I mean we attended the matches and took any opportunity we could find to get involved in fights. After the incident at the party, it became harder to meet up due to continued threats and possible attacks.

I grew up on a poor housing estate in the east side of Cardiff. My Mum and Dad divorced when I was about 8 and my brother was 5. Although my Mum, Jane, remarried a decent chap called Tony, not having our Dad around affected my brother and me. Tony was brave to take on my Mum with her two stroppy sons.

I didn't really know anything about the National Front, except that they seemed to be rather violent and they didn't like black people. As I was having trouble with a violent black gang at this time, I identified with them. I wrote to them. They sent me their newspaper and magazines, and booklets etc. And despite coming from a fairly left-wing family, one of my uncles even being an activist in the Trotskyite Socialist Workers Party, a lot of what the National Front (NF) said at the time seemed to make sense, and so I joined. Around this time, I also picked up *The Napoleon of Notting Hill* and *The Man Who Was Thursday*. So along with all the political books I was reading, I was also reading Chesterton, and then I moved on to Belloc.

About a year or so later, I went to visit Belfast, where my father comes from, for the first time. It felt like home. My mother had moved to Cardiff when she was a teenager and didn't have a strong sense of belonging, and my Belfast-born father had spent most of his life in England and Wales. However, my Nan would talk about "Home," and "Home" was Belfast! I loved it, the people were friendly, and my family name was not alien there like it was in Cardiff. I took photos of the

McCullough Bakery and then the McCullough Butchers and so on. I even met McCulloughs who were not related to me, not something that had ever happened to me in Wales. I visited my Nan's stepfather in the house where my father was born, in Ebor Street. I had a really great time, I made some good friends with some local members of the National Front and decided to move there. At that point, the National Front was campaigning for an independent Ulster, partly on the idealistic grounds that Ulster was a nation and thus deserved its' independence, but also from the pragmatic point of view, as a way of solving "The Troubles." Generally speaking, Catholics wanted a United Ireland while Protestants wanted to be part of the United Kingdom. The Catholics did not want to be ruled by London while the Protestants did not want to be ruled by Dublin. An Independent Ulster would have at least stopped both London and Dublin rule, thus we hoped giving both sides of the community something to be content with. Especially in the Catholic areas it was a huge uphill struggle as the National Front has always been seen as a Unionist party. When I stood in the local elections in East Belfast in the late 1980s, we had leaflets freely delivered to every voter as part of our campaign. We even printed the ones for the small Catholic enclave of Short Strand on green paper in an attempt to win Catholic supporters over to our idea!

Then there was a split in the National Front, and I went with the International Third Position (ITP) side of the argument. The split revolved around one individual issuing a public apology on behalf of the National Front to the Jewish Community for anything that the NF had ever done to offend them. I felt he did not have the authority to do this. I was also moving away from blaming non-white immigrants for the downfall of Europe and was now blaming what I would have called "International Jews" for everything. We launched our own local magazine, *Ulster Dawn*, a strange mixture of Ulster Nationalism, anti-Zionism and Paganism. I was, all this time, continuing to read Chesterton and Belloc, despite living in the staunchly Protestant Ballysillan area of North West Belfast. I remember going home from Belfast Central Library one day in the back of a loyalist run bus route, with a copy of Belloc's *Essays of a Catholic Layman in England* in my bag. And yet, becoming Catholic would not have occurred to me. I was a Vegan, heavily involved in the Animal Rights Movement and was even going out on Saturdays protesting against fox and stag hunting as a hunt-saboteur. I was also a Pagan, traveling to ancient sites such as Newgrange in Ireland and Stonehenge in England for the summer and winter solstices. At one point the police had put an exclusion zone around Stonehenge to stop Druids, Pagans and New Age hippies from descending on the site and causing chaos. I managed to avoid the cordon, run across the field and actually touch one of the stones before the police arrested me. I spent a few hours in the police cells, trying to explain that under some United Nations charter or other that I had a right to practice my "religion." I was released without charge.

On arrival back in Belfast after a trip home to Wales, I found a note through my door which said "Stuart McCullough, please call Captain — at the local RUC (Police) station." At first, I thought it was a joke from one of my friends, but I phoned the number. The Police Officer asked me to come to the Station and reassured me that I wasn't in any trouble. I went to see him and he sat me down and he told me rather formally that "We have reason to believe that the Provisional IRA are planning to kill you." He didn't know why. Did the IRA want rid of me because of my political activities? Had some British "spook" just said this to the police to put me out of the country? Or what else?

I didn't know. I thanked him and asked could I have the form to apply for a personal firearms license.

A few months later, a friend informed me that somebody from a Loyalist Paramilitary group wanted to talk to me, which made me wonder if the Loyalist side was going to threaten me, too. I started to think that it might be time to move to a safer environment and thus headed off to London for the time being. Around about this time one of my political associates had agreed to meet me in the tea room of the London Church he attended, after Mass, to discuss some projects we were working on. I have no doubt now that his intention was to get me to go to Mass, as knowing me quite well, he knew I would be early. When I arrived at St. Joseph's, it was raining and I was early, so I ducked in and sat in the back pew. I of course had no idea what was going on, so I just kept my head down and tried not to be noticed. I think the only part of the Mass that stood out for me was what I now know to be the Consecration, as there was quite a bit of bell ringing and everybody's head went down, as it was an Old Rite Mass. They had Exposition of the Blessed Sacrament after Mass, but I didn't know what this was either. In the tea-room afterwards, I rather foolishly asked my friend a question. I asked why the chap wearing black and white (cassock and cotta) had put his hand inside his white top to hold and carry out what I now know to be a monstrance rather than just pick it up with his hand. I then received a twenty-five-minute explanation of Transubstantiation, Sacred Vessels, the importance of laymen not touching these things, and why the Old Rite of Mass was better than the New Mass. It gave me much to think about, although not very consciously, as I wasn't really asking out of interest, only out of curiosity.

I was offered a job doing construction work for a political project in Spain. So, I packed a few belongings into a car and with a Polish comrade set off for Valencia. After a harrowing journey, we arrived and I spent the next 18 months or so living in the middle of nowhere, building houses. I was still reading a lot of Chesterton and Belloc and even bought a couple of GKC books in Spanish. The idea of moving to this project was to go back to the land and to put Distributism into practice. Most of those I was working with were traditional Catholics. Having read bits of history about the Spanish Civil War, Isabella La Catholica and Torquemada, the day-to-day reality of Spanish life was a bit of a disappointment.

While visiting the UK for Christmas, I spent some time working in a warehouse in London, with people mostly from former British colonies. Over lunch one day, a chap from Australia told two South African girls who were about to spend Christmas in Wales to speak to me as I was from what he called that "Godforsaken country." I told them a bit about Wales and then one of them said, "It will be strange to stay in a house with people who celebrate Christmas, as we have never done that because we are Jewish." And so, while still talking about Wales I proceeded to explain that Jesus Christ was the Messiah and the Catholic Church was the One True Church, and that they should both join. The Australian chap was totally bowled over and said that he didn't realize that I was a Catholic, to which I replied that I wasn't. He said "No, you definitely are, I was forced to go to a Catholic school by my devout mother, so I know what a Catholic is."

I wasn't as surprised by this as I might have been, because when reading Belloc's *Essays of a Catholic* some time before this incident, I felt Belloc was accusing me of already being a Catholic who just wouldn't admit it. I phoned a friend and asked him to get me "one of those Missals that you take to Church with you on Sunday," which he duly posted to me. I phoned him back after spending a couple of days looking at it to inform him that "No, that's not what I need. I need something else." After a brief discussion as to what I was thinking of, he sent me the Baltimore Catechism, number 4. Just before the following Christmas, on December 16, 1996, I was baptized by Fr. Michael Crowdy, in a small private chapel in Hampshire.

I remember a few days later in Cardiff trying to work out how I would tell my grandmother, a Belfast Protestant, that I had become a Catholic as I did not expect this to go down very well. Before I could do so, she told me the strange story of how her own father had become a Roman Catholic, six months before he died, while she was very young. I laughed, and she said she knew I had done the same, and said I was always just like him.

I was mostly attending Mass at churches and chapels of the Society of St. Pius X. Being the argumentative sort of person that I am, I spent a lot of time reading and arguing about the New Rite Mass versus the Old Rite Mass, and about whether the Society was in schism or not. But then one day, I was lecturing a Falange leader in Madrid, on why he should go to the Old Rite of Mass instead of the New Rite, he just said flatly that he could not see the point of going to church at all. I found that I had less arguments to counter this. I wasn't able to defend the Catholic faith at all, and so changed my reading habits. It wasn't long before I stopped going to the Society of St. Pius X. While I still prefer the Old Rite Mass (as officially sanctioned within the Church), I can stand up and declare the Creed in clear conscience as part of "One, Holy, Catholic, and Apostolic Church."

In the Jubilee year of 2000, I got engaged to my now long-suffering wife. I also decided that year to walk from Toul in France to Rome, following in Hilaire Belloc's footsteps, in part to thank him for his help in my conversion. I hadn't actually read his book *The Path to Rome* at that point, but my fiancée, Clare, did read it and made notes to help me work out the route. She even insisted on buying some maps, which to be honest, I hadn't thought of and wouldn't have bothered with, but she was right! Having walked 800 miles through France, Switzerland and Italy to Rome, and seen Pope John Paul II sitting a few hundred yards from the tomb of St. Peter, the reality of the continuity of the Church in spite of whatever problems and upheavals She may undergo was made very real to me.

For years when asked why I joined the Catholic Church, I would blame Belloc as his rather blunt approach was very clear to me. But it was Chesterton who introduced me to Belloc and it was Chesterton who was quietly working away in the background the whole time. And while I have done the one long walk in thanksgiving to Belloc, I have organized eight annual Chesterton Walking Pilgrimages and distributed tens of thousands of G.K. Chesterton prayer cards. We pray for many intentions on the Pilgrimage, which is a 27-mile one-day walk from St. George's Anglican Church, Notting Hill, London, where GKC was baptized as a baby, to his grave in Shepherds Lane, Beaconsfield. I'm pleased to say that we get answers to prayers and not just blisters.

I must also say that Chesterton stopped me hating Jews. He showed the nonsense of racial theories. He made it clear that Christendom was being destroyed from within, by an "inner ring" as he describes it in *The Man Who Was Thursday*, who "hate life itself." They call themselves liberal, but they hate freedom. They call themselves inclusive but they are elitist. They are doing their best to bring the moral order to ruin. They are anarchists, and they are made up of every race, creed and color, while people of the same race, creed and color are working to uphold the moral order. We need to be at Mass to preserve not only our faith but our culture. We need to say the Rosary daily and read Chesterton's poem *Lepanto*. We need to read and share Chesterton with others, and we need to pray and ask his intercession.

THE ROAD TO ROME BEGAN ON CARBERRY ROAD

By Clark Durant

I T WAS CHILLY OUTSIDE. Autumn was nearly over. Richly colored leaves blew in the wind. Squirrels were preparing for winter. A single street lamp burned on Carberry, a backroad two miles east of downtown Niles, Michigan, a town of twelve thousand nestled in the southwest corner of the state, ten miles north of the law school at The University of Notre Dame.

Carberry Road was not well traveled. On the corner of Carberry and Yankee Street there was a tiny two-story, two-bedroom, freshly painted green farmhouse with one bathroom on the first floor. With our meager savings Susan and I bought that farmhouse in August of 1973. As I sat at my well-worn light tanned oak banker's desk in the little library, night had long fallen. I was reading material for a law school class the next day. My dark wooden chair had a spindled back, an uneven swivel, and a tilt frame that adjusted irregularly. A brass floor lamp from my parents' basement provided the only reading light at night.

An old five-shelf wooden bookcase hugged the wall behind me. It was fully stocked with old favorites, most purchased from one or another used bookshop. Some C.S. Lewis, a few Wodehouse volumes, Hayek, Buckley, Read, Milton Friedman, Jaffa's book on a house divided, an OZ book or two, *Charlotte's Web*, Churchill's *My Early Life*, a couple of Allen Drury novels, Ayn Rand, a U.S. history textbook, Chambers' *Witness*, some reference books, Cash's *Mind of the South*, a Walker Percy novel, a mix of poetry, a volume of Shakespeare, and some recently purchased law books; but nothing by Gilbert Keith Chesterton.

The one double-hung library window was not sealed well and winter's chill seeped through. It did provide, though, a nice view out to the surrounding farmland and to the only house across Carberry, a white clapboard, well-constructed modest colonial with forest green shutters. A tall globe streetlamp from old Chicago lit the small circular pebble stone driveway. We called it "the moon."

In their mid-sixties, Harold Hunziker, a retired landscape architect, and his delightful wife Doris lived in that colonial. Over the three years we lived in the farmhouse Doris prepared many meals for us in her kitchen (I never tired of her strawberry shortcake!), and we often went out for Sunday brunch together. They were our only friends on Carberry Road until later that autumn night.

Susan and I were just beginning our life together. I was 24 and she 26. We had married in June that year in her hometown of Poland, Ohio, in an old stone Presbyterian church. Our newlywed Niles house was perfect for us. My drive was ten miles south to Notre Dame. Susan, who directed the music in high school plays and taught history and government at Buchanan High School, drove only five miles west to her school. She earned $11,000 a year, and I focused on law school.

Is not Notre Dame where all good Presbyterian boys attend law school? Raised a Congregationalist, I was at Notre Dame as a result of an unexpected encounter in New Orleans in May of 1971 with Father Theodore Hesburgh, then President of The University of Notre Dame. I was one of four Tulane University graduating seniors invited to attend a national foundation board dinner at the home of Dr. Herbert Longenecker, the President of Tulane. His majestic white multi-pillared antebellum residence was at the corner of St. Charles Avenue and Audubon Place. Father Ted and I were seated next to each other for dinner at the end of a long mahogany dining room table. That night our rich conversation and his kind invitation led me, a faithful Presbyterian, to apply to Notre Dame's law school. Frankly, this would have been an unthinkable option at an earlier time in my life. Yet this choice changed the whole trajectory of my life. I am grateful, even unto this day.

At law school I encountered faculty with a deep and abiding Catholic faith. An ND lawyer was encouraged to pursue a unique calling for good, to be a person for others, not just a skilled negotiator or talented trial lawyer. I audited courses of Dr. Gerhart Niemeyer, the distinguished graduate professor of political theory, and Joseph W. Evans, the Jacques Maritain scholar. For undergraduates I taught Collegiate Seminar, a great books course. Coming back one day from teaching, my constitutional law professor invited me to what I thought was only lunch. It turned out to be a noon encounter with Jesus in the Eucharist, long before Susan and I were to become Catholic... all, and more, because of a dinner conversation with a Holy

Cross priest who happened to be President of the Catholic university in America. A stanza in G.K. Chesterton's poem *The Arena* describes the place:

> I have seen, where a strange country
> Opened its secret plains about me,
> One great golden dome stands lonely with its golden image,
>   one
> Seen afar, in strange fulfillment,
> Through the sunlit Indian summer
> That Apocalyptic portent that has clothed her with the Sun.

GKC wrote and dedicated *The Arena* to Notre Dame during his 1930 six-week visit to campus to lecture on Victorian literature, a visit that included his presence with Knute Rockne and others at the dedication of Notre Dame's now classic football stadium. The stanza is an apt and beautiful description of the university, and the full poem compares the gladiators of ancient Rome with the young "untroubled" and "untortured" footballers of Notre Dame. I would not discover *The Arena* until many years after my graduation from the law school. In the autumn of 1973 however, I had not even discovered Gilbert Keith Chesterton. I was to meet him that night in a farmhouse on a lonely Carberry Road.

Law school reading assignments for the next few days were completed. It was easily after midnight, but I was not interested in going to bed. Instead I stared at three unread essays sitting in the upper right corner of my desk. My brother Peter had sent these essays to me earlier that week. They were authored by Chesterton. Peter believed they might be a refreshing break from the rigors of the law.

The once widely published writings of an English poet, playwright, essayist, journalist, and amateur illustrator had to be more interesting, thought my brother, than the dry language of the law. So with my dear bride sound asleep and my homework done, I picked up the essays thinking I could skim through them quickly. I laugh now. You don't skim Chesterton like a Petoskey stone skipping across the surface of the Bear River. You jump in and get all wet in the crisp clear waters. With a plunge that night I discovered a new friend in the library of our farmhouse on Carberry Road, Gilbert Chesterton. On my road to Rome he became a companion for life.

Oh, the three essays? They were "In Defense of Rash Vows," "The Twelve Men," and—unbelievably—I can't remember the third! "In Defense of Rash Vows" was so appropriate. Susan and I had exchanged our marriage vows less than five months before. Chesterton wrote: "The man who makes a vow makes an appointment with himself at some distant time or place. The danger of it is that he may not keep the appointment." I never thought of a vow that way, particularly when I was actually making one in that stone church under a blue-sky summer Saturday in Poland, Ohio. But I wish I had. In "Rash Vows" Chesterton critiques a modern age that looks for an out, a retreat, rather than a commitment that lasts. That night on Carberry Road Chesterton told me, "The revolt against vows has been carried on in our day even to the extent of a revolt against the typical vow of marriage." It is most amusing, he said, "to listen to the opponents of marriage on this subject. They appear to imagine that the ideal of constancy was a yoke mysteriously imposed on mankind by the devil, instead of being, as it is, a yoke consistently imposed by all lovers on themselves." Chesterton went on, "It is the nature of love to bind itself, and the institution of marriage merely paid the average man the compliment of taking him at his word. Modern sages offer to the lover, with an ill-flavoured grin, the largest liberties and the fullest irresponsibility; but they do not respect him as the old Church respected him; they do not write his oath upon the heavens, as the record of his highest moment."

Chesterton was on a roll. He knew the ancient wisdom. There must be no retreat from the deepest vows. I loved his closing metaphor. We must leave our ships and travel ashore. It is then that we will turn to witness a "towering flame rise from the harbor announcing that the reign of the cowards is over and a man is burning his ships." The sailor, the lover, who goes ashore, his way for retreat destroyed, will now work to taste the sweeter and richer fruit of a vow well kept, as a battle well fought, a marriage well lived. This was exhilarating stuff to imagine, late one brisk night on Carberry Road.

I then read "The Twelve Men." It was a perfect preface for a law student's appreciation of the jury, the men and women who make it up, and its special role in the framework of a civilized order. A specialist may catalogue the universe, transplant a heart, or compose a symphony, but only twelve ordinary people can determine another man's fate, something much more monumental than the knowledge or skill of the expert. And Chesterton takes the jury of twelve ordinary citizens to point us to the carpenter of Nazareth who changed the whole world, beginning with twelve common men.

I came to appreciate "The Twelve Men" in my Detroit law practice when I pleaded before "the Cs of Battersea" as Chesterton would first describe himself and his peers when selected for a Battersea jury in South London. I too counted on twelve ordinary citizens of Detroit when making my closing argument on behalf of some chap charged by the State for a crime, major or minor. *Nisi Dei gratia, sim* (Except for the grace of God, it might be me). It enhanced my trial preparation and success to think of these jurors as GKC did.

That night in a farmhouse on Carberry Road Gilbert Keith Chesterton introduced me to the gift of paradox. He encouraged me to see the divine in the ordinary. He knew the deeper truth of a thing not in plain sight, but ever so obvious. "One of the four or five paradoxes which should be taught to every infant prattling at his mother's knee is the following: the more a man looks at a thing, the less he can see it, and the more a man learns a thing, the less he knows it," said Chesterton in "The Twelve Men."

Paradox is not just a logician's art. It is every man's tool to understand the real world we inhabit for a short time, and how it shapes our everlasting life. Paradox is a tool so common that a carpenter once used it to explain the depth of our existence. We must die to live, give to receive, and wash the feet of others to lead. The carpenter told us too that we would find the very maker of all things, time and again, fully and forever with us, in the bread and wine, the simplest of elements. Do this in remembrance of me. Ponder that paradox. Ask what rash vow one must take? Way too tired, I could do neither that night. Awake to new things, I went upstairs to bed.

I tiptoed into the darkened bedroom. Trying hard not to wake a sleeping Susan I slipped under the covers beside her. I did not know it then but Chesterton's rash vows, twelve men, and paradoxes, joined with my priceless experiences at Notre Dame and after, would take us both from our little farmhouse on Carberry Road down a very old winding road to Rome, a journey fresh and new every morning. It was a journey to represent the poor and the voiceless, to build schools on the rough streets of Detroit, to know the Everlasting Man who emerged from a cave, and to be at the altar of the Eucharist in a Church established by a carpenter. Susan and I were to travel an open road to...better yet, let GKC tell you where we had arrived.

To an open house in the evening
Home shall men come,
To an older place than Eden
And a taller town than Rome.
To the end of the way of the wandering star,
To the things that cannot be and that are,
To the place where God was homeless
And all men are at home.

Thirty-two years later, Susan and I formally entered the Catholic Church. Father Ted Hesburgh, now in his late eighties and losing his eyesight, flew to Detroit in a Notre Dame plane. He blessed our Cornerstone Schools with a visit. Then in the late afternoon he concelebrated with Adam Cardinal Maida, the Archbishop of Detroit, our first Mass as new Catholics. The constitutional law professor with me at my first encounter with Jesus in the Eucharist so many years before, a gentle man of God, drove to Detroit from South Bend. Other friends and family gathered to be with us.

Gilbert came too. He sat unseen in the next to last row of the Cathedral's pews, his brilliant English blue eyes alive with joy. He chuckled; no, he laughed quietly, and said to no one in particular: "So very simple is the road, that we may stray from it," his voice trailing off. It was quiet now. Barely heard, the angels afar off were singing, "Hark! Laughter like a lion wakes to roar to the resounding plain…" Those assembled saw the Host rising reverently into the air. And as he lowered his head in veneration, Chesterton sang in a whisper with the angels, "And the whole heaven shouts and shakes, for God Himself is born again, and we are little children walking through the snow and rain."

At that moment the voices were heard of the friends who had gathered to celebrate this day with us. They quietly began to say the centurion's plea for us all, "Lord, I am not worthy that you should enter under my roof, but…," and as they finished, "only say the word and my soul shall be healed," Chesterton swiftly scribbled and sketched something on a brown piece of scrap paper pulled from his jacket side pocket. When he rose from the pew to go forward to the altar, his scrap paper was absentmindedly left behind. So too were three pieces of chalk. A child behind the last row looked down to see what the heavy-set man had drawn. She picked up the paper and stared for what seemed an eternity. She saw a serpent crawling away biting its own accursed tail, clearly beaten once more. A King, with sword drawn, stood nearby. And figures, signed of the cross of Christ, seemed to go gaily into the dark. Just then the two concelebrating priests were heard to say to all who had gathered, "Go in peace to love and serve the Lord." The little girl turned the scrap paper over. There in a distinctive hand was drawn the image of a white horse on a hillside. In the same white chalk Chesterton had written what seemed a personal note to Susan and me as one:

> I will go with you,
> As man with God has gone,
> And wander with a wandering star,
> The wandering heart of things that are,
> The fiery cross of love and war
> That like yourself, goes on.

LONGING FOR TERRA FIRMA

By Fr. Spencer J. Howe

*"They wanted to take him into the boat, but
the boat immediately arrived at the shore to
which they were heading"* – JOHN 6:21

I N ORDER TO FULLY APPRECIATE the awesome discovery of the feel of solidity beneath one's feet, it is helpful to imagine the sensation of making landfall after a precarious and life-threatening crossing of the sea. Whatever else might be said about the feeling of standing on *terra firma* it is unmistakably different from the mere *impression* of land. A mirage of solidity hovering over the surface of the water is not solid; nor can one plant a flag or build a home upon a distant scene of *fata morgana*. Christ's coming into the boat of the disciples was effectively—mystically even—their discovery and arrival at the secret port for which they longed. If we are honest with ourselves we too have this shared longing for the solid rock upon

MY NAME IS LAZARUS

which to build our lives. I hope to bear witness to this longing and its fulfilment by sharing my story of conversion to the Catholic Faith and my subsequent path to the Holy Priesthood.

G.K. Chesterton saved me from the unfortunate fate of being a fallen away Catholic. This is, of course, the fate of so many of my contemporaries and compatriots. I would fail in pride and presumption to suggest that I am invincible before the sad and widespread apostasy and blasé non-practicing of the Faith, but Chesterton is for me one of *the* great witnesses to the possibility of final perseverance and rock-steadiness in faith. Long before me, he had discovered in the Orthodoxy professed by the Roman Church a unique fulcrum which could change the world rather than be changed by it, and he energetically put all his weight upon the lever of his journalistic and evangelical career.

I must confess (as Protestants are *not* wont to do!) that I was a fallen away Catholic even before I consciously knew it—*beginning from infancy!* My parents had dutifully carried me to be baptized according to the Rites of the Church one particular Christ the King Sunday. The baptism was valid and efficacious even in the less than inspiring suburban Catholic environs of the mid-1980s. My father, having been raised a Unitarian in Oklahoma, was not at that time baptized into the life of the Trinity and would not be baptized until some years later. (*Spoiler Alert:* Some years after that he would receive Confirmation and Holy Communion shoulder to shoulder with me on December 13, 2001, the day of our common journey home to Catholicism). He had religious curiosities and for a time studied philosophy and even considered ministry of some sort. My mother, on the other hand, was raised in an intensely Catholic Cuban-Flemish home in small town Illinois. She was strongly conditioned and formed by her Catholic upbringing by devout parents and stalwart Benedictine school sisters, even though she came of age in the tumultuous late 60s and early 70s. Thankfully, Catholicism had seeped into her and acted as a preservative against cultural decay, saving her from the degrading slavery of being *merely* a child of her age—as Chesterton's phrase so beautifully has it. The children of that age were flower children, but my mother was somewhat more attune to the lily of St. Joseph at the side altar of St. Anthony of Padua's lovely little church in Atkinson, Illinois.

All of us come from somewhere and are made who we are by the formative experiences of a family of origin and upbringing. My mother was able to sniff out the 'straight stuff' when it came to faith. From what I understand of her itinerary of faith, her religious formation allowed her to weather the storms of one of the more chaotic ages of cultural revolution in recent times, still clinging to her childhood faith. Although she drifted in her college years towards a complacent mediocrity, she could never come to deny the sacramental ground of her being. Like so many others, it was having a family of her own that led her back to practicing Catholicism with *a twitch upon a thread.* Finding a church to get married in and one where she could attend Masses with her family, she actually took formal leave of the Catholic Church only when the crucifix at my baptismal church disappeared one week and a colorful kite appeared hanging in its place. Impelled to seek out authentic Christianity in an age of strange 'local uses' such as the disappearing crucifix act, my parents took refuge in an Evangelical Lutheran community, burgeoning in the wake of the Charismatic Renewal. Other families were doing the same and my parents were in good company. This became home for our family and was essentially the only form of Christianity to which I was exposed. The only exception being my semi-regular encounters with the

Catholicism of my maternal grandmother's world to which I would eventually owe my conversion. It was an altogether positive sort of Christianity which I came to experience and for that I am ever grateful.

Growing up I began to intuit a basic truth that could perhaps be stated as simply as this: *if life with God is hard, life apart from Him is futile and hopeless.* Our Lord had said as much, "In the world you will have trouble, but take courage, I have conquered the world" (John 16:33). Raised in a prayerful and God-fearing family, I was given an ability to see this gift of Christ's victory as something offered *to me*, a sort of bedrock upon which I could ground my life. Even before reaching high school I began to experience an unquenchable desire to understand my faith. Like the wise man building his house on rock in the Lord's parable, I wanted to discover the solid ground upon which I would be able to anchor my life to stand even through the storms that I knew would come.

When I eventually made a decision to become Catholic in 2001 as a freshman in high school, I was taken with learning about the solidity and depth of the Catholic Tradition: its history, its saints, its theology and wisdom tradition. I found a sound teacher of the fundamentals of Catholicism and was captivated. In addition to my parents who taught me the importance of prayerfully seeking truth in religion, my maternal grandmother and a few joyful priests and women religious that I came to know impelled me to delve into the rich Catholic patrimony that I was only vaguely familiar with but nonetheless enchanted by. My mother had found her way back onto Catholic terra firma in 1999 and proceeded to usher many across the bridge to a Catholic sacramental life flowing from the altar of sacrifice. My father, always guided by an active mind and intellectual appetite, also discovered his way home. Likewise, my sister and brother-in-law and now numerous other family friends. It was a glorious and humbling homecoming for some lapsed Catholics; discovery of a new homeland for those raised outside the Church. Seen with a time-lapse camera this migration might appear almost like a mass movement if not for the reverse taking place with ever more alarming rapidity: leave-taking of the Church that seems to be accelerating, at least if one gives credence to the mainstream media and certain 'experts' on demographic trends. But what are they finding as they follow the sign to the *Egress* of the Ancient Church? Freedom in self-actualization or boredom unto empty despair?

If the Catholic Faith is foundational and substantial, it is so by contrast with the world which is shifting, inconstant and (in one of Chesterton's favorite phrases) topsy-turvy. Inspired by Jesus' parable of the *wise man building his house on rock*, at a time in my life where I was seeking solid ground for the foundation upon which my life would stand, I discovered precisely what Chesterton discovered in Catholicism: *solid ground*. Why settle for less than this? A whole generation is preferring the shapeless and shifting existence of life at sea, bailing a sinking lifeboat, or worse, drowning in a sea of mire and pain as the barque of Peter keeping its homeward course passes by.

One of the most essential things that the Church provides is stability. Peter's being likened by Christ to a rock gets at this same basic truth. The Editors at MacMillan of Chesterton's *The Catholic Church and Conversion*—one of my personal favorites of GK's volumes—noted this fact in their introduction to his account of conversion:

> The Catholic Church is reality. If a distant mountain may be mistaken for a cloud by many, but is recognized for a stable part of the world (its outline fixed and its quality permanent)

by every sort of observer, and among these especially by men famous for their interest in the debate, for their acuteness of vision and for their earlier doubts, the overwhelming presumption is that the thing seen is a piece of objective reality. Fifty men on shipboard strain their eyes for land. Five, then ten, then twenty, make the land-fall and recognize it and establish it for their fellows. To the remainder, who see it not or who think it a bank of fog, there is replied the detail of the outline, the character of the points recognized, and that by the most varied and therefore convergent and convincing witnesses—by some who do not desire that land should be there at all, by some who dread its approach, as well as those who are glad to find it, by some who have long most ridiculed the idea that it was land at all—and it is in this convergence of witnesses that we have one out of the innumerable proofs upon which the rational basis of our religion reposes.

Man is not made to live on the water, that is why he becomes seasick more often than he becomes *landsick*. Man is made to live his life in keeping with reality, as it is, not as he might imagine or prefer it to be. It is a blinding delusion that reality—nature itself even—does not define a thing; that what a thing *is in itself* is more a suggestion than a given. For all the images that can be used for the Church, I think these lines from the forward to Chesterton's 1922 *The Catholic Church and Conversion* really point to what made Chesterton's conversion so satisfying and definitive. Once one has set feet on solid ground, there is no going back to life as it was before. That would be like exchanging the firm foundation beneath one's house for quicksand, quite a disappointing trade.

For me the reason to convert was based on my surmising that Catholic ground was sound and permanent, not shaky and shifting. Fads and fancies ebb and flow but the permanent truths that Catholicism stood for and valiantly defended drew my young heart, my mind and imagination. I was made for what this world could not offer and so I had to allow Christ into the little dinghy of my solitary and individual existence to lead me to the solid banks along the Tiber. I was made for absolute truth, not the changeable relativism which lures and beckons like the siren's song sounding from the citadel of a castle mirage—mere fata morgana—on the sea. Joseph Cardinal Ratzinger, on the eve of his election to the office of the Papacy in the spring of 2005 saw as much: "How many winds of doctrine have we known in recent decades, how many ideological currents, how many ways of thinking. The small boat of the thought of many Christians has often been tossed about by these waves—flung from one extreme to another...Today, having a clear faith based on the Creed of the Church is often labeled as fundamentalism. Whereas relativism, that is, letting oneself be 'tossed here and there, carried about by every wind of doctrine', seems the only attitude that can cope with modern times" (Joseph Cardinal Ratzinger, Mass *Pro Eligendo Romano Pontifice*, May 18, 2005). I remember hearing these words for the first time and having them resonate not only with right reason but with my experience of having come to embrace the Church's Creed in all of its staggering beauty, elegance and weightiness of demands.

I discovered at a young age, which our often condescending and coddling culture does not take seriously, that I was made to live upon the firm ground of reality. I made a decision for Catholicism as Chesterton had made a decision for it before and earlier converts before him. What I am certain of is that Chesterton bore witness to the truth of the solidity of Catholicism in a way that I could understand and follow suit. Through the vicissitudes that mark the modern age and with the shaking down of half-way houses and pseudo-stability of life at sea, the Church still beckons us home. And homeward we must carry on.

One of the ports-of-call of my early Catholic years was a pilgrimage to Merrie England with the American Chesterton Society in 2004. It was a decisive moment to take a step out on my own, apart from my parents. As our group coalesced as a band of pilgrims not only to Canterbury but to Beaconsfield and Fleet Street, too, Chesterton and his companions came alive to us in our coach bus conversations, pub sessions, cultural excursions and daily Masses. We met many of Chesterton's friends and disciples in a land of people who have largely forgotten their own prophet. Quite humorously, one historic pub reserved our tables for the *G.K. Chesterfield Party*. In the laughter and levity, in the staggering depth of history, in the beauty evoked by places immortalized by Chesterton's pen, and in all the friends we made along the way it was evident that this American pilgrimage had made landfall on a strange island but also a place that was somewhat *familiar*, even if new to most of us. There were special graces waiting for each of us. Although our focus was on Chesterton we could not help but hear about the terrible upheaval of Catholicism that had taken place beginning in the sixteenth century. As my young heart came face-to-face with the staggering truth that men my age had risked all to pursue studies for Holy Orders on the continent only to return as clandestine priest apostles who were hunted and dismembered for love of Christ, I began to sense a growing question emerging deep within. How could they have believed that the English Channel was worth crossing in order to shore up the stability of the ancient faith and win back lapsed souls to the Sacraments?

It was in the act of climbing down into a priest hole—a hidden chamber specially made for a hunted priest to hide as a house was searched by the authorities—that I came to discover the reality of a call upon which I too could risk all. There in the close quarters of the secret priest hole at Oxburgh Hall, a recusant manner house in Norfolk, I discovered that the gift of stability in faith was not for me to enjoy alone. The sense of conviction and purpose which I felt in that cramped and hallowed hiding place was something which I could not hide from. I had been found by God; I had been searched out; I was being summoned to answer a call to lay down my life for the flock of Christ and to help them experience the stability I had discovered in Catholicism. When I was ordained a Catholic priest on May 25, 2013, it was lying prostrate upon the polished marble sanctuary of the Cathedral and National Shrine of Saint Paul that I felt the whole stability of *the Catholic Thing* beneath me, and having been overshadowed by the Holy Spirit together with my classmates with whom I was ordained to go on mission for souls, I felt the firm ground beneath me and like Lazarus I stood and walked, wrapped in a linen alb and called forth into newness of life and service. *My name is Lazarus and I live.*

CLASSIC

By Bishop James Conley

I WAS A TYPICAL SUBURBAN 1970S TEENAGER who had the benefit of a horrible public education, not much grounding in anything substantial. I enrolled in the Integrated Humanities Program at the University of Kansas in 1973. It was a program that was led by John Senior, Dennis Quinn, and Frank Nelick: a Classics professor and two English Professors. I was kind of the student they were looking for because they realized there was a whole generation of students that hadn't been exposed to the great works of Western Literature. They came up with this program, and they even called it a "remedial" program. When I describe this program to people it sounds like it is an honors program. It was not an honors program. We were not honors students. We had simply been deprived of anything decent.

Editor's note: Edited from a transcription of a live interview with Dale Ahlquist, July 11, 2018.

So, there I was, a typical kid of the 70s into the Grateful Dead and rock and roll and all kinds of things that go along with that. Like the rest of my generation, I was just looking for something, and thought I might find it in music. When I discovered this two-year program for freshmen and sophomores at Kansas, I was attracted to the model. I saw the phrase: "Let them be born and wonder." That sounded pretty cool. And what is this all about? We plunged into the Great Books. We began with the *Iliad* and the *Odyssey* and Aesop's Fables and bits of Plato and the Greek Tragedies. Second semester we read Roman authors: *Caesar's Gallic Wars*, Ovid, Lucretius. The second year we started reading Christian authors. We read selections from the Bible, the *Confessions* of St. Augustine (that was a really pivotal book for me), *The Consolation of Philosophy* by Boethius, the life of Charlemagne, *Chronicles of the Crusades*, and then we finished with *The Little Flowers of St. Francis*. Then the fourth semester we read *Canterbury Tales* by Chaucer, *Don Quixote* by Cervantes, a few Shakespeare plays, then the modern philosophers: Rosseau, Descartes, Hume and Locke, and then Newman (which was another pivotal book).

Along with reading all these books, we memorized poetry, listened to music, learned to sing together, and studied rhetoric and debate, where we'd take a position and stand up for an hour and defend it. The Humanities Program satisfied a number of core requirements at the University of Kansas. English, Speech, Western Civics and they integrated all these elements together with history, poetry, and music. There were students pursuing a variety of majors, pre-med students, biology majors, all different disciplines, but they had to take the humanities core courses to get their degrees.

But in addition to reading these books and discussing them, we also had extra-curricular activities, which led to great friendship, friendships around great ideas and great ideals like truth and goodness and beauty. Every couple of weeks in the evening we would go out in groups and learn the constellations. That not only tied into the study of Greek mythology, it got us out of the city and out into the country, and got us to look up. "Let them be born and wonder."

Along the way, I discovered another writer of wonder. There was a supplemental course taught by Richard Hart that was called "Supernatural Fiction." It included authors such as George MacDonald, J.R.R. Tolkien, C.S. Lewis...and G.K. Chesterton. That was my introduction to Chesterton. I took this course in my sophomore year. The very first book I read by Chesterton was *The Man Who Was Thursday*. A whole new world was opened up to me. Chesterton is so delightful to read, but reading the classics before reading Chesterton was a great foundation. He takes you on an adventure, but he refers to the classics (he is clearly well-read in the classics), but he is thoroughly contemporary, looking at the world today, trying to make sense of the modern world.

I fell in love with Chesterton with the reading of that first book. We read *The Everlasting Man* next and then *Orthodoxy*. I read those books my sophomore year, and as I was going into my junior year I started asking, "Do I even believe in God?" I had been raised in the Presbyterian church. We went to church maybe on Christmas and Easter. We were believers in my family, but it wasn't a very formal religious training. At this point in my life I started church-hopping. I went to a Methodist church for a bit, but then after reading more Chesterton, Belloc, and Lewis, I started going to the Episcopal church. A lot my friends in the program were either converts or in the process of converting to Catholicism, but I think subconsciously I was afraid of the Catholic Church. It was looming very large on the horizon and I wasn't too ready to jump into that yet. So I was keeping in "safe territory" for a while. But then I realized it was inevitable that I would have to at least take a look at the Catholic Church. After all, I was very taken up with Newman and Newman's story, and how he became Catholic, and then, of course, Chesterton's story and how he converted.

Finally, in my junior year I decided I would look into the Catholic Church. There was a wonderful Irish priest in Lawrence who was the pastor for the Newman Center, and he was the pastor of the local parish church. He would tell stories like only the Irish can about the faith. And he also was familiar with Chesterton, Belloc and all these great writers, so it was a perfect segue into more formal inquiries. After about a couple of weeks of these instruction classes, it all made sense. All the pieces to the puzzle came together. At the same time I was reading more and more Chesterton and Belloc and Ronald Knox. They all combined to move me right into the Catholic Church. After a month or so I was ready: "Where do I sign up?" This is the place where I need to be.

Of course, boatloads of grace were poured down upon me, and that was another thing that was moving my heart. As I look back on it, there was just two things. Sometimes, and that's true to a certain extent, I tell people that I read my way into the Catholic Church. And that is true, because I had this intellectual journey that was taking place over those couple of years as a freshman, sophomore and junior in college. But at the same time there were these friendships that were developing in the heart, you know, and just falling in love with truth, and goodness and beauty, through the example of virtue in other people, to the example of joy and faith in other people. That was sort of using me as well. It wasn't merely an intellectual conversion, it was a conversion of the whole person, all coming together through this experience in my college years.

Obviously, there was almost nothing like this going on in the 1970s. In fact, one of the ironies about the program was that the professors got a grant from the National Endowment for the Humanities, which was not, shall we say, a very Catholic-friendly organization. But they built the whole project as an "experiment in tradition." It was such a crazy time in the 70s that these kinds of traditional ideas were avant-garde. A Chestertonian paradox.

But equally amazing was that it appealed to students, too. We really were fascinated with these ideas and we would learn things like how to write beautiful script with a calligraphy pen. Everything beautiful was incorporated into our studies, getting us to look up and to wonder at beauty and truth and goodness. That was really the key to the program. Plus, these professors were gifted professors. That was a huge part of it. They really knew how to teach. They loved what they taught, and they were great examples of men who believed in what they taught. They believed that there was a truth, an objective truth. It was one of the key things that resonated with the students.

I converted half way through my junior year and ended up graduating the following year with a degree in English literature. I didn't know what I wanted to do, and so, with a bunch of my friends who also didn't know what to do, we decided to go hitchhiking across Europe. While we were there, we stumbled across a Benedictine monastery in France called Our Lady of Fontgombault. They were still praying the office in Gregorian Chant. Since we had studied Latin under John Senior, we knew what we were hearing, and we were drawn to the place, and some of us wanted to spend more time there. Several of our classmates stayed and became monks there, and

I was considering it myself. But after about nine months there I decided that I didn't have a vocation to monastic life.

I went back to Kansas and worked for a couple of years with some friends of mine who were farmers. There were doing a lot of subsistence farming, which I loved. And I met a girl, thought I was supposed to settle down and raise a big Catholic family. But in 1979 Pope John Paul II came to the United States, and went to Des Moines, Iowa, which was close to us. So, we piled into the van and drove out to Des Moines to see this new Polish Pope. It was the Feast of St. Francis of Assisi, October 4, 1979. At the end, he made a plea to young men to consider the priesthood. I hadn't really thought about the parish priesthood; it was monastic life in France, or marriage. Those were the two things, so for the first time I starting thinking that maybe God was calling me to be a parish priest. I couldn't get it off my mind. I talked to my girlfriend about it. She was a wonderful Catholic girl, and she actually made an appointment for me to meet with her pastor. She was from Wichita, and her priest happened to the Vicar General of the diocese. By January of 1980, I was in seminary and never looked back. I love to think about those days, which seem like yesterday. But it was 40 years ago.

I just want to add that Chesterton continued to play a role in my life after my conversion. As a priest I would always direct young people to the writings of Chesterton. He is such a diverse writer. If someone was interested in the saints, of course I would give them one of Chesterton's wonderful biographies of either St. Francis of Assisi or St. Thomas Aquinas. If they were grappling with the big questions, *Orthodoxy*. If they were just wanting great stories, the Father Brown mysteries. I used Chesterton a lot to catechize. He was one of the authors I would always recommend people to read. As I continued in my priesthood I was a university chaplain, I taught at the University of Dallas, six and a half years in Rome and then taught at Christendom College in Rome for a couple of years, and I always found that Chesterton was great literature and a great author for college students. There was always a good way to begin a conversation with a Chesterton book.

Then as a bishop, I have been very involved in education, in Catholic schools, and trying to get students (and teachers) to rediscover the great traditions of western learning, the things that the historian Christopher Dawson talks about in his books. Chesterton always plays a role because Chesterton is the example of someone who was deeply immersed in liberal education. Chesterton continues to be a source of inspiration and in helping to enrich and strengthen our Catholic schools.

Ballade to G. K. Chesterton

By Reuben Slife

If I know (rather paradoxically)
That silk has no less beauty than a sow,
That wonder is our first necessity,
And sin makes sparks less bright; if I know how
To pay for sunsets or her lifted brow;
If I have found an honest and carefree
Delight in earthly, earthy ruck and row—
Then I will say you showed me how to see.

Do I know what abyss it is to *be*,
With Thomas, utmost that our minds allow?
That all things echo back Infinity
And there is but one topic—yes, somehow,
A girl's red hair, three acres and a cow,
And Nicaragua are one mystery—
And, thus, one conversation: with the Thou?
Then I will say you showed me how to see.

And since I found from you the wild key
Whose shape cannot be guessed, that can endow
Our reeling world with reeling sanity;
Since I have followed you to break and bow
And, named anew, the Holy Faith avow;
Since I am blessed to fill my poverty
With that divinest Fruit of earth and plough—
Then I will say you showed me how to see.

envoi

Prince, if I come to the eternal now
Of clear, rapt vision of the One-in-Three,
Before His glory—gratefully I vow—
Then I will say you showed me how to see.

—R.S.

"The things which are the simplest so long as they are un-
disputed invariably become the subtlest when once they are
disputed."   —G.K. CHESTERTON

A S I SIT DOWN TO TRY to tell the story of G.K. Chesterton's
influence on my life, that sentence (his sentence, of
course) comes to mind. How to make plain in fragmentary words what is so clear and whole in my mind? It would
be like tracing the source of a spring to prove that a river exists—belaboring the obvious; or like painting the portrait of a
memory so another could share it—ridiculous and impossible.
Yet it must be tried, to pay a debt.

I do not remember the first time I read Chesterton. In my
teens, I found several quotations by him and wrote them in
a notebook, with his name circled and the words "look him
up" scrawled in the margin. His wisdom demanded attention.

What kind of man could say such things? And what else had he said? At the nearest library, I found he'd written a book with the irresistible title of *The Man Who Was Thursday*. And the title, as it happened, was the least of its merits—every third page, at that age, struck me like a private revelation. "When you say 'thank you' for the salt, do you mean what you say?" "The most dangerous criminal now is the entirely lawless modern philosopher." "'Well, really,' said Syme, 'I don't know any profession of which mere willingness is the final test.' 'I do,' said the other—'martyrs. I am condemning you to death. Good day.'" Over a decade on, I can still remember the precise passages.

(Some time later, I discovered he had also written the Father Brown stories, which, strangely enough, I had already read without impression and forgotten. The fault must have been mine, I knew. I did not repeat it.)

After that, I began to devour everything I could find by Chesterton. The feast continues with no loss of appetite— though with some diminution of pace—to this day. But the discoveries of those early years cannot be equaled. Chesterton, then, was like a second self, who thought my own thoughts ahead of me, maturing my subterranean insights before they had begun to sprout. It's true to say, with C.S. Lewis, that "I loved him for his goodness." What was healthy and innocent in me saw itself reflected in him more brightly—in his poems "Femina Contra Mundum" and "Music," in the mystical pageantry of Sunday's country house, in Adam Wayne's love for the spear-topped railings of Notting Hill—and I trusted him implicitly.

That trust is strange. At that time in my life, especially, I was ensnared in intellectual pride, and no one could tell me what to do or how to think. I argued against people reflexively. A few other writers whom I respected, such as Lewis, could argue me into the truth; but Chesterton didn't have to argue—he pointed to things, and I saw them. He pushed out the horizon. He wrote somewhere that "What we really feel, naturally and casually, about the look of skies and trees and the face of friends, that and that alone will almost certainly remain our vital philosophy to our dying day." That is the kind of debt I owe him. He didn't give me conclusions: he renovated my first impressions. He enlarged my basic insights and rooted them more deeply.

Which is not to say that I agreed with him on everything. When I realized he was Catholic, I didn't know what to make of the fact. I recall telling someone at the time that even our difference of faith wasn't a disagreement, exactly, because he never talked directly about the doctrines I disagreed with. Of course, that isn't precisely true. I suppose I meant that he wasn't, like Lewis, making sustained arguments for particular theological propositions.

As you can gather from that, I was Protestant. My parents and family gave me the gift of faith, and led me to be spiritually serious and doctrinally-minded. (My debt to them, of course, is even deeper and harder to express than mine to Chesterton. But that is a task for another time.) Despite their irenicism, somehow I became inflexibly opposed to certain Catholic doctrines: particularly the belief that there was one, true, visible Church. Chesterton didn't directly change that. However, he started me on a journey (by leading me to Thomas Aquinas and a few other writers), and he made me expect Catholics to be wise, good people.

In my early twenties, I eventually did find direct explanations of the doctrines I disagreed with, and was received into full communion with the Catholic Church. I cannot speak of that fulfillment too strongly—though some words of Chesterton almost cover it: "The Church is the natural home of the Human

Spirit." There's no triumphalism in this. I can't think that when you find a career you disdain your previous occupations; nor can I think that when you find your wife you turn bitter against other women you have known. Certainly, when you find the Church, you don't regret the faith you had before full communion. It has not been abandoned, or even changed. For that reason, the precise words "full communion" are very important to me—it is a filling up of what is already present. It is far, far from an overthrow or a supplanting.

Though that great realization didn't come directly from Chesterton, I see little chance it would ever have taken place without his influence. The Spirit has His ways, of course—but for me Chesterton was one of His principal ways. He formed the cast of mind within which nothing but fullness made sense. And when the realization happened, I had a sudden, deep sense that it had come about because of his intercession: that he had been praying all along that I might receive without asking, find without seeking. So he was, in fact, the second saint whose intercession I sought—after St. Paul, whose letters had sustained me my whole life. I knew he cared and would want to hear from me.

But God forbid that anyone see this as some sectarian story. It is not that at all. Chesterton did not merely lay intellectual groundwork: he formed me as a person. His holistic common sense corrected my congenital drift to "the clean and well-lit prison of one idea"; his innocence, his unshaken joy and simplicity stand to me as a beacon. Indeed, this is not even a conversion story in the conventional sense, of coming to final views or to a definitive change of heart—because it has not yet ended. It is a story of a journey toward human fullness, in which Chesterton plays something like the role of magnetic north. I can honestly say that, without Chesterton, I have no idea who I would be. I am unable to imagine myself under those conditions, almost as I cannot imagine myself with different parents.

In the *Divine Comedy*, Dante calls Virgil many extravagant things, even, near the end of the *Purgatorio,* as the time draws on when Virgil must leave him, calling him "my more than father." Having taught the *Comedy*, I can say that many find his gushing regard baffling: how could Dante have such a deep attachment to a man he never met? But, making all allowance for Italian effusiveness, my experience with Chesterton has given me a touchstone of understanding. For my own reasons and in my own way, I know something of that sense of sonship, that illimitable debt.

And I do not think the one who has been my guide will be forced to retreat to the shadows as my faults are purged away. No. He, I am confident, has gone on before.

THE BEATIFIC VISION

By Dale Ahlquist

I ONCE GAVE A TALK ENTITLED "How G.K. Chesterton Ruined My Honeymoon." I didn't choose the title.

And the fact is, Chesterton did not ruin my honeymoon. One could argue that Pope John Paul II getting shot on my honeymoon ruined my honeymoon. Did I mention I was honeymooning in Rome? Did I mention I was Baptist? One could argue that Rome is no place for a Baptist, especially on his honeymoon, and especially when the Pope is getting shot. But none of those things ruined my honeymoon. Nothing ruined it. It was a great honeymoon, exciting, romantic and lots of fun. The start of a great marriage to a great woman, who somehow continues to put up with me. The start of a great adventure that still has not stopped. And yes, the start of reading G.K. Chesterton. Little did I know where it would all lead. It would lead all the way around the world back to Rome.

I was a comfortable and confident Baptist, though I did not want to be known as a Baptist. I only wanted to be known as a

Christian. My theology was Baptist, but I wanted to be known as something bigger than that denomination. At the same time, I made it clear that I was not a Catholic. Whatever I was, I was a Protestant. I was sure of Christ, and I was sure the Catholics had somehow gotten Christianity wrong.

But when I began my life with my wife, I also began my life with G.K. Chesterton. In Laura, I had found a woman who was everything to me, who could do just about anything: artist, accountant, seamstress, chef, problem-solver, fluent in four languages, an amazing mother, a vibrant personality, with a divine gift for cutting through the bovine surplus. In Chesterton, I found a writer who also could do just about anything, who could go deep and wide, who shocked me with the obvious and dazzled me with the subtle, artist, mentor, guide, friend, with a divine gift for dishing out common sense. Never mind that he was Catholic. I didn't.

But the more I read Chesterton, the more I faded from the Baptist church. In fact, I stopped going to church, even though I retained my belief in Christ. I knew that something was missing from all the churches I had gone to. I just didn't know what it was. Chesterton, in the meantime, led me to other Chestertonians. There didn't seem to be many of us back then, but most of them were Catholics, and some of them were...converts. This was new. A Protestant becoming a Catholic. I really could not believe that such a creature existed. Even though I was daily drinking in the words of a convert named G.K. Chesterton. Along with discovering converts, I also discovered the Church Fathers. They were profound and inspiring...and Catholic. How had these giants been kept hidden from me?

When Chesterton was in the process of converting, he told his mentor, Fr. John O'Connor (the inspiration for the priest-detective Father Brown), that he was no longer a Protestant, but

not yet Catholic. I don't know at what point this happened to
me, but it happened. As I learned about the sacraments, the
significance of rituals, the history of Western Civilization, I
moved from thinking that the Catholic Church had kept people ignorant to seeing that I had been kept ignorant about the
Catholic Church.

I went through the three stages of conversion described by
Chesterton, which he obviously went through: first being fair
to the Catholic Church (which is impossible because no one
is able to be fair to the Catholic Church: one is either for it or
against it); secondly, discovering the Catholic Church (which
is the thrilling part, a joyride, because there is no commitment
involved); and thirdly, running away from the Catholic Church
(which is the terrifying part, and which is what happens when
the head is convinced but the heart is still looking for a way out).

I went through the same two conversions as Chesterton
(and as many of the others in this book): first becoming a
Christian, then becoming a Catholic, or, as Chesterton puts
it, one incomplete conversion that was later completed. But
I also went through the same *six* conversions as Chesterton,
six stunning realizations that were like bursts of light: first
that Protestantism had lost its purpose; then that the Church
understood the world better than the world understood itself;
that the Church never takes the easy way out on the hard questions; that the Church knows more than I do; that materialism
does not accept its own conclusions; and that in the end there
are only two things: there is the Catholic Church, which is
"the one supremely inspiring and irritating institution in the
world," and there are its enemies, who will be for or against
anything as long as they are against the Church. Its enemies
set out to destroy the Church but only succeed in destroying
everything else.

And like Chesterton, my conversion took a long time. In his case, it took about twenty-two years. In my case, it was sixteen. And like Chesterton, in the end, the final obstacle was a woman. For Chesterton, it was his wife Frances. For me, it was Joseph's wife: Mary. This was where my Baptist theology held its ground. The last holdout. Except the theology was not the problem. Christ is the Savior, the Redeemer, the son of God, and, well, the son of Mary, and, since Christ is God in the flesh, that makes Mary the Mother of God. I was able to accept that. But all this veneration? All these prayers to her? All these statues? Where is that in the Bible?

Early on, a priest (one of the very few priests I knew) explained to me that you don't have to have a devotion to Mary in order to be Catholic. I suppose I sighed with relief. But it didn't move the needle. It would still be many years before I started getting any closer to the Catholic Church. And when I was nearing the threshold, still harboring my Marian objections, it was a different priest who looked me in the eye and said to this Baptist who knew his Bible: "Do you believe that her soul magnifies the Lord?"

I knew this verse, but of course I had never thought about it till that moment. "My soul makes God bigger." Something only Mary could say. In the Magnificat, she goes on to say, "All generations shall call me blessed." Why had I never called her blessed?

When I was re-evaluating my attitude towards Mary, I discovered that the Reformers did not dislike her. It was their heirs who banished her. And even though the earlier priest had assured me that Marian devotion was not a requirement to be a Catholic, I discovered that all of the great Catholic mystics had a particular devotion to Mary. And so had all the great saints. But what about Chesterton? After all, I certainly considered him a mystic. And a saint.

Did I just say I considered Chesterton a mystic? And a saint? Yes, I did. Neither is a term we associate with a joke-making, cigar-smoking, beer-drinking, untidy, absent-minded London journalist. But as to the latter, it was only when I heard the suggestion that Chesterton should be canonized that I had a complete and instantaneous understanding of the Communion of the Saints: saints bring us closer to Christ; saints are models of the Christian walk, showing us what it looks like to live a virtuous life; rather than interfering, they are interceding; and saints prove themselves to be your friend, suffering with you, laughing with you, talking to you, listening to you. For the first time in my life, a saint was real to me. As for the former, the mystic, I can say that once we enter into the architecture of Chesterton's words, we know we have stepped into a literary cathedral, we know we are being given glimpses of something transcendent, eternal, even in one paragraph or one sentence or one phrase. The mystic, says Chesterton, passes through the moment when there is nothing but God. This is an insight that one does not get out of a book; one has to experience it to know it. Chesterton obviously did. He also tells us that the true mystic does not conceal mysteries; he reveals them. He tries to put into words what he has seen. He does not mystify. He clarifies.

And though Chesterton reveals much about everything with his honesty and his grasp of the truth, there is one thing about himself about which he reveals very little. He has not completely kept it hidden, but he hardly ever writes about it, choosing even to put it into his poems rather than his prose. It is so well-veiled that I did not hesitate to fall in love with Chesterton because I did not know this thing about him. It is perhaps why so many other Protestants, especially Evangelicals, have been drawn to him, because like me, they might have been put off if they had known. Known what? That he had a devotion to Mary.

She appears in his epic poem *The Ballad of the White Horse.*

Her face was like an open word
When brave men speak and choose,
The very colours of her coat
Were better than good news.

That was written more than a decade before his conversion. And after he became Catholic, he wrote a whole book of poems, *The Queen of Seven Swords*, which he kept out of the volumes of his collected poems. The title refers to the "seven-fold splendour" surrounding Mary, corresponding to the seven wounds of Christ, and the book includes seven poems corresponding to the seven champions of Christendom. In one poem he muses that if all the statues of Mary were smashed, we would still carve her image with a song. The myriad of images are not idols, and there are so many because they portray an inexhaustible profundity, "Truths by their depth deceiving more than lies." The Master of Paradox meets the Matron of Paradox, for what could be more paradoxical than the epithet, "Mother of God"?

In one of his only essays about Mary ("Mary and the Convert" in *The Well and the Shallows*) he says that he never had to overcome the standard Protestant objections to the Blessed Virgin Mother. But he understood that Mary is what sets the Catholic Church apart from all the others. And in his own conversion, he realized that when he was thinking of her, he was thinking of the Catholic Church; when he was trying not to think about her, he was trying not to think about the Catholic Church.

Every convert and certainly every "revert" has the sense of coming home when becoming Catholic, and Mary is part of the home in Rome, because every home needs a mother. Protestantism will always be something less than the Catholic

Church. If it has not left out the sacraments and the saints, it has left out the fullness of history and culture. It has even left out part of the Bible which it touts as its own authority. But the ultimate emptiness of Protestantism is due to the fact that it has no place for the Mother of God. It does not call her blessed.

If we were to set aside the question of Chesterton's holiness, of his potential sainthood, which will be the decision of the Catholic Church, we can still maintain the claim that he is a mystic. He once let drop the line that it is embarrassing to speak with God, face-to-face, as with a friend. Even the cynical Franz Kafka wondered at Chesterton's happiness, musing that that he "has found God." In any case, I could not deny it, and I had to admit that Chesterton, the convert and the mystic, had a devotion to Mary. And Mary played in a role in his conversion and in his mystical insight.

What is the Beatific Vision? It is what we shall perceive of God when we are in the ultimate state of blessedness. It is what we see in Heaven. Dante tries to describe it in the *Paradiso*, to be in the presence of God in his unveiled majesty. Some on this earth have been granted a glimpse of heaven. But of all those who have had a mystical experience with the Ultimate, surely Mary stands alone. What Christian can dispute that Mary has enjoyed a unique relationship with the Triune God? When the Angel of God, Gabriel, salutes Mary, proclaiming that she is full of grace, and that the Holy Spirit will come upon her and she will conceive God Incarnate, she says, "Let it be done." She is directly connected to the Most High in a way no other human will ever experience, and that is a mystery to be contemplated over and over.

But in a small way, less profound, less dramatic, but still very real, her ultimate communion with God can be shared by us in our communion. We can say "Amen" and God can touch our

lips and we can carry Christ, the Body and Blood, within us at
the altar. We can have a brief glimpse of the Beatific Vision, the
blessed sight. Taste and see that the Lord is good.

G.K. Chesterton says The Beatific Vision is astonishment.
And he wrote a poem under this title.

The Beatific Vision

Through what fierce incarnations, furled
In fire and darkness, did I go,
Ere I was worthy in the world
To see a dandelion grow?

Well, if in any woes or wars
I bought my naked right to be,
Grew worthy of the grass, nor gave
The wren, my brother, shame for me.

But what shall God not ask of him
In the last time when all is told,
Who saw her stand beside the hearth,
The firelight garbing her in gold?

I read this poem just before I was received into the Catholic
Church. It is the expression of someone who understands that
he is not worthy of the great gift of existence itself, not worthy "to see a dandelion grow." He has to gone through "fierce
incarnations" to behold even the birds of the air and the lilies
of the field (or in this case, wrens and grass). But then he has
a vision. A vision of a woman. Bathed in a mystical light. Who
did Chesterton see beside the hearth, "the firelight garbing her
in gold"? It may be a vision of sacramental love (which, being
sacramental, is both human and divine). It may also be a vision
of the woman clothed with the sun. Like any good poem, it
works on multiple levels. But certainly the Beatific Vision here
is of a woman. And she is called blessed. And the conclusion

is that once we've had the Beatific Vision, there is nothing that God could ask of us that we will not be ready to do.

So much for my problem with Joseph's wife. As for *my* wife, when I told her that we had to start attending church again… but the Catholic Church, it was the one moment in our marriage where this woman who could read me like a book, and who could predict the end of a movie before the end of the opening credits, was caught off guard. Even though I had dropped a thousand hints, she didn't see this one coming. She had actually been raised Catholic but was not in communion with the Church when we met in college. She embraced my Evangelical faith when she embraced me, and we were married in the Baptist church. Naturally, when I made my Catholic announcement, she had some questions. I was ready. "Here," I said, handing her a stack of books, "Read these." She did. Not only did she reconcile with the Church, she went on to became a fervent Catholic. We had the wonderful experience of getting married again, this time by a priest. Our two oldest children were the witnesses. Though we were in the massive Cathedral of Saint Paul, we were in a side chapel with nothing more than the minimum five needed for the sacrament. After we had been Catholic for a while, Laura reminded me of the verse she had recited to me at our Baptist wedding. It was from the Book of Ruth. "Where you go I will go, and your people shall be my people, and your God my God." She pointed out that she followed me into the Baptist Church and then into the Catholic Church (and she has since followed me in other wild pursuits, starting the Chesterton Society and then starting Chesterton Academy), but, she said, if I ever left the Catholic Church, she would not follow me out. Even though no question was asked, I told her that was the right answer.

ABOUT THE CONTRIBUTORS

DALE AHLQUIST is the President of the American Chesterton Society and the Society of Gilbert Keith Chesterton and the Creator and Host of the EWTN series "G.K. Chesterton: The Apostle of Common Sense." Even though he is a Scandinavian from Minnesota, he is not a former Lutheran, but a former Baptist.

ROBERT ASCH is the co-founder and former co-editor of the *St. Austin Review.* He helped start Chavagnes International College, an English Catholic boarding school in France. He is a Jewish convert.

THE MOST REVEREND JAMES CONLEY is Bishop of Lincoln, Nebraska. He is a former Presbyterian, Methodist, and Episcopalian.

BR. NEIL B. CONLISK, O.CARM. was raised religion-lessly. He is now a Carmelite teaching high school in Chicago.

NOEL CULBERTSON lives on an island in Washington State's Puget Sound where she and her husband attempt to take on the gigantic task of teaching their two daughters about the universe. She also runs the Pacific Northwest Chesterton Society. She is a former Baptist.

VICTORIA DARKEY lives near Pittsburgh where she runs the Western Pennsylvania Chesterton Society and writes for *Gilbert!* She is a former Evangelical.

CLARK DURANT is the co-founder and former CEO of the Cornerstone Schools in Detroit and is a board member of the Society of Gilbert Keith Chesterton. He is a former Presbyterian.

DAVID W. FAGERBERG is a theology professor at the University of Notre Dame and columnist for *Gilbert!* He is a former Lutheran pastor.

BRENT FORREST is a former professional magician and runs a private investment company. He lives in San Antonio and is a member of the American Chesterton Society Board of Directors. He is a former just about everything.

TITO GALINDO and his family live near Seattle, Washington, where they attend the North American Martyrs parish. He is a former member of The Church of God Seventh Day.

FR. SIMON HEANS is a priest in Ramsgate, England. He is a former Jehovah's Witness, a former Marxist, and a former Anglican priest.

FR. SPENCER J. HOWE, is Parochial Administrator of Holy Cross Catholic Church, Minneapolis, and a Director of the Society of Gilbert Keith Chesterton. He is a former Lutheran.

B. FREDERICK JUUL grew up in Christian Science. After wandering the whole world, he is now retired and living in Sausalito, California.

DR. STUART J. KOLNER is a retired dermatologist living in Ames, Iowa. He runs the Des Moines Chesterton Society and serves on the Board of Directors for the American Chesterton Society. He is a former Presbyterian.

PETER KREEFT is a professor of philosophy at Boston College and a widely-published author. He is a former Calvinist.

LEAH LIBRESCO SARGEANT is the author of *Arriving at Amen* and *Building the Benedict Option* and lives in New York City. She is a former atheist.

ARTHUR LIVINGSTON is a retired librarian living in Chicago. He is a founding member (and the last one standing) of the Midwest Chesterton Society, which started the national Chesterton conference that has been held annually for over 37 years. He is a former Episcopalian.

FR. DWIGHT LONGENECKER is a former Fundamentalist Protestant and also a former Anglican priest. He is now a Roman Catholic priest, who serves as pastor of Our Lady of the Rosary Church in Greenville, South Carolina.

STUART MCCULLOUGH and his wife run The Good Counsel Network in London, and he is the head of the Catholic G.K. Chesterton Society. He is a former Pagan.

KEVIN O'BRIEN is the Director of Theatre of the Word Incorporated and Upstage Productions, and the author of *An Actor Bows*. He lives in St. Louis. He is a former atheist.

THEODORE OLSEN is a lawyer and financial advisor in St. Paul, Minnesota, and a member of the American Chesterton Society Board of Directors. He is a former Lutheran.

CARL OLSON is the editor of *Catholic World Report*. He lives in Eugene, Oregon. He is a former Fundamentalist Protestant.

JOSEPH PEARCE is a prolific author who has penned acclaimed biographies of Chesterton, Belloc, Solzhenitsyn, Tolkien, Lewis, Oscar Wilde and Roy Campbell. He is a former member of the militant anti-Catholic Orange Order. Originally from London, he now lives in South Carolina.

YASHA AND DENISE RENNER live near Portland, Oregon. Yasha was raised in no faith by a secular Muslim mother and Denise was raised Lutheran.

LAURIE ROBINSON is a writer and the founder of the Greater Wichita Area G.K. Chesterton Society. She is a former Mennonite.

ZUBAIR SIMONSON is a writer living in New York City. He is a former Muslim.

REUBEN SLIFE is a poet, playwright, and philosopher, and has taught at Canongate Catholic High School in Fletcher, North Carolina. He is a former Methodist.

THOMAS STORCK'S latest book is *An Economics of Justice and Charity: Catholic Social Teaching, Its Development and Contemporary Relevance.* He is a former atheist and a former Episcopalian (though not at the same time).

MATT SWAIM is the host of The Son Rise Morning Show on EWTN Radio and Communications Coordinator for The Coming Home Network International. He lives near Cincinnati. He is a former Free Methodist, Nazarene, Emergent Church and a couple of others.

BRANDON VOGT is a best-selling author and the Content Director for Bishop Robert Barron's Word on Fire Ministries. He lives outside of Orlando, where he runs the Central Florida

Chesterton Society. He is a former Methodist.

EMMA FOX WILSON lives in Birmingham, England and is editing *The Letters of G.K. Chesterton*. She is a former unbeliever on all levels.

PETER WILSON is a retired teacher of English (when it was once taught in the schools), and an unofficial oblate at St. Benedict's Abbey in Still River, Massachusetts. He is a former Unitarian.

DR. TOD WORNER is an internist with Abbott Northwestern Hospital in Minneapolis, Minnesota and is a frequent contributor to *The National Catholic Register*. He is a former Lutheran.

ALSO AVAILABLE
FROM ACS BOOKS

All Roads by Dale Ahlquist

The Hound of Distributism edited by Richard Aleman

The Catechism of Hockey by Alyssa Bormes

The Woman Who Was Chesterton by Nancy Carpentier Brown

Jousting with the Devil by Fr. Robert Wild

The Four Men by Hilaire Belloc, with annotations by Deacon Nathan Allen

Justice and Charity by Fulton Sheen, with afterword by Richard Aleman

The Scrappy Evangelist by Fr. Paul Rowan

Get Louie Stigs by Larry Pavlicek

The Satisfied Crocodile by Fr. James Schall, SJ

Reading Between the Signs by Rhonda Zweber

An Actor Bows by Kevin O'Brien